Good As Her Word

Good As Her Word

———

Selected Journalism

LORNA SAGE

FOURTH ESTATE • *London* and *New York*

For Olivia

First published in Great Britain in 2003 by
Fourth Estate
A Division of HarperCollins*Publishers*
77–85 Fulham Palace Road
London W6 8JB
www.4thestate.com

1 3 5 7 9 10 8 6 4 2

These articles first appeared in various UK and US publications, details of which
are given on the contents page

Extract from 'Living on Writing' by Lorna Sage, from Grub Street and The Ivory Tower
edited by B. Bennett and J. Treglown (1998).
Reprinted by permission of Oxford University Press.

A catalogue record for this book is available from the British Library

ISBN 0-00-715779-7

Designed by Geoff Green Book Design

Typeset by Rowland Phototypesetting Ltd, Bury St Edmunds, Suffolk

Printed in Great Britain by
Clays Ltd, St Ives plc

Contents

II POST-WAR LIFE WRITING

Contents

III THE WOMEN'S CAMP

Contents

IV CLASSICS

V CRITICAL TRADITION

VI ITALY

Contents

Introduction

LIKE CERTAIN PHOTOGRAPHS, WHICH hint at the gap between themselves and their future, posthumous books often have a slightly thin, accidental irony about them. This effect depends on how much they are designed to render their author's intentions, how narrowly those intentions are inscribed in the book's form: the stricter the author's plan, the more the unfinished nature of the text becomes an issue. Here, there are no ghostly plans left on the desk, nothing was left unfinished. Instead, the work itself – perhaps a million and a half words written over thirty years – is just too vivid and alive to be left merely dispersed. What strikes us now, having made our selection, is how intimate a portrait of a mind and personality it provides, and how unexpectedly fresh, how new, that portrait is. As Lorna puts it in 'Death of the Author', her unflinching tribute to her friend Angela Carter: 'Nothing stays, endings are final, which is why they are also beginnings'.

We have selected Lorna's journalism to display the sheer range and diversity of her writing. During the seventies and eighties, while making her reputation as a contemporary fiction-reviewer, Lorna was also writing in many of the other newspaper and magazine genres. From the days of *The New Review* in the early 1970s under Ian Hamilton, she continued this diverse practice all her working life: profiles, short notices, interviews, multiple book reviews, essayistic pieces and, more latterly, obituaries. In the late 1970s, she started writing for the *TLS*, a long-time 'home' (branching out briefly into the *New Statesman*), and settled at the *Observer*, with Terry Kilmartin, under whose subtle tutelage she learned the tricks of the trade. In the last years, she wrote for the *Independent*, the *London Review of Books* and the *New York Review of Books*.

In a late essay called 'Living on Writing' from 1998, Lorna rebels against what she calls a 'conspiracy of reflexiveness' in literary journalism:

> Barthes's famous saying went: 'The birth of the reader must be at the cost of the death of the Author'. But the Author's death has led to the birth of endless lower-case authors. If you want to speak with authority as a reader, in other words, you do it first by saying that you are a writer. I have always preferred to be a hack, it seems less of a mystification.

'Hack' is a theatrical double-take: Lorna dressed up in her hack persona to create an outside position for herself, from which she was able to concentrate on the work of other people. She thought of herself as a correspondent, sending in urgent bulletins from the front line of reading, not a 'lower-case writer'.

The urgency of her dialogue with books is one of the distinctive aspects of her voice as a reviewer. She liked the commitment deadlines forced. She also increasingly wrote for money, needed to work, and was proud of the way her pen could supplement her income. Lorna began as an instinctive reader (voracious, indiscriminate) and this trait never left her throughout her life: during the fine contempt of adolescence, the prentice years of scholarship in the Renaissance and seventeenth century, the later years of teaching and constant reviewing, and even finally the last, hand-over-fist period in which she started to edit and write books herself, the curiosity, the primary thrill of the reader, never left her – that what she had in her hand was new; even *Don Quixote* felt to her passionately curious eyes like a tract of snow that no one else had walked upon. She was able rapidly to read one book after another, without pauses for assimilation, ritual movements or changes of place. Her attention was absolute. She did not appear to digest books at all. She read like this late into the night and began again early in the morning: she simply picked up the next volume, whether it was the *Corpus Hermeticum* or *Tarzan of the Apes*, propped it in front of her, her thin, long-nailed thumb creasing down the top three inches as she turned the page, and sped away in a trance of rapid eye-movement, dog-earing the leaves as she went whenever something was memorable. When laid aside, paperbacks, in particular, always had a subtly pot-bellied aspect, as if somehow they had more in them: the persistent creasing at the top caused their pages to bell out slightly. They looked as if they had been filled with reading.

To write your reading was equally direct. Lorna's habit of accuracy was like a religious devotion and her unusual memory, into which books sank, apparently whole, not a feather of their print disturbed, combined with a jesuitical kind of mischievousness, meant that she was a formidable opponent indeed in a literary discussion. She positively wielded quotation and was very canny about lines of argument. So: this very 'directness' is a paradox. When she was young, one of Lorna's favourite quotations was Polonius's 'by indirections find directions out'. To represent your reading so directly is certainly a craft and a pleasure, to say nothing of the service it performs for your authors and readers. But that directness is the product of much meditation, a labour of indirection. When reviewing a book, Lorna would usually read the rest of the author's works and whatever she could find (often whatever there was) of biography and criticism. Marina Warner has spoken of what it felt like as a writer to receive a Lorna Sage review. Before starting to stab, hunched and one-fingered, at the old Olivetti, or later, the little Toshiba, whose keyboard was transformed into rows of letterless cups by the furious battering it had taken, she liked to make sure she had an intimate grasp of the text. This meant picking out the one-liners she made emblematic of the whole. She often did this by ear, not eye; reading out loud with the special emphasis she put into even the smallest of phrases. The quality of her attention, witnessed by the letters and cards she used to receive from writers, came from the detailed work she put in, to represent not only that intimate grasp but also its logic, where it was heading, its implications in a wider context. Many reviewers, of course, work in this way, but what is different about Lorna's writing is precisely what was different about her reading: a rare combination of warmth and sophistication, in which she mimes with strange fidelity the act of reading a text, while tactically holding it at arm's length at the same time. The details eventually click to make an unexpected drift of argument that was, if you look back, there all along. There is always a lot more going on in a Lorna Sage review than the ostensible, but she is always uncannily faithful to the ostensible.

The fact that her directness is also a rhetorical performance is what makes a lot of this writing so eerily coherent and readable. The articles and essays we've chosen seem not to develop, but to spring into print, fully fledged from the beginning. Lorna was a seasoned teacher and scholar by the time she started seriously writing for the papers in her late twenties. The development of her voice does not really take place in these pieces – it takes place offstage, earlier. It was curiously literal: a struggle against the lapidary written style of male academics – a kind of Attic dialect – which all students, regardless of gender, still had to acquire by the early sixties. You can see faint signs of that rebellion in the earlier pieces from the late seventies; the need to put the limp mandarin gesture in brackets as she speaks. When she began, Lorna would write out scripts for her voice. It was not long, however, before that's how she spoke. The brackets were in her speech, often indicated by a switch of the gaze or a fleeting rise in pitch, to throw away the important point. This voice was the one she wanted, the one that did for all purposes, including public speaking, and writing became a staging of her own mercurial speech. When that happened, she rapidly developed the capacity to make a discussion out of an account.

This work when put together has all the pleasure and risk of her bracing talk. Dialogue (between pieces, texts, authors, readers, different parts of herself) is everywhere like good sea air. Lorna pioneered for herself an informality of style that she used to translate into clear and accessible terms any form of perversity, jargon, or learned obscurity. She learned this defence of the common space of culture early on from Plato and it continually informs the 'attack' of these pieces. For all her tactical agility, that knack she has of seizing the acute angle, she is not to be deflected, always on a search for what is really there in front of her, its particularity.

Our title comes from Lorna's 1980 review of J. A. V. Chapple's *Elizabeth Gaskell: A Portrait in Letters*. 'Goodness' was part of the politics of intimacy, a special preoccupation in Lorna's writing about the lives of women, who can so easily become lost in what she calls, ironically, after George Eliot, 'the womanly duty to mediate'. Lorna was acutely aware of the mystification of the personal life, something which was for her a spurious self-confirming logic, by which women cast themselves as appendages. She is suspicious in this piece. Gaskell is almost *too* normal. She must have a hidden, inner life. You can hear Lorna probing for this telltale flaw of self, calling her, cajolingly, 'an almost infinitely divisible woman'. But in the end Gaskell's fund of empathy seems to have matched her own, for she concedes: 'Most good women turn out on closer inspection to be hypocritical, envious or dim (or of course bad), while she genuinely delights in living in and with others.'

As with books, so with people. Intimacy was another paradoxical aspect of Lorna's character. She disliked formal lecturing, but was a riveting public speaker, converting even her own shortness of breath to an intimate style. She read, wrote and received visitors at the kitchen table, her ear almost imperceptibly turned towards the door. She had a gift for intimacy, a trick of 'seeing the point' of people (a favourite phrase of hers in later years), especially outsiders. This was compounded of a genuine curiosity about the lives of others and a talent for benignly picking them up. She liked to keep open-house, sixties-style, often passing the latest apparition at the door a draft of what she had just finished. You were expected to read it on the spot, while she watched your face keenly for reactions. A conspiratorial need for close contact ran through all her relationships – intimacy was her style, but it was a public style, an argumentative style, a performative component of the writing life.

We have split the pieces into six sections, each arranged according to an internal, chronological order of publication: 'Pre-War Life Writing'; 'Post-War Life Writing'; 'The Women's Camp'; 'Classics'; 'Critical Tradition'; and 'Italy'. These divisions are essentially a shaping device – loose, but inclusive – intended to allow the reader to follow chronological development on one front, or on several at once. In the first two sections we have given prominence to biography, autobiography, memoirs, letters and sketches. From the mid-nineties on, while issuing bulletins from *Bad Blood* and then editing *The Cambridge Guide to Women's Writing in English*, Lorna had been reflecting on the whole question of 'Life-Writing'. The project she had begun to work on after *Moments of Truth* was a book entitled *Writing Lives*. She was fascinated by the links between lives and work; in much of what she writes she traces the cuspid points between inner and outer lives: in Dickens, for example, whose manic 'busyness' with people kept them away so that he could work, and Angus Wilson, whose 'inner life was lived on the outside'. Even in the other central sections, which contain a more familiar range of materials, this theme can often be found surfacing too. Finally, 'Italy' collects a number of different pieces Lorna wrote over the years about the culture in which she spent so many springs and summers from the seventies on. A good Latinist from childhood, her familiarity with Italian was another means of subverting binary imprisonment. It gave zest to her Renaissance interests, and with the help of the language she also kept the texts and authors of the modern tradition in view, outside the canonical effect of their English packaging. You can feel this direct contact with the language in her pieces on Calvino, and in the punning connection ('sapere'/'sapore') she spots in the Italian between knowledge and appetite. She's amused, here, to be outside and inside at once.

The readerly pleasures of these pieces are many and they are tied to Lorna's personality. Her hawk's eye for detail and her almost Dickensian penchant for the grotesque turn up some wonderful things. On St Theresa: 'her ecstasy was contagious. And not only to artists . . . General Franco carried her left hand around with him for 40 years.' Or take this brisk paraphrase of Lawrence's disgust at the thought of Shelley: 'A fairy slug is at once unmanly, irrational and grossly slimy: or, in short, a bit of a woman.' Byron's attempts to slim: 'I wear *seven* Waistcoats, & a Great Coat, run & play at cricket', which becomes a metaphor for the mawkish ghastliness of his juvenilia. Giantess Emma Hamilton who could 'impersonate Goddesses because she was nobody, or worse' declined, apparently, into 'a Juno lumbering among sceptics'.

And of Flora Tristan, she writes: 'Who else (except a Sterne) would have a chapter on pockets? Or report on a mud-splashing service for huntsmen too poor to hunt? Now there's an idea for a small business.'

The world of these writings is a generous, but not a frictionless one. Lorna is sceptical of both puritanism and realism in just about equal measures. Both overlap with the claustrophilia of women's personal lives. The point of writing is not to reproduce the world, but to change it. Women, she argues, have enough problems with reproduction without being locked into it as an aesthetic mode as well. And she is also suspicious of the exclusionary mechanisms of canon-making. She champions outsiders, writers who (as she used to put it) 'have no reason to exist', who invent themselves. The most important task of criticism for her is the act of finding a vocabulary for the value of those who are awkward and hard to define, like Elizabeth Smart, for example, whose writerly career, says Lorna, safety-pinning two reproductive functions in one phrase, 'came to a sticky end in low mimetic prose, and babies'. Yet she still feels, despite the slenderness of her *œuvre*, that Smart's prodigal, high lyricism, her offence to the quotidian, has a chance of being read when other, more plausible writers are not. Outsiders count.

Lorna's critical prejudices embrace anything writerly that she feels gets women out of the jails of biology, sex and gender. She's on the watch for 'stickiness', reproduction, fake authenticity, false being, instrumentality, and bad faith. The positive values that support this running critique come in various forms, but are usually performative, theatrical versions of 'inauthenticity': camp, pastiche, carnivalesque, perverse, decadent, even self-destructive or contradictory gestures. She was attracted by the idea, long before Queer Theory, that all women 'are' female impersonators.

Agency in the world, above all, is what she is committed to in these writings, and a resistance to myths of propriety and self-absorption. All writing for her was a form of 'doing', not talking about it. Or talking about the possibility of talking about it. The postponement of the object of knowledge, she observes in her pieces on Shere Hite and Linda Grant, has infected the space of mediatised culture: 'privatised emotions [lead] further into therapy-speak, and oral and masturbatory culture, of which the Hite reports are themselves a part'. Before all, she abhors 'loss of nerve'. The test of theory is the production of real (i.e. particular, different) things – they always bite back the theoretical hand.

The consistent feature of Lorna's proliferation of roles between Grub Street and Academe is her knowingness about her own potentially divided position. She writes for what's left of the common reader in us. She mimes, performs, re-presents the manoeuvres of her authors, not to 'reproduce' them, but to expose them for contemplation. Her convictions cross the line between authors and readers, and all theory to her, even the most shrinkingly narcissistic, is a form of (political) practice, which conforms to the same rules as any other species of persuasive writing, including fiction, where much of the thinking gets done. Cultural space is not like physical space: in writing you can (and need to) be in more than one place at once. There's always more room than you think. She's instinctively against identity politics from the start, because it literalises cultural space. Her appreciative piece on Susan Gubar's 1999 *Critical Condition* demonstrates the nature of this retreat: 'Has "What is to be done?" been replaced by "Who am I?" she asks, and the answer must be partly yes.' Her response to Gubar's remarks about the factionalising of women in the academy is characteristic of what Lorna stands for: 'There is room to live intellectually, in other words, without having to compete over who's more marginal than whom.'

Like many another thought in this heartening body of work, it's a good place to start.

Sharon & Victor Sage, 2003

I

Pre-War Life Writing

Grave-side story

Moon in Eclipse: A Life of Mary Shelley

JANE DUNN

JANE DUNN'S TITLE SETS out the glaring problem for Mary Shelley's biographers: that she exists more as the child of Mary Wollstonecraft and William Godwin, and as Shelley's satellite, than as her own focus of interest. For much of her life she was, even to herself, a lesser light, so that although we know a lot about her, the information hasn't ever quite added up.

Her other relationships, too, were oblique, filtered through Shelley: (Byron, Hogg, Claire Clairmont, Jane Williams); and after his death the pattern if anything intensified: with her fantasy-relation to Washington Irving and her indiscreet letters to the blackmailing Gatteschi look very like sad attempts to re-create scenes from the drama of her marriage. She was, as Jane Dunn says, intensely lonely for most of her 53 years, precisely because of her talent for intimacy.

She had of course, other talents: 'my dreams,' she wrote in her introduction to *Frankenstein*, 'were all my own; I accounted for them to nobody; they were my refuge when annoyed – my dearest pleasure when free.' For once (or almost twice, if you count *The Last Man*, the only other of her novels with something of this force) she contrived to build the contradictions of her experience – her agonies about parenthood as child and mother (or indeed, both simultaneously), the depressing human debris that surrounded her passionate marriage – into a fantasy that would dominate other people's imaginations.

Frankenstein toiling away in his charnel-house laboratory ('my workshop of filthy creation') grew out of what was for her a natural association of creativity with destruction. There were the circumstances of her own birth, which killed her mother; then her father's chilly and increasingly groundless and absurd performance of the role of 'great man' ('You have it in your power,' he wrote once to a prospective second wife, 'to give me new life . . . to raise me from the grave in which my heart is buried. You are invited to form the sole happiness of one of the best-known men of the age'). Her first assignations with Shelley took place round her mother's grave in St Pancras churchyard; and the way he seems to have talked of rejecting his first wife, Harriet – 'I felt as if a dead and living body had been linked together in loathsome and horrible communion' – reveals a truly Frankensteinish capacity to switch from enthusiastic consciousness-raising to revulsion.

By the time Mary finished the first draft of the book, Harriet's suicide had lent a more literal horror to Shelley's cruel metaphor ('Poor Harriet,' she wrote years later in her journal, 'to whose sad fate I attribute so many of my own heavy sorrows, as the atonement claimed by fate for her death'). Her half-sister Fanny Imlay, Mary Wollstone-craft's illegitimate daughter, put an apologetic end to her drab, unwanted existence with an overdose of laudanum, leaving nothing to identify her body but her mother's initials on her stays. Further shades of the charnel-house were supplied by the death (the year before) of Mary's first child: the way she talks about the book ('my hideous progeny' and so on) shows that she made that connection too.

Her own life, for the moment, was going well (was, in other words, only routinely precarious, dogged with money worries, begging letters from Godwin, and Shelley's relation to Claire) and that seems to have enabled her to create the elaborate mythic mix of loneliness, guilt and innocent outrage that makes the novel such a splendid focus for every-one's nightmares.

Usually, though, and almost always in the long years of her widow-hood (she was 24 when Shelley died), her complex inner life was consigned to the amorphous, unhappy pages of her journal, where it came to nothing: 'It has struck me what a very imperfect picture these querulous pages afford of *me*. This arises from their being a record of my feelings, and not of my imagination . . . my Kubla Khan, my pleasure grounds.' She seems to have played her part courageously, but (as though the playing of it exhausted her, as well it might) she became more and more unable to imagine. Her losses and her memories isolated, as she said 'islanded', her, 'sunk me in a state of loneliness no other human being ever before, I believe, endured except Robinson Crusoe.'

There were compensations – her surviving son Percy Florence (reassuringly ordinary), her socialising: she was abused by Shelley's friends for her lack of radical fire, but she could reassure herself that while she couldn't deal with abstractions (except in symbols), she practised liberation ('I have never written to vindicate the rights of women, I have ever befriended women when oppressed').

A very clever, perceptive woman. And yet still in eclipse. Jane Dunn retells the story fairly straightforwardly, but that's not enough to rescue Mary Shelley from unreality. It was a mistake, too, to underplay the fiction and the intellectual issues (references to 'Shelley and his philosophising, and his ideas' just won't do) as if they weren't part of the life. All too often Jane Dunn gets stuck on the conventional surface of her narrative (Byron was 'worldly, red-blooded and extravagant', Paolo 'a hard-working but amoral Italian') when what's needed is precisely the boldness and inventiveness to delve underneath and challenge that ready-made perspective; and I suspect that her assumptions are too common-sensical and un-literary for such a venture.

Good as her word

Elizabeth Gaskell: A Portrait in Letters

J. A. V. CHAPPLE ASSISTED BY L. G. SHARPS

MRS GASKELL'S VICTORIAN REPUTATION for goodness has survived modern scholarship. Most of her writer-contemporaries have long been satisfactorily shown up as selfish, obsessive, perverse, quirky or inadequate: her all-round human decency seems simply confirmed by what we learn about her. She disapproved of introspection (it was 'morbid' and narcissistic, a form of hypochondria) but no commentator since has seriously claimed she had an 'other' secret self. She remains bewilderingly nice.

The result is that a book like *Elizabeth Gaskell: A Portrait in Letters* is bound to seem at first insipid. Her 'Cranford' (Knutsford) childhood may have had its sadnesses – she was after all motherless, and in effect fatherless, living with her aunt – but no letters survive to say so, and there is much fictional evidence to the contrary. Her marriage to Unitarian minister William Gaskell at 21 sounds happy enough, even if it didn't sustain the first honeymoon rapture; she worked with him; she loved her four daughters dearly; and though the death of her baby son in 1846 was a dreadful sorrow, she turned from personal grief to chronicle the sufferings of the Manchester working classes in her first novel *Mary Barton*.

Her writing thus came to seem an extension of her indefatigable social and charitable work in her husband's parish and beyond – exactly what, in contemporary terms, it should have been. And she has of course (true to her anti-self-consciousness line) little to say about the processes of imagination, or the art of writing: 'a good writer of fiction,' she says to an aspiring authoress, 'must have *lived* an active and sympathetic life if she wishes her books to have strength and vitality in them. When you are forty. . . .'

The *Portrait in Letters*, in short, is hardly a self-portrait. But from another angle, this very omission is fascinating. What we get is a picture of a 'self' diffused, a 'self' distributed and absorbed in the family, and in society at large – an unperson surprisingly like Mrs Ramsay in Virginia Woolf's *To the Lighthouse*, or even Mrs Dalloway. Mrs Gaskell is sturdier and much more worthy, but there is something of a stream of consciousness in her letters, especially those to her eldest daughter. This one starts off on a charitable project:

> We have got up to £2,236, and have more in hand. And I have had a letter from Mr Walpole (brother to the Home Secy) saying his brother will help on the Government pension, and the Hornbys (cousins of Lord Derby) are stirring *him* up; so we are in good hopes. I should think any air of Mendelssohn's must be beautiful. *Don't* call Shifts chemises. Take the pretty *English* word whenever you can . . . independently of the word we shall be most glad of the *thing*. Flossie is at her last shifts in two senses. . . .

'Shifts' indeed. She's a brilliant lateral thinker, an almost infinitely divisible woman: 'One of my me's is, I do believe, a true Christian (only other people call her socialist and communist), another of my me's is a wife and mother . . . that's my "social" self I suppose. Then again I've another self with a full taste for beauty . . .' One is not, however, to imagine these selves squabbling or repressing one another (this is not introspection); they are all equally present, equally vocal.

Her reaction to literary fame was not to concentrate herself, but to spread her energies yet further. She travelled to Paris, to Italy, to Germany (as well as to the Lake District and Oxford), acquiring more and more connections, without shedding those in Manchester or London or Knutsford. Henry James, a friend of friends, recognised in her the social spirit that held fictions – and people – together: 'Clear echoes of a "good time" (as we have lived on to call it) break out in her full, close page. . . .' She saw what she was not – she admired George Eliot from a distance, and paid tribute in her *Life of Charlotte*

Brontë to the woman writer who most questioned her values. She believed implicitly in the importance of the individual, though in certain senses she wasn't one.

She was, perhaps, something more rare. Most good women turn out on closer inspection to be hypocritical, envious or dim (or of course bad), while she genuinely delights in living in and with others. Professor Chapple and Mr Sharps, in assembling the book (and doing an admirable job in making material from the 1966 Manchester University Press *Collected Letters* practically available) make no great claims. Professor Chapple ends indeed by quoting Charlotte Brontë on Mrs Gaskell: 'Do you who have so many friends – so large a circle of acquaintance – find it easy, when you sit down to write, to isolate yourself from all those ties, and their sweet associations, so as to be your *own woman* . . . ?' The answer was no. You couldn't and be good.

Flora by gaslight

The London Journal of Flora Tristan

TRANSLATED, ANNOTATED AND INTRODUCED
BY JEAN HAWKES

FLORA TRISTAN'S INTEREST AS an investigator of nineteenth-century London starts with the fact that she is so un-English – so utterly immune, that is, to the atmosphere of decorum and common sense that covered the English public women of her time like a veil.

It's not just that she is French, or at least it's more complicated than that: her parents were a French *émigrée* and a Peruvian grandee; she was dubiously legitimate and certainly disinherited; her own marriage failed, and when, after a battle for the children, she won a court separation, her husband shot her in the back and got 20 years – all of which she rushed into print, along with an account of her voyage to Peru to claim kin. Unsuccessfully – hence her hand-to-mouth career as a wandering socialist prophet, and hence the *London Journal*, based on her visits in the 1820s and 1830s. She was also Gauguin's grandmother, as the most recent biography (C. N. Gattey's *Gauguin's Astonishing Grandmother*) chauvinistically announces.

However, here she is in her own right, in a new translation by Jean Hawkes, who admits to removing some exclamation marks and dashes, but has otherwise splendidly preserved an original *collage* of romance, realism, high feeling and visionary prejudice.

We start from the Port of London, bamboozled by sheer size – the world's biggest city – and mesmerized by the glamour of gaslight; but within a couple of pages we adjust to the English pace: it's nearly impossible to get from A to B, which is why people are so churlish and weary, not to mention the climate, which is what drives them to drink ... In short, Londoners are glum, snobbish, sycophantic, inhospitable, punctual (very sinister this, since journeys take hours) and appallingly conventional:

> If a daguerreotype were made of the public in Regent Street or Hyde Park it would be remarkable for the same artificial expressions and submissive demeanour that characterise the crude figures in Chinese painting.

Flora, on the other hand, is a woman of spirit, labouring under the burden of reporting British Podsnappery for the sake of posterity (England is the shape of things to come, if we're not careful). She is also *very French*, and blissfully unaware of it – 'Thank God I long ago renounced any notion of *nationality*, a mean and narrow concept.' She also doesn't exactly believe in God (a mean and narrow concept).

'Beer and gas are the two main products consumed in London.' Can it have been true? Could it be still? The link between debauchery and drunkenness is obvious: '*The sober Englishman is chaste to the point of prudery.*' But other equally incautious remarks give one pause – on the connection between Protestantism, free enterprise and insanity, for instance, or on religious education ('in the Bible criminals can find good reason for persisting in their life of crime'). And if she's altogether of her time when she visits prisons looking out for criminal physiognomy and 'bumps,' she soars into wilder regions when she confesses: 'I see prostitution as either an appalling madness or an act so sublime that my mortal understanding cannot comprehend it.' Her section on the need for infant schools from the age of two, on the other hand, is so prosaic, sane and obvious, it quite takes one's breath away in our neo-Victorian age.

Volatile as she is, however (she is inconsistent *on principle*), it's not hard to see how she reads England. Its commercial supremacy is founded on India (sharp of her in the 1830s?). It abolished the Slave Trade to prevent other countries founding colonies, and has proletarianised the West Indian Negroes, who are now almost as wretched as the English working class. London itself – the final exposure of British 'humanitarianism' – is a slave market, where young children (of both sexes, she observed coolly) are sold for prostitution. England is imperialist, materialist, masculine. Hope lies with the Chartists and the women, then, logically enough.

Her account of a Chartist meeting is in deliberate contrast with her visit to Parliament (squalid boredom, quite apart from the fact that she had to disguise herself as a Turk to get in). The Chartist delegates are alive, eager, visionary, and hopeful – 'You can see that the poor boy believes in God, in Woman, in self-sacrifice' – as are the women writers, though perhaps they *write* because their lives are so socially null:

> In France, and any country which prides itself on being civilised, the most honoured of living creatures is woman. In England it is the horse . . .

Her profundities and inanities alike spring from the weird acuteness of the angle at which she approaches England. Who (except a Sterne) would have a chapter on pockets? Or report on a mud-splashing service for huntsmen too poor to hunt? Now there's an idea for a small business. You never know, though, with this wild lady, when she'll turn out to be timely. A final thought for the day:

> Oh! The railways, the railways! In them I see the means whereby every base attempt to prevent the growth of union and brotherhood will be utterly confounded.

Life stories

A Need to Testify: Four Portraits

IRIS ORIGO

THIS BOOK IS A SET of variations on the theme of biography: its dubious credentials, its delights and pieties, and – Iris Origo would argue, hence her title – its necessity. The four portraits here, all of people involved in resisting Italian fascism, make space for the quiddities and peculiarities of their subjects (whom she knew), but serve at the same time as statements of faith in 'character'. Her people may be merely particular, but they are also stubborn and courageous; they are loners who none the less feel for and with one another, and many others.

The first of her subjects, Lauro de Bosis, is the hardest for her to make real, partly because he seems to have lived out his brief life as mythology. He was aristocratic, half-American, brought up on Shelley and Whitman, a bard and a chemist who advocated a conservative (King and Church) take-over from Mussolini. At 26 he wrote a verse drama about Icarus, and at 30, in 1931, he flew over Rome in a small plane, scattering anti-fascist leaflets, and vanished west to crash into the sea.

His style, in every sense, was excessive – though he did, in one letter, locate the twist in history that would lend him substance. 'If the American Revolution had failed, Washington and Jefferson would be considered as seditious Bolsheviks,' he reflected. When, 12 years later, Mussolini fell in (roughly) the way he had planned, de Bosis's story returned to earth.

It was never, anyway, as Marchesa Origo points out, just his story: three years before his terminal gesture he had fallen in love with a celebrated American actress, Ruth Draper, whose long life comes next, linked with his. Here the biographer's brief is different, for Ruth Draper not only came from a densely sociable background ('old New York,' very Edith Wharton), but had monologued her way through a multitude of characters, and round the world, before she met de Bosis, in middle age. She was all life-wish and, though savaged by his death, went on adding to her repertoire and her friends for a quarter of a century.

Her practical belief in his cause outlived him too: among other things, she endowed a chair in Italian history at Harvard, which was occupied by a man unlike de Bosis in every way but one, Gaetano Salvemini, socialist, republican, sceptic – and anti-fascist. Salvemini is the anchor man of the book, 'the man who would not conform' though events battered him grotesquely. In 1908 his wife and their five children died in the Messina earthquake; in the years that followed his whole generation, it almost seemed, was dispersed and destroyed – murdered on fascist orders, murdered in Spain, driven (like himself) into exile. In 1946, as the world repaired itself, the stepson of his second marriage was tried and executed as a collaborator in France. He comes through it all, in this portrait, suffering, resilient and mocking, with just a hint of secular sainthood.

Here Iris Origo's conviction that 'Every individual life is also the story of *Everyman*' occupies the foreground. Her last subject, Ignazio Silone, is allowed to characterise himself, in passages from *Fontamara*, *Bread and Wine* and *Emergency Exit*, but at the same time the book's structure quietly manoeuvres him into an exemplary role, as the priest of a non-existent church. Silone's defection from the Communist Party, his long exile and his even longer wait for recognition in his own country, even the form of his final illness, in 1978, when agraphia scrambled words for him with a last irony – all of this piles up as evidence of 'the need to testify'.

Strategy for survival

Secrets of a Woman's Heart: The Later Life of Ivy Compton-Burnett

HILARY SPURLING

'I AM ILL AT ease with people whose lives are an open book' – so says Felix (aptly and most deliberately named) in *More Women Than Men* (1933). Ivy Compton-Burnett's happiest, wisest and most uncharitably perspicacious characters are all convinced of the virtue of concealment. As, famously, was their creator, who was apt in her later years to regale learned and inquiring fans with tea, toast, Gentleman's Relish and advice on (say) how to mend holes in rugs. Her 'inner' life – the obsessive family scenarios that fed her fiction – seemed to belong, like her clothes and hairstyle, to a period before the First World War, locked away in the past.

Hilary Spurling, in her splendid biography of 10 years ago, *Ivy When Young*, rather shared this carefully fostered impression. The tragic passions she unravelled in the lives of the Compton-Burnetts seemed more than sufficient to account for an after-life spent, as it were, writing them up. However, as she says, there turned out to be another story to tell, with its own rather different fascination: the story of how, when 'family life was in ruins, her last link with the only world she knew had been snapped by the death of her brother Noel on the Somme in 1916, and she herself had nearly died in the great influenza episode of 1918', Ivy reinvented herself as a woman and as a novelist.

The title Mrs Spurling has chosen – *Secrets of a Woman's Heart* – has a teasing irony about it, since what she's doing this time is exploring secretiveness itself as a strategy for survival. It is, as she shows, by evolving 'layer by layer the extraordinary protective armour' that Ivy became so subtle and radical a writer.

The relationship with Margaret Jourdain which sustained her, and which ended only with Margaret's death in 1951, seems to have held no 'secrets' of the sexual sort (they adopted each other, they weren't lovers). Only, shockingly, it was based on the assumption that *living* in any ambitious or indeed 'normal' way was hideously dangerous. To start with, Ivy played the invalid – there were 'months, even years, when she lay about the flat eating sweets, reading Wilkie Collins and silently watching Margaret's callers' before producing *Pastors and Masters* in 1925. They perfected what one might call, travestying F. R. Leavis, an irreverent closedness before life. Not in the social sense (their tea parties, like the Mad Hatter's, were never-ending) but in the sense of an offensive neutrality ('we are neuters') in the midst of the permanent state of hostilities represented by marriage and the family.

Like Ivy, Margaret Jourdain was a veteran of that battlefield. Her vicarage family was large, proud, almost penniless and wretchedly quarrelsome, though full of energy and talent. Three elder sisters were teachers (Eleanor eventually became Principal of St Hugh's College, Oxford), Margaret herself became an eminent historian of furniture and the domestic arts, brother Frank was a founding father of British ornithology, and Philip was a distinguished mathematician though afflicted, like the youngest sister, Milly, with multiple sclerosis, thought to be hereditary.

Mrs Spurling, who is especially good on this kind of thing, traces their histories in some detail: Margaret's early poetical leanings, suppressed in favour of furniture; the family's disgust at Philip's marriage; Eleanor's intrigues and forced retirement; Milly's lucid poems on her own decay. The final score is daunting:

> Margaret died, like her four sisters, unmarried, and though the five brothers each took a wife ... only Frank had children: they were born before the disease affecting Philip and Milly had declared itself fully, and all three died ... without issue, so that by the middle of the century it was clear that the Jourdains like the Compton-Burnetts – families of 10 and 13 children respectively – drew the line at reproducing themselves.

Margaret – formidable, mocking, protective – had had other protégés, though none so (eventually), successful as Ivy. Though it's clearly not the case, as she once confided to a strange man from Gollancz on a bus, that she was the real author ('I write all her books'), her strength and her acid wit helped stake out Ivy's special 'no-man's-land'. As did her 1920s *Country Life* set, which included Firbankian figures like Ernest Thesiger, cousin to the Viceroy of India, actor, narcissist and needleman (nothing was more terrible, wrote Beverley Nichols, than to see Ernest 'sitting under the lamplight doing this embroidery'), or interior decorator Herman Schrijver (whom Margaret referred to as 'Ivy's Jewish friend') who bet Ivy she couldn't name one heterosexual male among their acquaintance. The bleak, unillusioned tone of the novels was, as Mrs Spurling points out, part forged in this heretical set, for all 'Ivy's old-world style'.

In fact, it matched the times increasingly well. As Edward Sackville-West wrote in 1946, 'Apart from physical violence and starvation, there is no feature of the totalitarian regime which has not its counterpart in the atrocious families depicted in these books.' Or, as Mrs Spurling more moderately puts it, 'the moral economy of Ivy's books had always been organised on a war footing'. After the war her fame burgeoned. People at the tea parties included Angus Wilson, Nathalie Sarraute, Mary McCarthy . . . and Ivy perfected her techniques of evasion.

She did, however (especially after Margaret's death), unbend to some of the younger writers who sought her out, like Robert Liddell, Elizabeth Taylor and Kay Dick, who provide evidence of her kindness and generosity as well as her more 'frightening' habits, like interspersing conversations with muttered asides to imaginary characters. In 1967, two years before her death, she was made a Dame, which it's hard not to see as a tribute to her tea-table persona, as much as to her writing. She had kept her counsel; her atrocities were committed in the books. Hilary Spurling's brilliant and meticulous account – studded with scones, sticky with honey – is a study in secret survivalism.

Honest woman

Selections from George Eliot's Letters

EDITED BY GORDON S. HAIGHT

G EORGE ELIOT'S PERSONAL LIFE is one of the grand anomalies of Victorian culture. She ought to have been an outsider, a Bohemian, a George like George Sand, whereas of course she made her way to the centre of things, to become the lion of her day and its literary conscience.

Boston Brahmin Charles Eliot Norton, nervously contemplating paying a call on her at 'The Priory' in 1869, described her position with such comic, twitching refinement that it's worth quoting the whole passage:

> She is an object of great interest and great curiosity to society here. She is not received in general society, and the women who visit her are either so *emancipée* as not to mind what the world says about them, or have no social position to maintain. Lewes dines out a good deal, and some of the men with whom he dines go without their wives to his house on Sundays. No one whom I have heard speak, speaks in other than terms of respect of Mrs Lewes, but the common feeling is that it will not do.

However, as you can tell from his tone (he protests altogether too much), he managed to transcend 'common feeling' and not only go along to one of 'Mrs Lewes's Sundays' but to take Mrs Norton too. George Eliot's enormous critical prestige and popular success had overborne the old story that years before someone called Mary Ann Evans openly set up house with George Henry Lewes when he couldn't divorce his wife. But it wasn't just that: she had a special authority precisely because people came to her on her own terms, *as* an author, which they wouldn't have done anything like so much if she had been 'received in general society'. She was condemned – and freed – to live in a world more concentratedly literary than that of any of her female contemporaries.

In the letters, selected by Gordon S. Haight from his monumental nine-volume edition (1954–78), you can see the effects of this. Instead of (say) Jane Austen's network of family ties, here there's a surrogate family of colleagues, peers and (latterly) admirers. She did salvage a few old friends, and she developed a motherly relationship with Lewes's sons, but for the most part these are personal bonds created around the writing, and the warmth and respect it generated.

She had, as people remarked, a talent for friendship, and apart from a few early, preachy and pretentious letters addressed to school-friends and an ex-teacher from her evangelical days, she's a generous, concerned, thoroughly unselfish correspondent. She even worries about the egoism of not wanting to seem an egoist: '. . . my anxiety not to appear what I should *hate to be* . . . is surely not an ignoble egoistic anxiety . . .' And this is the way she hides herself. Or rather, the way she contrives to remain pseudonymous, removed from the mere market-place of prejudices and opinions and controversy. This must have been part of the secret of her impressive 'rightness' – that she questioned conventional rigidities less by what she said than by what she *was*.

The other side of this is that there is always – nearly always – an embargo on intimacy. Only one letter here reveals the passionate and needy self she kept to herself, the woman who found fulfilment with Lewes, and it is, ironically enough, a letter not to him but to that cold fish Herbert Spencer with whom she had fallen horribly in love in pre-Lewes days:

> I want to know if you can assure me that you will not forsake me, that you will always be with me as much as you can . . . I find it impossible to contemplate life under any other conditions . . . I have struggled – indeed I have – to renounce everything and be entirely unselfish, but I find myself utterly unequal to it . . . I suppose no other woman ever before wrote such a letter as this – but I am not ashamed.

One is grateful that Spencer was cad enough to preserve this explosive, desperate stuff, because it enables one to measure something of the achievement of the creation of 'George Eliot,' the person she became with Lewes. As do, more indirectly, the letters to friends and publishers in which he figures as Muse, critic and go-between, her constant and loving companion.

Their union (too close for letters) is the unspoken theme of the collection, the necessary condition for the warmth and sanity she is able to summon on topics as diverse as women's suffrage, table-rapping or the Franco-Prussian war. Their mutual solitude, as she knew, was what enabled her range and freedom as a writer. 'I prefer excommunication,' she wrote to one of her closest women friends, Barbara Bodichon, who had suggested that perhaps Lewes might be able to get a dubious divorce abroad. 'I have no earthly thing I care for, to gain by being brought within the pale of people's personal attention, and I have many things to care for that I should lose – my freedom from petty worldly torments . . . and that isolation which really keeps my charity warm . . .

Not that 'petty wordly torments' are lacking. The letters are splendidly domestic in their running commentary on the myriad, wracking changes of the weather and touchingly ordinary and wifely – and ominous – in their concern with Lewes's fragile health. His death (in 1878) is marked by a wordless gap, as though she ceased to exist for weeks on end. When she comes back she seems stunned, and only recovers herself when she can replace him (it's hard to see it in any other light) with their young friend, her devoted admirer, John Cross.

Their marriage was more shocking, in its way, than the years with Lewes had been. But as Anne Ritchie (Thackeray's daughter, who had herself married a man 17 years her junior) wrote: 'She is an honest woman, and goes in with all her might for what she is about.' It's this honesty of need, perhaps, that makes her so eloquent an advocate of what she calls, in one letter, the 'impersonal life', the life that we identify with the George Eliot of the novels:

I try to delight in the sunshine that will be when I shall never see it any more. And I think it is possible for this sort of impersonal life to attain great intensity – possible for us to gain much more independence, than is usually believed, of the small bundle of facts that make our own personality.

The girl from Mrs Kelly's

Beloved Emma: The Life of Emma Lady Hamilton

FLORA FRASER

EMMA HAMILTON WAS ENDLESSLY gossiped about, in every tone imaginable from awe to contempt. The best quick summing-up seems to have been Lady Elgin's: 'She is indeed a Whapper!' This was in 1799, in Emma's hour of triumph, when a lifetime's posing in classical attitudes paid off on the stage of world history, in her affair with Nelson. She was a heroine, larger than life, sublimely improbable and very possibly absurd. Flora Fraser's biography, which mostly lets Emma and her contemporaries speak for themselves, produces an impression of a generous giantess, a woman constructed from the outside in.

Romney's portraits of her in her teens already show her as somehow on a different scale from ordinary sitters. As of course she was – she had no social identity to speak of, and could impersonate goddesses partly because she was 'nobody', or worse. The first extraordinary thing about her is that she survived at all in the world of three dimensions, that she wasn't just a vanishing 'model' sucked down into poverty and whoredom. It seems (the early years are very murky) that her beauty was so striking, as well as classically fashionable, that she brought out the Pygmalion in people.

Sir Harry Fetherstonhaugh plucked her out of Mrs Kelly's brothel (a 'nunnery' in the style of the brothel in *Fanny Hill*) and passed her on to his friend Charles Greville, a dilettante and collector who set her up in domestic seclusion in the Edgware Road and began the process of educating her into a largeness of spirit that would match her splendid physique. She was a collector's item, 'a modern piece of virtu' as he proclaimed her ('ridiculous man' says Ms Fraser with unusual sternness), and he watched over his investment. It was he who introduced her to Romney; it was he who, when his finances became chronically embarrassed, passed her on to a more kindly and civilised collector, his uncle, the British ambassador in Naples, Sir William Hamilton.

This part of the story is always fascinating. Greville seems to have conned Emma into believing that her trip to Naples was part of her education, while to Sir William (recently widowed) he represented it as a mutually beneficial arrangement – he would be free to look for an heiress, his uncle would become the possessor of an enviable *objet*, who was also pleasantly domesticated and quite likeable in bed.

Greville is here a study in himself, the quintessential dilettante — 'the whole art of going through life tolerably is to keep oneself eager about anything'. He also seems to have been hoping to distract Sir William from a second marriage, since he was his uncle's heir. In the event (served him right) Sir William became so attached to Emma that he made her Lady Hamilton, and forced English society to acknowledge her, though at the convenient distance of Naples.

Emma's injured and statuesque innocence throughout the whole episode is (again) extraordinary. For a girl from Mrs Kelly's she had already come a long way, and now she moved from a heroic passion of resentment against Greville ('If I was with you, I would murder you and myself boath') to a fervent attachment to Sir William in the grandest, most unhesitating style.

To the astonishment of her protectors, she took herself seriously: the classical 'Attitudes' in which Sir William perfected her (and which she performed for the company after dinner) were reflected in an awesome personal straightforwardness that made people accept her as a brilliant exception, outside the rules. Greville had written to Sir William that she was 'capable of anything grand, masculine or feminine'; and Sir William, justifying his marriage, described her as 'an extraordinary being' – 'It has often been remarked that a reformed rake makes the best husband, *Why not vice versa*?' Visitors to Naples saw in her classical antiquities brought to life. This is Goethe, one of the after-dinner audience:

> The spectator . . . sees what thousands of artists would have liked to express realised before him in movements and surprising transformations . . . in her [Sir William] has found all the antiquities, all the profiles of Sicilian coins, even the Apollo Belvedere.

And so the stage was set for her apotheosis as Nelson's consort. Here the sublime teeters on the edge of the ridiculous: he came along only just in time (she was getting dangerously large in her thirties) and few observers could quite take the real life enactment of a passion on the Olympian scale. Spiteful Mrs Trench was only one of many unbelievers – 'She is bold, forward, coarse, assuming, and vain. Her figure is colossal . . . Lord Nelson is a little man, without any dignity.'

Suddenly she is a Juno lumbering among sceptics, her grandeur turned to grossness like one of Swift's simple-minded Brobdingnagians. With Nelson's death, her claims to heroic stature fell away, and the story leads with a sad inevitability to the boozy death in Calais, embittered further by the clause in Nelson's will which bequeathed her (as though she were indeed a great work of art) to the nation.

Flora Fraser doesn't moralise over the ending – not even over the nastiest part of it, Emma's failure to acknowledge her daughter by Nelson, Horatia, who watched her die, repelled and mystified. 'Why she should so fascinate is difficult to answer' is the nearest we get to a conclusion.

Ms Fraser lays out the evidence in a conscientious, noncommittal fashion that reminds one that she's a third-generation biographer, following in the footsteps of mother, and of grandmother Elizabeth Longford, and so confident (perhaps a touch too confident) that 200-year-old gossip will prove sufficiently riveting. But she has chosen her subject well – deeper speculation, one suspects, would be out of place with a character so entirely public property from the start.

Half of Shandy

Laurence Sterne: The Later Years

ARTHUR H. CASH

'HE IS IN VOGUE. He is the man of Humour, he is the toast of the British nation.' So reported Yorkshireman Sir Thomas Robinson from London in May 1760. Laurence Sterne, the vicar of Coxwold, was the hero of the hour, famous to a degree literary men seldom manage – like an actor, or a saint.

The second volume of Arthur H. Cash's Sterne biography covers the years when he became public property, following the publication of the first euphoric instalment of *Tristram Shandy*. Sterne and his creature Tristram merged into one tricksy and titillating 'character', larger than life and twice as odd, a prodigy, a 'phenomenon'. Lapdogs and racehorses were named after Tristram; Garrick befriended him; Sir Joshua Reynolds painted him; 19-year-old James Boswell, looking for someone to hero-worship, tried him out for size in a 'poetical Epistle':

> He runs about from place to place
> Now with my Lord, then with his Grace . . .
> A budding whisper flys about,
> Where'er he comes they point him out.

Boswell, though, went on to settle on someone quite different, soundly three-dimensional Dr Johnson, whose maggots and eccentricities were ballasted with moral authority. Sterne was slippery, skinny and ambiguous, his fascination tied up with his contradictions – the obscenity with the sentiment, the tears with the wit, the clergyman with the buffoon.

Moreover, he had stage-managed his own début, ghosting a letter from his mistress to Garrick ('The Author . . . is a kind and generous friend of mine') and arranging for Hogarth to be shown another letter to a third party, in which Sterne wished – all innocently – for a Hogarth illustration for his book . . . and so forth. Small wonder it soon became the height of fashion to complain about how fashionable he was: 'A very insipid and tedious performance,' opined Horace Walpole enviously; and the classics tutor at Emmanuel, one Richard Farmer, solemnly predicted that 'in the course of 20 years, should anyone wish to refer to the book in question, he will be obliged to go to an antiquary for it'.

There was more to his respectable contemporaries' distaste than fashion, however. One of Sterne's most lasting friendships was with dangerous John Wilkes, atheist, rake, and proto-revolutionary; and his admirers included d'Holbach, Diderot and the Encyclopaedists. The philosopher David Hume pronounced *Tristram Shandy* 'the best Book that has been writ by any Englishman these 30 years . . . bad as it is'. Shameless Shandy was a subversive, all the more effective because he posed as a humble jester ('alas, poor Yorick!'), and threw off his jibes against authority with a whimsical air. He was profoundly, irretrievably *indecorous* – not just in the matter of *doubles entendres,* smut and playing with dirt ('a naughty boy, and a little apt to dirty his *frock,*' said motherly blue stocking Elizabeth Montagu), but in the way he upset hierarchies and categories of meaning. He was an intellectual, but he refused to sweep out his mind, or spring-clean his imagination – and (worse) he persuaded his readers to collude with him in his nastiness and irreverence.

It's this promiscuous closeness with strangers – on or off the page – that's perhaps the most striking and extraordinary thing about him. Professor Cash, after patiently tracing and identifying hundreds of friends and contacts, sums it up this way: 'Sterne had a knack for intimacy, in his letters, his life and his fiction. His letters to his bankers . . . read as though written to brothers.'

The cumulative effect is close, cloying, a touch repulsive even – a whisper in one's ear, a breath on one's neck, a thumb in one's buttonhole. One of Professor Cash's most telling exhibits is a caricature in oils by the historical painter John Hamilton Mortimer reproduced on the handsome dustjacket. It shows a boozy, dishevelled and unshaven group of boon companions of the 1760s – all flushed faces, grey jowls, hectic, rolling eyes – with a grinning, emaciated wigless Sterne baring his breast to display the locket that holds the picture of his last chaste and sentimental love, Eliza Draper.

It's an image that is at once comically congenial and somehow chilling. Sterne was, of course, dying of TB, and he knew it; indeed, he'd been dying all his life a lot more consciously than most of us (he had his first major haemorrhage as a student at Cambridge) and it was that awareness that gave the edge of urgency to his jokes – especially the ones about sex.

Professor Cash is not given to elaborate theorising about Sterne's subconscious goings-on, but he does point out that the sentimental affairs (and the wretched quarrels with his wife) were not about love (or hate) but the desperate desire for *health*. Sex 'straight' reminded Sterne of his own mortality; only postponed, avoided, played with did it promise life. He regularly compared writing with childbirth ('I miscarried of my tenth volume') and he played both father and mother to his own creations. His wife Elizabeth and his daughter Lydia were, in the end, excised like rejected chapters, less real to him than the life on paper.

In effect, and ironically enough, this means that this splendid biography makes him *less* real, and a lot more distant, than he is in his fiction. In the books he is everyone's closest friend; here, he is a bit of a monster, a man who bled black ink for posterity, and wrote out his death. There's a macabre appropriateness about the postscript: Sterne's body was snatched from the grave for an anatomy lesson almost as soon as he was laid to rest, by those experts in immortality known as resurrection men.

Nothing by halves

The Letters of Edith Wharton

EDITED BY R. W. B. LEWIS AND NANCY LEWIS

EDITH WHARTON'S POWERS OF mobilising people and making things happen extended, famously, far beyond her fiction. Her good friend Henry James pretended awe in the face of her energy, wealth and social appetites and heard in the sound of her car-horn ('your silver-sounding toot') an echo of the Last Trump. He consented, of course, to be called back to life every time, but got his revenge by portraying her as a comic figure, a matron of misrule.

This picture was given new depth by the revelations about her passionate affair (at 45) with fellow expatriate journalist and writer W. Morton Fullerton, in R. W. B. Lewis's 1975 biography; and in this book of the letters he's able to reveal more by printing letters to Fullerton which came mysteriously to light only in 1980. The intensity of her response to Fullerton took her by surprise ('you woke me from a long lethargy . . . all one side of me was asleep') and so did his absences, mystifications and lies:

> Dear, won't you tell me the meaning of this silence . . . this aching uncertainty . . . we might have had together, at least for a short time, a life of exquisite collaborations . . .

But it was not to be.

Morton seems to have been a practised juggler, who liked to keep several ladies in the air at once, so that Edith found herself, humiliatingly, elaborating a whole love-story round a man who only wanted the occasional intimate episode:

> What you wish, apparently, is to take of my life the inmost & uttermost that a woman – a woman like me – can give, for an hour, now & then,

when it suits you; & when the hour is over, to leave me out of your
mind & out of your life. I think I am worth more than that . . .

Professor Lewis suggests that these complaints 'cannot but strike a
disquieting note for a reader in the late 1980s', but I'm not sure why.
It isn't as if this particular problem has dated. It's true that Edith
revealed her vulnerability, but she also copes with it splendidly. In the
end, you feel, she proves that she was simply better at loving than
Fullerton – more able to rise to the occasion, rather as she did when
she set about gruelling war-work six years later in 1914. She did nothing
by halves (this was what terrorised James) but she was very good at
patching up disasters, and before long she'd rewritten Morton as one
of her entourage of friends.

She had already radically rearranged most parts of her life; it only
remained to divorce mindless and increasingly manic-depressive Teddy
Wharton, who'd married her as 'Pussy' Jones back in Old New York
and whom she'd long left behind in the senses that counted. She could
look back on the ready-made, dull distinction that stifled her so long
with brisk aversion: '. . . for 12 years I seldom knew what it was to be,
for more than an hour or two of the 24, without an intense feeling of
nausea . . . this form of neurasthenia consumed the best years of my
youth . . . *Mais quoi*! I worked through it, & came out on the other
side . . .'

Born to a fortune, she earned a bigger one from her writing; born
into a monstrous network of cousins and snobbish connections, she
invented her own (equally snobbish it has to be said) cultural and
literary world; born American, she improved her heritage by settling
in France the better to celebrate and satirise her native land. Rumour
even had it that she was illegitimate, based, it seems, mainly on the
fact that there was not the slightest precedent in her family for her
talent or energy.

Energy is the key word. Given the busyness of her social life, and
the impression left by the photos (semi-regal, all corseted curves, pearl
chokers and small dogs), it's easy to conclude that she merely swapped
one established role for another. However, the letters tell a different

story: she designed and sustained her personal world rather as she restored houses and made gardens.

The letters aren't mostly meditative or analytic (she never wrote much about her writing); instead they're a vivid jumble of plans, *aperçus*, provocations, descriptions. Gossip she prized; and over the years the writer she came to feel closest to was Trollope. 'I'm trying now to think out his case in relation to his contemporaries,' she wrote to Bernard Berenson in 1934 '& a strange and interesting one it is. To them he was simply a good story-teller, whose books one could "leave about."'

She felt the same fate overtaking her work. Would the novels have been better if she hadn't had to invent her life alongside them? She would have thought not, would have said – unlike most of her modernist, male contemporaries – that you can't separate the two.

The bright, ferocious flames of his internal ether

The Letters of Charles Dickens: Volume VII, 1853–1855, The Pilgrim Edition

EDITED BY GRAHAM STOREY, KATHLEEN TILLOTSON
AND ANGUS EASSON

NO WONDER DICKENS BELIEVED in spontaneous combustion. The three years covered by this volume are so absurdly full of life that he seems himself in danger of burning up or flying apart.

The labours of the Oxford editors have retrieved 1,271 letters from this brief period, bearing witness to the extraordinary balancing-act he was managing: the public man and do-gooder, the man of letters, the crony and diner-out, the amateur actor, the editor (*Household Words*), the friend, the mentor, the traveller writing home. Not to mention the novelist. At the beginning of the volume he's finishing *Bleak House*, in the middle he writes *Hard Times*, and by the end he has started *Little Dorrit*.

At the height of his powers, he is ebullient, sentimental, a practised and hard-nosed literary entrepreneur. If he believes in unrealities – like spontaneous combustion – he does it with shameless conviction. The victims go up in flames because they're old and gin-soaked, he assures a sceptical George Henry Lewes. His own fuel is altogether more mysterious stuff – seemingly inexhaustible psychic energy.

Except that he did get ill, for about a week, and frightened himself, in the last stages of *Bleak House*: 'I have been shaving a man every morning – a stranger to me – with big gaunt eyes and a hollow cheek', he wrote to Lady Eastlake. And he finished the book in relative retreat in Boulogne, away from the teeming London that gave it its epic shape. In fact, he hardly notices London any more in the letters, now that he's got it onto the page so triumphantly. Only the occasional casual afterthought registers the city – 'Today there is a great thaw, and London looks as if it had a gigantic dirty nose' – where it's a familiar grubby urchin, for all its immensity. Nor does he comment on the creative process, though he *does* confess to *not* having invented the character of Harold Skimpole in *Bleak House*, who is not merely based on, but is, Leigh Hunt: 'I suppose he is the most exact portrait that ever was painted in words! . . . It is an absolute reproduction of a real man.' (Later on we find him apologising to the original – 'I am deeply sorry, and . . . I feel I did wrong in doing it'. But in fact he got the egregious effrontery of Hunt so right, that he didn't care, and their friendship was hardly affected at all.)

Escaping for a while from novel-writing in the autumn of 1853 he goes on a continental jaunt with Wilkie Collins and painter Augustus Egg, whipping through Italy with impatient zest. It's wonderful in this pretty land, of course, *but*:

> I am so restless to be doing – and always shall be, I think, so long as I have any portion in Time – that if I were to stay more than a week in any one city here, I believe I should be half desperate to begin some new story!!

So by his own frenetic logic he has to stay on the move in order to 'rest' from writing. It's the same story a little less than a year later, when he's finished *Hard Times* and is troubled by 'dreadful thoughts of getting away somewhere':

> *Restlessness*, you will say. Whatever it is, it is always driving me, and I cannot help it . . . If I couldn't walk fast and far, I should just explode and perish.

His travels are mostly described in the comic vein, though. On the earlier journey's channel crossing, for instance, he describes, courtesy of Collins's malicious eye-view ('raised aloft on a high pile of luggage') a deckfull of sick ladies 'wet through . . . like an immense picnic party with everybody intent upon a pigeon pie of her own – from the immense number of white basins'. He celebrates discomfort wherever he finds it, in fact – 'We have been in the most extraordinary vehicles – like

Swings, like boats, like Noah's arks, like barges and enormous bed-
steads.'

And wherever he goes he not only sends letters, but demands them.
Writing to Georgina Howarth from Naples he bewails the absence of
mail – 'I wish I had arranged ... to find some letters here. It is a
blank to stay for five days in a place without any.' For of course he lives
on words, anybody's and everybody's. He may cruelly reject aspiring
contributors to *Household Words*, but he very much enjoys doing it:

> People don't plunge into Churches and play the Organs, without knowing
> the notes or having the ghost of an ear. Yet fifty people a day will rush
> into manuscript ... who have no earthly qualification but the actual
> physical act of writing.

With real writers he is circumspect. Mrs Gaskell, whose *Cranford* and
North and South he serialised, brought him out in facetious-but-furious
asides ('If I were Mr G. O Heaven how I would beat her!'). He professed
to think Collins's apprentice *Hide and Seek* 'much beyond Mrs Gaskell',
and was even a touch gratified that circulation went down during *North
and South* – 'Mrs Gaskell's story, so divided, is wearisome in the last
degree.' In *Hard Times* he kept out of her way, plot-wise ('I am not
striking'), and in general of course their styles couldn't have been more
different. When she writes about working people, and about the north,
she's calling on her intimate observation, and she does it in the
mediating anti-excess tones of the realist. Whereas he is melodramatic
by conviction.

He was, at the same time, indefatigable in his efforts on behalf of
Miss Coutts's Home for reclaiming fallen women, and many of these
letters are to her, and are eminently practical. Still there's the characteristic note ('one more chance in this bitter weather') even here; and
perhaps it's not unfair to note that it was in mass *readings* (an audience
of 3,700 in St George's Hall in Bradford) that he seems to have come
closest to working people.

These years are of course only an arbitrary slice of his life. However,
the volume does acquire an almost fictional plot of its own when,
towards the end, one finds him writing to Forster, gestating *Little Dorrit*:

> Am altogether in a dishevelled state of mind – motes of new books in
> the dirty air, miseries of older growth threatening to close upon me . . .

And, seemingly summoned from the ether by this mood, his old adolescent love Maria Beadnell (now, slightly ominously, middle-aged Mrs Winter) resurfaces suddenly in a letter – 'the remembrance of your hand, came upon me with an influence that I cannot express to you. Three or four and twenty years vanished like a dream.' Her reappearance provokes a kind of self-analysis that's rare with him – 'the wasted tenderness of those hard years . . . I refer to it the habit of suppression which now belongs to me . . . which makes me chary of showing my affections, even to my children, except when they are very young.' All sorts of discontents and anxieties begin to surface, and although Mrs Winter herself is soon fobbed off, the excuse he uses (that his work demands all his time and energy) rings true:

> A necessity upon me now – as at most times – of wandering about in
> my own wild way, to think . . . I hold my inventive capacity on the
> stern condition that it must master my whole life, often have complete
> possession of me . . .

Despite the many-sidedness of his life, this makes sense. His sociability by the end almost looks like a way of keeping people at a distance, while he gets on with the job.

II

Post-War Life Writing

First person singular

Sleepless Nights

ELIZABETH HARDWICK

T HIS IS A FICTIONAL autobiography – an autobiography of just such a scrupulous, reticent, cunning kind as one might expect from Elizabeth Hardwick. All her critic's experience and discrimination, all her scepticism about making life over into stories and people into characters ('People do not live their biographies') has been turned on herself. And the result is an impressively personal book that manages to fit none of the formulas.

In looking back over a life that led from Kentucky (religion and racehorses) to literary/artistic New York, and many worlds between, her point of view is dictated by a sense – a conviction, even – of her own present aloneness. This seems to have worked back on the past so that she recalls other people too as fundamentally and vividly *alone*, their lifelines broken into fragments.

So the book is populated by isolates, people encapsulated in their own settings and idioms from suave literary bachelors to exhausted Irish cleaning ladies, and from Billie Holiday seen in Harlem to careful, saving senior citizens in country retreats. It is a lone person's life, outlined through friends, acquaintances and neighbours, the outer circle. As for the inner circle, the attempt to cure loneliness with love, or with marriage – that has slipped away. 'I was then a "we,"' she writes, referring to her marriage to Robert Lowell, doubly broken by their divorce and his death – as if to say that the 'we' could never have written this book, and so can't really appear in it.

Homes seem to have turned into hotels, people into hotel-dwellers, 'undomestic, restless, unreliable, changeable, disloyal'. And yet there is a regard, and a generosity, in her portrayal of them that make even the saddest or most brittle seem possibly heroic. Miss Cramer, for instance, once a music teacher, a snob, a genteel traveller, now a derelict in 'dreadful freedom', with her 'dress of printed silk, soiled here and there with a new pattern of damage and no stockings to cover her bruised, discoloured legs'. Or a survivor of another sort, spoiled, desiccated, once-promising Alex who suddenly 'is radical again and has the beard of a terrorist. The students like him and the faculty does not. He lives in a dreadful house and mows the lawn – starting over, poor, *on time* as it were.' The breaks and new directions in people's lives don't at all point one way (there's a very good section on variegated 1940s Marxists trying to cope with this, in their personal histories). Miss Hardwick is scrupulous always to tell other lives, that add up differently.

Thus, New York's savage divorces are balanced comically (it's often a very humorous book) with the way they arrange things in Amsterdam:–

> There, first husbands and first wives are always at the same dinner parties and birthday celebrations with their second husbands and wives. Divorces and fractured loves mingled together as if the past were a sort of vinegar blending with the oil of the present.

The care she takes with this salad simile is characteristic too. It's often said, sometimes rightly, that critics write fiction badly, because they're hopelessly self-conscious. Elizabeth Hardwick, however, has contrived to turn her critic's virtues – a generous interest in others, a sharp sense of the boundaries between literature and living – into novelistic assets.

There *is* a sense of strain in *Sleepless Nights*, of tight-strung, nervous energy, but that's essential to its effect of individuality and honesty. It's also, curiously, a hopeful book, because it suggests that aloneness, the absence or loss of intimacy, doesn't mean the loss of humanity.

Client relationships

An English Madam: The Life and Work of Cynthia Payne

PAUL BAILEY

'MADAME CYN', SHOUTED THE headlines: 'luncheon vouchers', 'Streatham'. It was somehow obvious from the start that Cynthia Payne's 'disorderly house' was not the usual kind: that it was, on the contrary, bizarrely orderly. As details of Cynthia's domestic economy emerged the curious subculture of 'Cranmore' looked, in fact, so exactly an inversion of the banalities of middle-class existence that legal outrage seemed absurd. It wasn't just a matter of the 10p and 15p vouchers clutched by the queue of middle-aged-to-elderly clients on the stairs (though these puzzled the police); nor of the clients' own professions – church, civil service, politics, the bar. As Cynthia's trial and appeal (plus her recent confessions in the *News of the World*) have revealed, her Streatham brothel was not a house but a Home, a place where the repressions of everyday life were reflected in a fun-house mirror. And she herself was that most English of institutions, a 'character'. Hence Paul Bailey's splendid study, *An English Madam*, which removes Cynthia (with her willing cooperation) out of the commercial underworld, and installs her in a niche in the Dickensian tradition of social fantasy.

There is after all, Mr Bailey insinuates, a certain similarity between Cynthia's role and that of, say, Mrs Todgers in *Martin Chuzzlewit*. She is the landlady as comic genius loci, the 'hostess' restored to matronly dignity. Consider the management skills involved: the house, for instance, was cleaned by 'Philip', who paid Cynthia a modest sum to stand over him with a switch and complain when he (always accidentally) missed a tiny corner. Roughly the same arrangement, with 'Rodney', took care of the large garden. Drinks were served by the ex-Squadron leader, disguised as the butler or (judging from his photo-graph) Theda Bara as the mood took him. Sometimes a noted political commentator helped out as 'Tweeny', and was spanked by Theda Bara for answering back. 'Gregory' provided an advice-sheet on the apparatus of domination ('WIG: as most dominants are blonde, a platinum wig or hairpiece worn to show below the helmet, as stated'). Once, the bank manager, a difficult customer who could never be humiliated enough, was brought to the verge of ecstasy when pelted with the contents of the hoover, which Philip had been warned to fill to bursting. More conventional clients watched blue movies, and 'went upstairs' when they felt like it. The party atmosphere was maintained by a system of paying (£25) on entry (hence the famous vouchers), with discounts for pensioners and the impotent. It all sounds like an inspired experiment in energy saving, with Cynthia ('Lady Domina' as she was known to the help, though the Squadron Leader, an old friend, called her 'Madam Baloney') orchestrating the follies like a benevolent deity.

The carnival spirit however, depended – as carnival spirit tends to – on the conviction, shared by Cynthia and her party-goers, that the world outside Cranmore was an alien, bleak, unaccommodating place. If Mr Bailey's instincts as a writer led him back to the nineteenth century it must have been partly because Cranmore was a kind of time-machine, a refuge from the present where, for example, second childhoods were catered for (again very Dickensian), and where it was taken for granted that your little ways and wants might be entirely out of sync with the greyish person who'd 'settled down' or 'grown old'. It's not exactly that the set-up *resembles* a Victorian comedy of humours: a lot of the time it *is* one, and the intensity of the illusion is a measure of the futuristic bleakness, to Cranmorians, of the supposedly permissive society. What they wanted was the delirious unfreedom – queueing in their socks, with tickets, poached eggs on toast afterwards – of living in the past, not necessarily their own pasts, though some of the fantasies are very specific, but a collective daydream of early life.

Cynthia understood all this so well, apparently, because her own early life (in fact, her first thirty-odd years) had been fairly unrelievedly awful. As the book's hilarious account of the historic police raid modulates into the story of her experiences before she found her vocation and acquired her house, the party atmosphere is rapidly dissipated. In many ways we still seem to be in the nineteenth century, but now the ambience is less English, more Maupassant. Cynthia's mother died young, in 1943, and her father, whom she and her sister hardly knew (he'd been a hairdresser on the cruise liners) wasn't well-equipped to cope alone, though he had to, since potential second wives found his girls too difficult, and his own conscious respectability cut him off from the sort of surrounding support his working-class background might have provided. Each sister reacted in her own way – Cynthia 'ran wild', used bad language, and displayed a generous curiosity about sex, Melanie became sensible and 'posh' (and married a police inspector). As 'Cinders' drifted away from home on the south-east coast and into London (failed hairdresser, waitress, unmarried mother) she seems, by her own account, to have lost control of her life with frightening speed. She semi-starved for a season in a slum basement with a derelict who 'looked like Christie', though all he did was, harmlessly, to collect other social casualties into a family of sorts. Her men seem to have been either father-substitutes (though penniless and inept – she only managed one 'sugar daddy') or sexy spivs like 'Sam', who worked in the amusement arcade, and got her pregnant with nightmarish regularity.

This is a twilight world of female drudgery (waitressing, preg-nancies), of more-or-less lost children (for her first son she arranged fostering, her second was adopted), of abortions and sexual fear. Only as she nears her destiny as a Madam does Cynthia seem to be a person at all. Indeed, she never is quite a person; she moves from unperson to personage (via a short and unpleasant spell on the game herself) in a most disconcerting fashion. As a casualty of family life, and an exile from it, she is a self-made expert in the weird, nostalgic fantasies about domesticity that set the tone at Cranmore. Perhaps the point is made most painfully and absurdly when her long-estranged father, lonelier than ever, and now an old man, becomes one of her party-goers, and joins the queue on the stairs. This is, in a way, Cynthia's moment of triumph, the closing of the magic circle. She provides the home from home, a haven for refugees from the respectable world she couldn't live in, and becomes herself a motherless Mother Superior. (House rules excluded men under forty – 'Old men are more appreciative' – and her 'girls' were chosen because they did it for love as well as money.)

And so we return to the domain of Madam Baloney, the hilarity by now slightly shadowed, the humour blacker. Cynthia has preserved letters from her clients specifying their wants, and a selection of the most picturesque of these forms the funniest part of the book. A methodical diplomat describes in enormous detail how the lady of his dreams ('aged 38–46 if possible, and preferably English [including Jewish], otherwise European, blonde or brunette') is to create the precise quality that turns him on: 'a *very* strong, *natural* odour coming through her blouse from under her arms'. After instructions about not washing and so on, he continues.

> My request is really quite a simple one and not really all that demanding, if you consider that less than 100 years ago, when ladies seldom took a bath and scent was too costly for most people to afford, it was considered perfectly normal for ladies to smell of 'B.O' . . .

And he hints darkly at tortures of the damned on the rush-hour tube of a hot summer's evening. Others are briefer, and perhaps less sincere:

> Honoured Partygiver.
> Can you supply a nun at your next shindig? Severe face and Irish accent for preference.
> Yours beatifically,
> 'Decameron George'

What they all have in common is longing for that lost past, that time before they grew up and became insurance men or vicars or whatever, when women dominated and enveloped them.

Many can only do it when reminded of Nanny ('Who's been a naughty boy then?'). Some hanker after housework as the only really exciting thing, like the retired police superintendent who pursues one of Cynthia's 'girls' back home to Somerset to clean her oven in the nude while 'Agatha' whips away. 'Agatha', in fact, comes dangerously close to enjoying her work: 'I thought of all those years washing my husband's socks and underpants, cooking his meals, waiting on him hand and foot, and it suddenly gave me a lovely feeling, punishing that policeman.' But this isn't Cynthia's line: she never married, after all, and is more disinterested, 'unswervingly loyal', indeed, Bailey discovers, 'to the curious notion that the male is the superior of the species'. When they left her house, they returned to their dog-collared or pin-striped adult disguises, and (you realize, with a dazed feeling) to running the society we live in.

Paul Bailey, I think, relished his task because he saw in Cranmore's alternative economy a satire on normalcy, and more specifically on the family as an institution. Cynthia provided a place where 'earnest obsessionists' could painlessly (unless they insisted) act out their quirky emendations on the family scenario, and thus unwittingly proclaim (as it turned out) the quiet insanity of English life and manners. The satiric effect is, however, in the end overlaid with a rather different one: a sense that this particular comic subculture is autonomous, endemic, changeless. Cranmore's world reflects remarkably few of the things that are supposed to have happened to relations between the sexes in the last hundred years. Except of course that they can be written about – something Bailey here does marvellously well. For the rest it's as though the only testimonies to a century of hectic change are roll-on deodorants, Philip's hoover, and assorted electronic gadgets, littering a family mansion still really inhabited by our great-grandfathers in short trousers, or, possibly, skirts.

Orient of the mind

Profile of Lesley Blanch

LESLEY BLANCH HAD JUST returned to the south of France from a visit to Turkey. 'I'm at home anywhere and nowhere,' she'd said, and I saw why when I climbed through the jungly tunnel of foliage in her steep little garden and stepped through the looking-glass into her Persian parlour, all latticed windows, low divans and overlapping rugs. 'The Orient of my mind,' she announced jokily, with nonetheless something of the air of a satisfied magician – a small, ageless, quicksilver woman in a striped cotton jellaba, who reclined leaning on an elbow to answer my questions.

These were, first, inevitably, about her style of living. She must be a ruthlessly practical dreamer, I realised, to have stamped her desires so clearly on everything surrounding her. So we started with gardens. The romantic green twilight, she said, is achieved by concentrating not on flowers but on leaves – 'leaves of every kind, mimosa, cypress, fig, jasmine, thickets of bamboo, oranges and lemons and datura . . . If you sleep under the datura it's supposed to send you mad for love, but, she added with an air of gallant regret, 'there's no one sleeping under mine.'

She has lived here alone now for 10 years, but it's not the first house she's 'made Turkish': there was an earlier one up the hill in Roquebrune village which she shared with her husband writer-diplomat Romain Gary 30 years ago. After their divorce she tried Paris but hated its greyness so settled again for the south. 'I craved the sun. I never feel the need for people, or much else, if it shines on me . . .'

Her love of sunshine is not the only reason, however, why she has not returned to England. (She became a French citizen on marrying dashing Gary in 1946.) Animal quarantine regulations of 'pig-headed rigidity' (I'm to make sure to put this in my piece) also keep her pets and hence herself out. She loves animals – 'but for my travels there'd be a menagerie'. Indeed, pictures of animals are everywhere : an Indian painting of a tree-bear, a pathetic Victorian spaniel needing a home, stray naïve paintings, taken in, 'out of charity'.

And it seems to be true that her things are her pets, as it were. The room is furnished with fetish-objects; everything has a story, a sentimental footnote, a personal 'point' – 'I prefer things to people, you don't have to entertain things, they keep you company and they're loyal . . .'

She's not, of course, a mere armchair traveller herself, but she knows how they tick. That was the secret of her first book and surprise best-seller *The Wilder Shores of Love* in 1954, with its shamelessly romantic evocation of the lives of French and English women who turned their backs on the grey North ('comfort maybe, but hysterical comfort') and chose the passionate East. 'At the time Romain was First Secretary to the French Embassy at Berne in Switzerland – which I found a place of absolutely hallucinatory boredom – and I took off to North Africa, to the Sahara, and began thinking about other ladies who'd turned East. The East attracted them romantically and adventurously; they willed things into a pattern they liked. It's rare . . . You need imagination and will combined for this sort of transformation of your life – not into fiction exactly, but into something which becomes fact in the living of it.'

Her new biography on French writer Pierre Loti – traveller, romantic, egocentric and shameless and passionate poseur, who was admired by the adolescent Proust and even by an ironic Henry James – is again an intimate portrait, a kind of conspiracy with her dubious and nowadays rather discredited hero. 'A wonderful combination of subject and author,' says her publisher Philip Ziegler of Collins, with the air of a man who perhaps got more than he bargained for. Not that Lesley Blanch idolises Loti as his contemporary fans did: 'I would have found him maddening, not at all attractive, despite all the women . . . imagine, a midget charmer.'

What she recognises in Pierre Loti is the completeness of his dedication to fantasy: the house in provincial Rochefort that concealed a lavish private mosque behind its quiet, bourgeois frontage; the discontented spirit that sent him off again and again on new journeys, new affairs of the heart; the romantic hubris that drove him to reject his own appearance ('I was not my type,' is his immortal line) and to try every means from gymnastics to lifts and cosmetics to transform it. She does, of course, find him frequently funny, whereas he seems to have found himself grandly pathetic. Nonetheless, the identification is close.

One thing she certainly shares with Loti is his hatred of the colonising culture he himself (as a French naval officer) was a part of. Like him, she is fierce against the West's arrogant materialism – what she sums up in shorthand as 'machine-mindedness, big business': 'West' spells true alienation to her.

Her response to this is a combination of domestic retreat and rebellion. She will rhapsodise about clothes: 'I've a beautiful collection of exotica ... gold-embroidered velvet jackets, pantaloons, Turkish court robes, men's kaftans and burnous...' She's a skilled needle-woman, too, and used to create pictures in *gros point* of places she'd visited. 'I'd do the picture as I'd go, no tracing in advance, just stick in the needle and start on the Nile or a tea-house in Afghanistan ... Like the heroines of *Wilder Shores*, she finds the habits of submission exciting because they're strange – a role to play.

Otherwise, she's all for rebellion: 'I've been a rebel throughout my life. I *am* disciplined about some things, but I've no social disciplines ... I haven't wanted to be as selfish as I probably am; I do have regrets that I haven't been more understanding of certain people – the few I've really cared about.

Again, she finds parallels with Loti – 'he had nearly everything, but there's something that makes people miserable' – and with Romain Gary, who committed suicide two years ago: 'Adventurous people cut and run'.

As my time with her ran out, and I was about to plunge again into the green pool of her garden, she suddenly sounded hungry for change, as though she might strike camp any minute: 'I might live in Turkey, I'm very tempted, I long to have a house-slave, someone who'd make me more time to write . . . North Africa perhaps? They do cherish the old, which is a very glorious thought.'

But then, her great gift to her readers has all along been her romantic restlessness and sheer dissatisfaction. It's this quality that makes her writing addictive – what she calls in a nice phrase from the new book, 'the habit of faraway places'.

Last testament

Adieux: A Farewell to Sartre

SIMONE DE BEAUVOIR TRANSLATED BY PATRICK O'BRIAN

This book is a deliberate affront to conventional notions of privacy and dignity. It's an exact, stoical account of Sartre's disintegration during his last 10 years, and in writing it Simone de Beauvoir is testifying, with a kind of obstinate scrupulosity, to their shared freedom from all such conventional decencies as would – for example – keep a great man's image 'intact'.

'Honesty suited us,' she said in a 1973 interview – as though too much truth might be damaging in less extraordinary lives. And there's something of the same pride in the writing here. Sartre's dying, you are meant to feel, is watchable because he had himself unfolded the possibilities of his experience (in the books, in his political life) so honestly. The book is as much a matter of keeping the record straight as a labour of love, from this point of view, and indeed the refusal of sentimental language is itself part of the pain of the thing.

We start in 1970, with Sartre at 65, in a frenzy of activity, involved with the militants, the Maoists in particular. Protest meetings, speeches, articles, manifestos, demonstrations, jostle with his work on Flaubert. He is working to redefine the role of the intellectual, in terms of 'decentralising and concrete' alliances when, out of the blue, come the first cruel intimations that old age means to decentralise him in its own way: at the start only hints of dizziness and vertigo; then in May of the following year a slight stroke, that pulls his mouth sideways in the night; and in July, another.

Still, he's most inconvenienced by terminal problems with his remaining teeth. He resurrects himself, almost magically. At the same time, he suffers from incontinence, leaving behind occasional small puddles that could be blamed on the cat, if there was a cat. You get the sense that the people around him now start to divide into two groups – those intimate (mostly women) friends, de Beauvoir above all, who read the signs; and the activists and literary contacts who see him as a figurehead, a spokesman, a signatory, and through whom he maintains a kind of collusion with youth.

Since de Beauvoir insists on the material truth, her focus shifts more and more onto the daily business of living (dying), away from the political life and the projects. They go on, but at a painful distance after the third stroke, in 1973, which leaves him for the first time undeniably mentally damaged, 'wandering', haunted by phantom appointments, and wearing 'a fixed smile of universal kindness' upon his face, 'caused by a slight paralysis of the facial muscles'. Worse blows follow: the progressive failure of his eyesight, which divorces him from the world of books; the last cigarette, the never-quite-last whisky; the diabetes. All this interspersed with happy but no longer believable periods of recovery, travel, talk.

One of the things that de Beauvoir most wants to insist on is the way the style of life they'd evolved held up under the strain. The women friends that surrounded Sartre shared him with her, as usual, and shared something of her dread. And he was helped, supported, 'coddled' even, without being immobilised or isolated. Until nearly the end he lived in 'vagrant' style, which removes some of the bitterness from her account of the closing stages of his public career – the legs that won't carry him on marches, his being increasingly 'spoken for' by others, in particular by Pierre Victor, under the guise of the 'dialogue' with a new generation he so prized.

She tried, she says, to persuade herself that he had somehow 'chosen' his death, but she failed. True, he had driven himself obsessively, but he was not 'the master of his fate'. When the end came in 1980 she wanted him lied to, and was grateful for the drugs that blurred his consciousness. At the funeral, 'I told myself that this was exactly the funeral Sartre had wanted, and that he would never know about it.'

His dispersal was finally complete. The only kind of consolation

she allows herself is his afterlife in words: here (in the second part of
the book) she transcribes a series of taped conversations they had in
1974, as a substitute for the work he could no longer do, in which she
prompted him to gather his thoughts, once again, on writing, childhood,
sexuality, and time.

It is a sceptic's testament – a sort of upside-down version of those
confessions and conversions priests like to extract from atheists on
their death-beds. What de Beauvoir extracts is a set of casual and
irreverent reflections on the necessity of living in the present. Or even
the future:

> I've always thought . . . that you don't have experience, that you don't
> grow older. The slow accumulation of events and experiences that gradu-
> ally create a character is one of the myths of the late nineteenth century.

He congratulates himself on belonging to old age, at least in the sense
that 'I'm not an adult any more' and 'only faintly' male. 'Adult,' 'male'
sex, we learn, he never really enjoyed ('I was more a masturbator of
women than a copulator') perhaps because he disliked 'letting go' –
ideally 'the other person was yielded up and I was not'.

He connects his writings with his general predilection for what is
against nature, humanly invented: even in the matter of food, it's always
been the cooked for him, not the raw. He goes into a comic ecstasy of
squeamishness at the thought of fresh fruit. 'It's lying on the ground,
in the grass. It's not there for me; it doesn't come from me.' Nature,
fecundity – 'all that' – constitute 'a philosophical problem'.

Perhaps I am exaggerating the lightness of the conversation. Certainly graver matters are touched on: 'I wrote, which has been the
essence of my life. I've succeeded in what I longed for from the age of
seven or eight . . .' But what de Beauvoir gives here (and, surely, what
she wanted) is the specifically, even absurdly, human. She ends with a
dialogue about God – that 'infinite intermediary' Sartre and she had
learnt to do without, though His Almighty absence explained why one
must face one's freedom, why one must write everything out again,
including, or especially, age and death:

> You and I, for example, have lived without paying attention to the

problem [of God]. And yet we've lived; we feel that we've taken an interest in our world . . .

To keep God out, you need to deconstruct the myth of 'the great man', too. This, or something like it, is de Beauvoir's logic, and she's probably right. 'Adieu' – except that *le bon Dieu* has nothing to do with it, 'this life owes nothing to God'.

What a frightful bore it is to be Gore

Profile of Gore Vidal

GORE VIDAL IS ON the brink of immortality. He must be, he has a biographer, and so will soon have a Life. Or will he? True, he's lately taken to writing down luminous, pastoral reminiscences about his boyhood age of innocence (which did not last long, and he couldn't wait to get it over with) – going brown and barefoot into the Senate to visit his grandfather, blind Senator Gore from Oklahoma, and flying across the States in the Thirties with his dashing aviator father, Gene. But for the rest? 'Most biographies are about love and marriage and divorce and children, the more autistic the better, and alcoholism and suicide. The usual American writer's life. I seem to have missed most of the Great Things . . .'

About the only way in which he's a rounded character is physical. These days he's, well, large, and indeed looks magisterial, not entirely unlike the Senator. ('All the senators were fat – I always thought everybody's grandfather was fat and a senator.') He's disappointed in himself. 'I never thought I would lose my beauty,' he says, waving it away with sincere regret. He likes people's outsides and (worse, much worse) says so, instead of claiming to be interested in their souls. His new novel, *Empire*, about the rise of Theodore Roosevelt, is one of his respectable ones, but nonetheless continues in its own way his scandalous polemic against inwardness, niceness, the mystification of the personal, 'real folks', unconscious destiny and such. The style, in keeping with the period, has a whiff of Edith Wharton, a writer he admires. 'I like Wharton's wit, and her toughness. She knows her world, and there is nothing soft or romantic in her approach. One must look to men,' he adds nastily, 'for those feminine qualities.'

He is a moralist: he believes that heterosexist, imperialist, born-again Americans are wicked. Or rather, he would if he believed in sin. Instead he thinks them hypocritical, deluded and dangerous, their gospel very Bad News. So clear is he about this that he himself is in danger of preaching. 'The American Empire is one of the most success-ful inventions in history, and all the more remarkable because no one knows it's there. Now the economy is coming apart and the locus of the world's economy has shifted to our far eastern province of Japan. There will be wars of liberation in due course.' He relishes all this stuff, playing the prophet of doom, Cassandra-to-whom-no-one-paid-attention-until-it-was-too-late.

What saves him from his own opinions is, first, that in fact he hates not being listened to, and knows it's the jokes and the inventions that spellbind; and secondly, that his impulse to mock and his sense of absurdity are in any case out of his control. In conversation he's a mimic, with a repertoire of voices ranging from the wise man's drawl, complete with pauses for deep thought, to an ecstatic tweetie-pie babble used for talking to the animals and cutting out the humans. In his work the propensity for mimicry famously displays itself in the variety of his styles and genres – theatre, television, film scripts, essays, histori-cal novels and satires, not in that order, nor in any particular order at all. Even his soberest third-person voice in the fiction has a doubleness about it (now *be* serious) and of course his regal first persons include the Emperor Julian and Myra Breckinridge, so ably plagiarised by our own Dame Edna.

Vidal thinks, or says he thinks, that it may all have something to do with his granny. 'I don't know where my voices come from, and I don't try to find out. All I know is that they start and I write down what they say, the way my grandmother went in for automatic writing. She was in touch with the dead, of course. As they don't exist for me, I hear from the living . . . it's probably Shirley Maclaine, anyway. She was given several hundred hours (it seemed) on television to tell us about her extra-terrestrial adventures and the fact that *she* is God.

Which of course she is, but isn't it a bit immodest to say so on television? Even the dread Jesus did a bit of shit-kicking when Pontius Pilate started asking him snooping questions. "You have said it," has always been my own way of handling Godhood.'

Myra B., megastar and living legend, came out in 1968 ('Has literary decency fallen so low?' – *Time*) and has now been resurrected, revised, and reissued back to back, or whatever is the right way to put it, with *Myron*, in a bumper edition. Both books seem to have been meticulously dirtied up by the author. Anyone who couldn't work out before exactly how Myra unmanned Rusty Godowski as part of her neo-Malthusian plot to control population and dominate the world, or what a prostate is for, will now be enlightened. With *Myron* the operation was simpler: in the original Vidal wittily excised all the bad words and replaced them with the names of the members of the Supreme Court who'd just decided (1974) to privatise censorship, and allow local communities to do it themselves. That joke lost its topicality and has been abandoned, so that readers will no longer have to puzzle over the translation of (for example) 'the whizzer whites that are cutting our powells off'.

Not that these changes really signal a slackening of censorship, rather (something that fills him with despair) the fact that books are so relatively unread that they simply don't matter. Book-readers are a tiny minority, and probably perverts anyway. The censorship has shifted with the majority, to television, whose programme-makers are increasingly urged to produce uplifting fibs, as in Plato's Spartan Republic. Vidal is somewhat tempted by TV, too: he wrote a lot of drama for the box in the Fifties when he was making his money and smarting from the reception of his homosexual novel, *The City and the Pillar*, and he still returns from time to time. He recently scripted a much-watched 'mini-series' (the kind of word he really relishes) about a murder at West Point. He wrote film scripts too, and points out that he was in on the end of the great studios.

He also, of course, performs. He's very good (which in his case means bad, Bad Taste, scene-stealing and so on) at being interviewed, confronted, chatted up, and inclines to be sceptical about other people's desire to stay pure. He tells a story of two Britishers: 'In Moscow I had a late dinner with Graham Greene. There had been a *froideur* between him and his neighbour, Anthony Burgess. As I quite like both, I am tactful. Greene suddenly said, "I saw him on television. In France. I don't do television, you know." I pointed out that in Moscow the two of us had not been off television for four days. "Well, this is Eastern," he said. "It won't get back. I hate having one's face known, and talking on television." I said sternly that I liked television very much because it was my only opportunity to talk about politics directly, without the discrediting mediation of a journalist. "Of course," I said, "I never talk about my books if I can help it. What did Anthony talk about?" Greene shuddered, and whispered, as if something too obscene for others, "His books." Greene's eyes were wide with horror. "In French."'

Vidal himself belongs in a less squeamish club (the late Truman Capote and Tennessee Williams spring to mind, as does Norman Mailer) – the author as celebrity: 'Modesty is a British invention that has never had much of a market in the United States. I do note at times a sort of dismay amongst your deep critics when faced with a writer who contemplates actual power in this world and does not blush and apologise. Different cultures. You are too modest – in a very vain way. We are too busy – in a very humble way, of course.'

He is interested in 'actual power' and has several times been tempted to cut corners and go into politics – in 1972 he joined Dr Spock in the People's Party, in 1982 he polled half a million votes for the Senate, in California. A few years back he explained to Michael Billington that politics seemed to him a family firm – 'most of those who write about politics are essentially provincials, journalists from the provinces who arrive with big round eyes. To me it's the family business, like being brought up in a tannery. I know exactly what the smells are, and how the leather's made.'

However, since he also knows the world of the media inside out – and since politics now happens in the media – what might once upon a time have been a public career has been turned inside out. Vidal is one of the age's most scathing commentators on the way in which newspapers and television, especially television, have changed the political process, emptied it out, filled it with fictions, 'public images' and lies. In the new novel, *Empire*, the front man is Teddy Roosevelt, but the power belongs to William Randolph Hearst's newspapers. 'Hearst is the great original. If there is no news you invent it. While I was "inventing" him, I kept thinking of that passage in *Oblomov* where the hero starts his slide into perfect sloth by giving up newspapers and coffee houses, where everyone talks about (say) the political situation in Turkey. But is there really such a place as Turkey? My Hearst wouldn't care. If there was no Turkey he'd make one up. What does one ever know about anything?'

The general sloth, passivity, delight in being lied to, is his great topic. And he brings to it an urgency of outrage that must have a lot to do with his conviction that in a parallel universe, on another channel somewhere, he could have been one of the actors. His most savage satire yet, *Duluth* (1983), one of his best and most frenziedly inventive books, has characters entirely enmeshed in third-rate dreams. On a more practical level, he foresaw long before it happened that the logical presidential candidate would be an actor; and more recently, in *Newsweek*, he exactly prophesied the effect Ollie North would have via the networks. When we learn from Bob Woodward's *Veil: The Secret Wars of the CIA* that 'since Ronald Reagan did not read many books but watched movies the CIA began to produce profiles of leaders that could be shown to the President ... soon the CIA began providing a classified travelogue of all countries that Reagan planned to visit', then we're in Vidal's territory. Not only is the President in a movie, but everyone else has to join him there.

Duluth, though, was only a book. Vidal's satires are fuelled with frustration. 'Myra Breckinridge is very much a frustrated power figure who takes charge of her admittedly fictive universe.' He flourishes in gloomy triumph a sheet of statistics thoughtfully compiled by the British Public Lending Right people, which shows that last year 30,000 people borrowed *Duluth*, but you feel that 30,000 strikes him as not very many. He likes to point out (his own statistics) that at least one third of Americans are functionally illiterate.

So he is back to his public/private dilemma. 'The public self is just that – the extent to which one wants to get involved with politics or whatever. The private self does the writing. I don't think I bring the two together. I certainly try not to.' But what about the Life? Well, his writing self lives, and has done for more than 30 years, with Howard Austen, who is even less of a sentimentalist (were that possible) than Vidal. They – he – used to explain to romantically 'programmed' interviewers that it wasn't a marriage – 'none of the assumptions are there. Each marriage I know of starts on the assumption of sexual exclusivity'; however, as time's gone by, the distinctions seem to have lapsed, perhaps because marriages in any case tend to become companionable. The house in Ravello, Italy, where I talked with him is out on a promontory, islanded from the town by gardens, vines, walks. He was entertained to discover that it had been built by my husband's first cousin twice-removed, Lucille Beckett – 'Welcome to your patrimony . . . How are the mighty fallen.' Some of the Thirties furniture is still there, the floors are tiled, the walls white, with 18th-century paintings and a Roman mosaic. There is the patter of tiny feet (two dogs, a cat) and there are books, books, books. They have an apartment in Rome and another place in Los Angeles, but this, increasingly, is where the writing gets done.

The hapless biographer will have to dig deep to come up with the inner Life, there's so much on the surface. Vidal has long ago published his selected indiscretions – for instance, Anaïs Nin ('Well she was exotic, I must say; and I was 20, she was 42, and she had a radiant act'). Then there was the conquest of Jack Kerouac. He is, he says, distracting his biographer with famous friends – 'Greta Garbo, Eleanor Roosevelt, Edith Sitwell, Hannah Arendt, Elizabeth Taylor', not to mention Paul Newman and Joanne Woodward and other assorted celebrities. 'I have lived in many different worlds . . . I didn't even try to meet anyone. I give my biographer all sorts of fascinating names to track down, hoping he'll forget all about me.'

Mary McCarthy

Obituary

M ARY McCARTHY DIED, IT'S safe to assume, unreconciled and unconciliated. The salad of genes and traditions that went into her making – Catholic on father's side, Jewish and Protestant on mother's – was a good start for a life-long balancing-act, and also for laying claim forcefully to the elusive middle ground of American cultural life. She was a liberal. She was *the* liberal, it sometimes seemed, but then the very label had already joined the ranks of near-unusable words, degenerated into a term of abuse. She was to compile, during her life in literature and politics, a sort of informal lexicon of these, rising to heights of comic indignation during the Watergate hearings when she realised that Haldeman, Ehrlichman, Krogh and company thought of themselves as an intellectual elite. Her characteristic tone was cool, fastidious, reasonable and despairing. And this may have had to do with the other basic autobiographical datum – that she was orphaned in early childhood, which was what led to being passed around the various sides of the family, and perhaps helps to account for her deep distaste for dramatics, shows of sincerity and breast-beating.

She cut her teeth and honed her pen during the McCarthy era. The eerie coincidence of the name was itself a portent of a career of needling the histrionic public figures by getting inside *their* rhetoric and gutting it. Her essays from the period – like 'The Contagion of Ideas' from 1952 – are a series of extraordinary and almost exotic exercises in 'balance'. For her, the real casualty was not so much the Left as the language of sanity and criticism, drowned out by the clamour of accusations, betrayals, confessions, excommunications and conversions. It was in the midst of this collective paranoia that she became (to quote an ironic Norman Mailer) 'our saint, our umpire, our lit. arbiter', and uttered one of her most memorable sentences – 'the liberal's only problem is to avoid succumbing to the illusion of "having to choose"'. She makes the whole thing sound like a bad movie, a vulgar and untruthful projection of private grey areas into public technicolour. The leading characteristic of the modern world, she said a bit later, was its 'irreality', by which she meant the packaging and marketing of life-styles and the erosion of cultural common ground which had made democracy a media event.

In her own account of her early years she attributes her style to having fallen in love with Julius Caesar in the Latin class. (In real life she fell in love with Edmund Wilson, not quite the same thing.) Caesar was, she said, 'the first piercing contact with an impersonal reality . . . just, laconic, severe, magnanimous, detached'. He wrote about himself, moreover, in the third person ('the very grammar . . . was beatified by the objective temperament that ordered it'). In our times, though, more desperate and satiric measures were called for. Her first fiction is characteristed by acts of near-Swiftean impersonation, where she puts on the voice of the detested enemy in order to expose him, and where the ironies are compounded by the fact that the plot is about the defeat of 'the ordinary liberal imagination' by some authoritarian, devious *poseur*. I'm thinking about *The Groves of Academe* in 1953, in particular, where a boring right-winger gets tenure by insinuating that he's a secret Red and so enlisting all the campus wets in his defence. McCarthy is of course 'dry' about all this; though during these years she wrote several pieces on the death of the novel, or at least the realist novel, dedicated as it used to be to common sense and characters who were more solid than the bright, grotesque types the present threw up. Comic characters, for her, were always secret codes for authorial despair, just as the abuse of the word 'hopefully' was a sign of the utter absence of hope.

Once upon a time novelists had heroes who, however flawed, represented our subjective conviction of human freedom. She was to have no heroes on the page, nor heroines either, though in life she admired and loved Hannah Arendt, Philip Rahv, Nicola Chiaramonte and many others. Her greatest novel, *The Group*, is structured around *absences* – the absentee hero/heroine, the (unwritable) novel of the common ground, and it still has the dangerous flavour of savage laughter about it. At the time (1963) she managed to get furious reviews from *both* Norman Mailer *and* Norman Podhoretz (those failed male Norms): Podhoretz grandly accused her of being 'wilfully blind to the spirit of moral ambition and the dream of self-transcendence' (though he was talking about the Thirties, when the novel was set); Mailer accused her of not being a 'good enough woman' to write a great book, because she devalued 'the horror beneath', and had 'no root' (so wasn't a good enough man either). Her power to offend couldn't have been more graphically illustrated. It was, and remains, a marvellous book about the transmogrification of life, and style, into 'life-style' and meaningless freedoms. It was also a prophetic book, which set the scene – the theatrical metaphor is appropriate – for the novels of protest and Liberation in the next decade, where women writers rose up to demand to be listened to in their own first persons, the 'I' without the irony.

She, on the other hand, might well have taken refuge in nostalgia – nostalgia for the cultural conditions that would give a voice like hers a more direct part in the script. The thing was, I suppose, that she could never reconcile herself to the notion that literature and life should fall apart, nor to the notion (which she'd have thought utopian in the extreme) that they could come together again. Like Humpty Dumpty, the realist novel and the high liberal tradition, were irretrievably shattered, and you almost feel that it was a point of honour with her not to pretend otherwise. During the Seventies she became more what she had always been, an 'occasional' writer – that is, more essayistic, more concerned to inject the sceptical, cajoling, quizzical tone into the turn of events. In one piece about visiting a press-briefing in Vietnam she'd declared 'If I had dropped straight from Mars . . . I would have known from the periphrastic, circumspect way our spokesmen expressed themselves that an indefensible action of some sort was going on . . .' It's a characteristic thought, she was a bit of a Martian, but then the Martian perspective is precisely the one favoured by sceptics from Socrates to

Swift, who set themselves up as public eyes, and she doesn't dishonour that great tradition. For her creation and criticism were inseparable, and circumstances saw to it that she was more of a critic when she created than the other way around. She *paid attention* unwaveringly, wittily, and without bitterness. She was in public more admired than liked. Gore Vidal says about her, 'She was our most brilliant literary critic, uncorrupted by compassion' – and says it with admiration, without irony.

The deb who caught her muse

Necessary Secrets: The Journals of Elizabeth Smart

EDITED BY ALICE VAN WART

The Assumption of the Rogues and Rascals
By Grand Central Station I Sat Down and Wept

ELIZABETH SMART

ELIZABETH SMART DIED IN 1986. Her extraordinary novel, *By Grand Central Station I Sat Down and Wept*, first published in 1945, had already been resurrected a couple of times by then. Now it is republished again, along with its companion piece, *The Assumption of the Rogues and Rascals*. Together these two slim and surreal volumes constitute her fictional *oeuvre*; and yet she has a better chance of being read in a century's time than many of her more solid, conventional contemporaries. She keeps being rediscovered, and each time the vividness and panache of the writing are more striking.

Weirdly enough, she anticipated fate – reached out to posterity, rather than her contemporaries. Being jilted by it is her theme. *By Grand Central Station* is the story of her love affair with the high style, and with the poet George Barker, which came to a sticky end in low-mimetic prose, and babies. As the blurbs used to put it: 'They never married but Elizabeth bore George four children', and then worked in advertising and journalism to support them. *Necessary Secrets*, made up of excerpts from her journals from 1933 to 1941, covers her pre-Barker twenties and shows how she transformed herself from a rather bored Canadian deb into the passionate and intransigent Bohemian of the books.

It makes fascinating reading. The journals more than confirm the novels' picture of Smart as plotting her grand passion before she even met Barker, 'when he, when he was only a word'. First she buys a Barker manuscript; then she dreams greedily about him ('If Barker should appear now I would eat him up with eagerness'); finally, she organises a 'rescue' package to help him and his wife leave Japan (this is 1940) and come to California, where she plays hostess Lady Macbeth-fashion, conspiring relentlessly to break up his marriage.

The resulting mess is what she made over into a shapely, poetical agony. Brigid Brophy, prefacing the first Smart reissue in 1966, said that 'the entire book is like a wound', and she's been echoed by many commentators since. It's a misleading description, though, unless you remember that Brophy (like Smart) is a shameless formalist. 'Every scar', says Smart's narrator, 'will have a satin covering and be new glitter to attack his heart' – which pretty well describes the erotic artifice she goes in for. One reason she published so little is that she wouldn't write the kind of modest prose you can fit in round the edges of domestic life. It was all or nothing for her: eloquent moments of blazing intensity (pain or pleasure, either would do), otherwise silence:

> I cannot write a novel – the form needs padding, the form needs to be filled up with air – for no truth can last so long or be so boringly consistent. I want each word to be essence . . .

In the event, she produces her own eccentric form. In the journals she uses metaphors of sex and birth continuously: 'Each word must rip up virgin ground. No past effort must ease the new birth.' (Male writers had talked like this for centuries, of course, but they didn't proceed to get *literally* pregnant by their Muse.)

Editor Alice Van Wart says that this edition represents less than a third of the journals. She seems to have done a good job of selecting the material that illuminates Smart the writer, as she pillages seventeenth-century metaphysical poets (Donne, Herbert) and contemporary sex-mongers (Anaïs Nin, Henry Miller) to concoct her own heady style. Smart isn't a good travel writer (she went round the world, improbably, with a matron who was addressing Women's Institutes); what's interesting is her egocentric habit of making everything grist to her mill. 'Sculpture. Mummies. Jewellery. Shoes' all serve her purpose.

Wars and atrocities turn to imagery – 'I will *not* be taken like Abyssinia.'

This arrogant ingestion of the world is her great strength. She takes things impossibly personally, as sensation on her skin, 'something only the body's language can say, oiled by the tides of mysterious passion'. No wonder one of her favourite quotations was Donne's line from 'The Canonisation', about lovers epitomising the world. The journals, at least in this selection, show her mythologising herself even in private.

Death of the Author

Obituary Essay on Angela Carter

THERE'S A PIECE ON Byron by William Hazlitt in which, as he's routinely and genially abusing the latest instalment of *Don Juan*, he learns that Byron is dead. Well, of course, Hazlitt says, he *was* the greatest writer of the age. The sudden deaths of contemporaries wrong-foot us: we have to turn too quickly into posterity's representatives. A living writer is part of the unsatisfying, provisional, myopic, linear, altogether human present, but add a full stop and you can read the work backwards, sideways, whatever, because now it's an *oeuvre*, truly finished.

Angela Carter annoyed people quite a lot when she was alive ('I certainly don't seem to get the sympathy vote,' she observed with more than a shadow of satisfaction when last year's big prizes were announced). But when she died everyone scrambled to make up for it, and perhaps there was more than a shadow of satisfaction behind some of those glowing obituaries, too: she isn't going to come up with any more surprises; that disturbing sense of someone making it up as she went along will fade; Literature can take its course. For the first time I see that there's at least one virtue in literary biography: a 'Life' can demythologize the work in the best sense, preserving its fallibility, which is also the condition for its brilliance.

This has been critical heresy for a long time. Writers' lives merely distract us from the true slipperiness and anonymity of any text worth its salt. A text is a text is a text. Angela, of course, was of the generation nourished on the Death of the Author (Barthes, 1968 vintage), as was I.

Looking back, she recaptured some of the euphoria of that time:

> Truly, it felt like Year One ... all that was holy was in the process of being profaned ... I can date to that time ... and to that sense of heightened awareness of the society around me in the summer of 1968, my own questioning of the nature of my reality as a *woman*. How that social fiction of my 'femininity' was created, by means outside my control, and palmed off on me as the real thing.

But she went on to qualify the 'sense of limitless freedom' you get by sloughing off the myths with a sentence which ought to stand as the epigraph to any attempt at a biography of her: 'I am the pure product of an advanced, industrialized, post-imperialist country in decline.' Well, perhaps not. But it is a remark that captures her tone pretty exactly: I can just see the *moue* of amused disgust (but also *disgusted* disgust at the same time, morally and intellectually fastidious disgust) with which she'd greet the notion that you could somehow levitate out of history.

A Life doesn't have to reinvent its subject as a 'real' person. Angela Carter's life – the background of social mobility, the teenage anorexia, the education and self-education, the early marriage and divorce, the role-playing and shape-shifting, the travels, the choice of a man much younger, the baby in her forties – is the story of someone walking a tightrope. It's all happening 'on the edge', in no man's land, among the debris of past convictions. By the end, her life fitted her more or less like a glove, but that's because she'd put it together, by trial and error, *bricolage*, all in the (conventionally) wrong order. Her genius for estrangement came out of a thin-skinned extremity of response to the circumstances of her life and to the signs of the times. She was, indeed, literally thin-skinned: her skin was very fair, pink and white; she weathered quite a bit but never tanned, and you could see the veins easily. You might almost say her body *thought*. She had very good bones and was photogenic, so that it didn't matter that she'd stopped looking in mirrors and painting her face. She let her hair grow out white in wisps two or three years before she got pregnant. I could have been a grandmother by the time she was a mother, and I was younger than she. The shape a woman's life takes now is a lot less determined than once it was. Or: the determinations are more subtle, you're *sentenced* to assemble your own version.

Beginning

> There's a theory, one I find persuasive, that the quest for knowledge is, at bottom, the search for the answer to the question: 'Where was I before I was born?'
>
> In the beginning was . . . what?
>
> Perhaps, in the beginning, there was a curious room, a room like this one, crammed with wonders . . .
>
> Angela Carter, 'The Curious Room', *SPELL* (*Swiss Papers in English Language and Literature*), 1990

She cultivated the role of fairy godmother and/or witch, and – in *The Bloody Chamber* (1979) – rewrote the Bluebeard story with pistol-toting Mother riding to the rescue at the last minute. However, it was not her own mother, one of a family of 'great examination-passers' (a scholarship girl who'd left school at fifteen to work at Selfridges) who provided the model for this kind of figure, but her maternal grandmother, who'd come originally from South Yorkshire. Granny came to the rescue in the year of Angela's birth (1940) and evacuated herself and her grandchildren from south London back to the gritty coal-mining village of Wath-upon-Dearne, kidnapping them safely into the past for the duration of the war.

Skipping a generation took Angela back to 'Votes for Women', working-class radicalism, outside lavatories and coal-dust coughs. Granny ought, perhaps, to have surfaced in the fiction as the spirit of social realism, though actually it makes sense that she's in the magical mode, since her brand of eccentric toughness was already thoroughly archaic from the point of view of the post-war and the south of England. In Angela's last novel, *Wise Children*, the granny-figure is killed in the Blitz, but bequeaths to her adoptive grand-daughters Dora and Nora the Brixton house that offers them a safe haven when they have to retire from the stage. 'When the bombardments began, Grandma would go outside and shake her fist at the old men in the sky . . . She was our air-raid shelter; she was our entertainment; she was our breast,' says Dora.

Grandma figures *as* the house in this book, the matriarchal space of the Carter house of fiction – 'but the whole place never looked *plausible*' (Dora again). In a *New Review* series on 'Family Life' back in 1976, Angela wrote that her grandmother 'was a woman of such physical and spiritual heaviness she seemed to have been born with a greater degree of gravity than most people'.

> Her personality had an architectonic quality; I think of her when I see some of the great London railway termini, especially Saint Pancras, with its soot and turrets, and she overshadowed her own daughters, whom she did not understand – my mother, who liked things to be nice; my dotty aunt . . .

Grandmother is a larger-than-life 'character' for her – Leninist Lizzie, the heroine's minder in *Nights at the Circus*, looks like another avatar – but mother is almost a missing person. Not unusual this, at all, particularly for daughters growing up in the 1940s and 1950s, with upwardly socially mobile mothers who'd given up work: women girlified, exiled and isolated in domesticity, who hadn't 'done anything' with their education. She wrote about her Scottish journalist father with obvious pleasure: 'very little to do with the stern, fearful face of the Father in patriarchy . . . there was no fear' ('Sugar Daddy' in *Fathers*, Virago, 1983). Whereas about her mother, who was younger but died first, she was wry, oblique, regretful, protective: 'There was to be no struggle for my mother, who married herself young to an adoring husband who indulged her, who was subject to ill-health, who spoke standard English, who continued to wear fancy clothes.' Angela was supposed to do something with her own education, so instead of course she married young herself, in reaction against what her mother wanted for her, though it didn't last long. If you look for the provenance of the feminist writer, mother is the key. The women who really nailed patriarchy weren't on the whole the ones with authoritarian fathers, but the ones with troubled, contradictory mothers: you aim your feminism less at men than at the picture of the woman you don't want to be, the enemy within. In this case, the girl-wife. Hence (again) a motive for skipping a generation, in imagination. Back to Gran.

It wasn't a card she openly played until she got older, when she took to fairy tales and ribaldry. However, the whole *camp* quality of writing of the 1960s derives from this sense of a lost (deliberately distanced) reality: working-class, northern, matriarchal. None of this could she *be*, or speak directly for, but she could do it in pastiche – and she did, writing in ghostly quotation marks. If there was nearly nothing 'natural' about her style, this was perhaps because her kind of family background introduced her early on to the notion that the culture was a dressing-up box and to the bliss and nightmare of turning the clock back. That is what *The Magic Toyshop* (1967) is about – slipping out of your precarious middle-classness into the house of (superficial) horrors and (libidinal) mirrors. Ten years after that she said to me in an interview (I'd asked, 'Do you think your environment shaped you?'):

> Well, my brother and I speculate endlessly on this point. We often say to one another, How is it possible such camp little flowers as ourselves emanated from Balham via Wath-upon-Dearne and the places my father comes from, north Aberdeenshire, stark, bleak and apparently lugubriously Calvinistic, witch-burning country? But obviously, something in this peculiar rootless, upward, downward, sideways socially mobile family, living in twilight zones . . .

This is not about nostalgia but connects with a quite different contemporary sensation: of coming at the end, mopping up, having the freedom of anomie.

'Perhaps, in the beginning, there was a curious room . . .' Crammed with wonders? The beginning, for Carter, is a magical lumber-room. Over the years her own south London house came rather to resemble this cabinet of curiosities. It was a toy-box long before her son Alexander arrived, though he completed its transformation so that there was hardly room to swing a cat. Indeed, the cats were eventually exiled to the garden. A letter she wrote to me just after that first 1977 interview records the beginnings of this process:

The NEW REVIEW piece is smashing. Thanks. The only snag, as far as I'm concerned, is that I only have the one script, alas, so that a number of the details of my autobiography are repeated in the 'Family Life' piece – repeated word for word, what's more. Which is a great tribute to my internal consistency, I suppose; only, my childhood, boyhood and youth is a kind of cabaret turn performed, nowadays, with such a practised style it comes out engine-turned on demand. What a creep I am.

And I always get cast down by my own pusillanimity. The notion that one day the red dawn will indeed break over Clapham is the one thing that keeps me going. Of course, I have my own private lists prepared for the purges but ... I'm more interested in socialist reconstruction *after* the revolution than the revolution itself, which seems to mark me out from my peers. We have just had the exterior of this house painted quite a jolly red, by the way. The front steps look as if the Valentine's Day massacre had been performed on them. However, I also managed to persuade Christine downstairs to have a *black* front door so it is the jolly old red & black & VIVA LA MUERTE & sucks boo to Snoo's barley and bamboos; we're going to have a *real* Clapham front garden, the anarchist colours & pieces of motorcycle & broken bottles & used condoms lightly scattered over all ...

PS I didn't manage to post this until today, Sunday, or rather 00.30 Monday morning, after a brisk search for the letter (in Portuguese) inviting me to this ruddy do [a Festival of Free Art], which begins to look more and more like a nightmare. Chris ['Christine downstairs'] wants me to bring home a 6 ft. ceramic cockerel. I have house-guests, just arrived, having driven from Nepal – the sister of a Korean ex-boyfriend of mine plus her bloke. Mark has strained a muscle in his back – I'd planned to have him push me around in my wheelchair in 20 years time; what if I have to push *him* around in one in 5 years time? It's like a soap opera in this house, an everyday story of alternative folk, I suppose.

You can see in the discussion of the decor here something of her inverted dandyism; also the self-consciousness which was her inheritance, for better and for worse. The whole place 'never looked *plausible*'.

Middle

They seemed to have made the entire city into a cold hall of mirrors which continually proliferated whole galleries of constantly changing appearances, all marvellous but none tangible ... One morning, we woke to find the house next door reduced to nothing but a heap of sticks and a pile of newspapers neatly tied with string, left out for the garbage collector.

Angela Carter, 'A Souvenir of Japan', *Fireworks*, 1974

Japan (1969–72) had been her rite of passage in between, the place where she lost and found herself. Being young was traumatic: she'd been anorexic, her tall, big-boned body and her intransigent spirit had been at odds with the ways women were expected to be, inside or outside. Looking back to her teenage years, she always made the same joke:

I now [1983] recall this period with intense embarrassment, because my parents' concern to protect me from predatory boys was only equalled by the enthusiasm with which the boys I did indeed occasionally meet protected themselves against me.

Her first marriage she portrayed as a more or less desperate measure, with her making the running ('Somebody who would go to Godard movies with me and on CND marches and even have sexual intercourse with me, though he insisted we should be engaged first'). And in her five 1960s novels the point of view is interestingly vagrant – as readily male as female.

When she impersonated a girl she described the boys as sex objects; when she went in for cross-dressing she did it, she later remarked, with almost 'sinister' effectiveness: 'I was, as a girl, suffering a degree of colonialization of the mind. Especially in the journalism I was writing then, I'd – quite unconsciously – posit a male point of view as the general one. So there was an element of the male impersonator about this young person as she was finding herself.' That is one way to put it. Perhaps she adopted the male point of view also because, under the mask of the 'general', it was more aggressive, more licensed, more *authorial*. At any rate, the result is that in the early fiction her boys and girls look into each others' eyes and see – themselves. Then in 1969 she broke the pattern. She and her husband parted company, and she went to live with a Japanese lover, in Japan.

And there her size – and her colour – made her utterly foreign. She compounded her oddity when she stepped into the looking-glass world of a culture that reflected her back to herself as an alien, 'learning the hard way that most people on this planet are *not* Caucasian and have no reason to either love or respect Caucasians'. Her 1974 collection, *Fireworks*, contains three stories that, most uncharacteristically, are hardly fictionalized at all. She must have felt that their built-in strangeness provided sufficient distance, and it does:

> I had never been so absolutely the mysterious other. I had become a kind of phoenix, a fabulous beast; I was an outlandish jewel. He found me, I think, inexpressibly exotic. But I often felt like a female impersonator.
>
> In the department store there was a rack of dresses labelled: 'For Young and Cute Girls Only'. When I looked at them, I felt as gross as Glumdalclitch. I wore men's sandals . . . the largest size. My pink cheeks, blue eyes and blatant yellow hair made of me, in the visual orchestration of this city . . . an instrument which played upon an alien scale . . . He was so delicately put together that I thought his skeleton must have the airy elegance of a bird's and I was sometimes afraid that I might smash him.

Feeling a freak was a kind of rehearsal for the invention of her lumpen winged aerealiste Fevvers years later. At the time, in Tokyo, whatever she was looking for, she discovered the truthfulness *and finality* of appearances, images emptied of their usual freight of recognition and guilt. This wasn't, in other words, old-fashioned orientalism, but the new-fangled sort that denied you access to any *essence* of otherness. Tokyo offered cruel but cleansing reflections. In another piece called

'Flesh and the Mirror', she described an erotic encounter so impersonal it left no room at all for soul-searching: 'This mirror refused to conspire with me.'

Self-consciousness had been her bane from the start, hence the anorexia. But while most women come out the other side and learn to act naturally, she somehow managed not to, and Japan is the shorthand, I think, for how. She discovered and retained a way of looking at herself, and other people, as unnatural. She was, even in ordinary and relaxed situations, a touch unlikely on principle. Her hair went through all the colours of the rainbow before becoming white at the moment when decorum would have suggested a discreet, still-youthful streaked mouse. Once, when I was staying at her house, I discovered I had mislaid my make-up and she dug out a paintbox from Japan, some kind of actor's or geisha's kit, which was all slick purple, rusty carmine and green grease.

She escaped the character expected of the woman writer by similar strategies. That is, she substituted work for inwardness. She'd once wanted, in adolescence, to be an actress; when I talked with her in 1977, she insisted that writing was *public*: 'Sometimes when you say to people you're a writer, they say, "Have you had anything published?" Which is a bit like saying to an actor, "Have you ever been on the stage?" Because if it's not published it doesn't exist.' And the same point, made more succinctly: 'I mean, it's like the right true end of love.'

Not that she stopped consulting the mirror. A small allegory: Plotinus and later Neoplatonists suggested mischievously that you could draw a subversive moral from the fate of Narcissus – it's not self-obsession that destroys you, but the failure to love yourself coolly and intelligently and sceptically enough. If he'd recognized his own image in the water he could have made a real beginning on knowing himself. Angela looked into some dangerous mirrors—for instance, de Sade's (in *The Sadeian Woman*, 1979), but by then she'd stepped through the Japanese looking-glass and could say, 'Flesh comes to us out of history.' When she came back to England she had her career to build all over again, and that's what she did, with help from journalism and an Arts Council Fellowship in Sheffield. She was hard up and marginalized in ways she didn't at all relish. She had no secure relationship with a publisher – between 1971 and 1977 she moved from Hart-Davis to Quartet to Gollancz – she couldn't make enough money out of her fiction to live on and she didn't fit easily into the classic outsider role. She never accepted the madwoman-in-the-attic school of thought about the woman writer, particularly not about the Gothic or fantastical writer: freaks and fairies, she believed, were as much socially determined as anyone else; our 'symbols' are of course *ours*. Theory apart, however, she had a thin time during the 1970s, and she was painfully prickly about her reputation. When she filled in an author's publicity form for Gollancz (who published *The Passion of New Eve* in 1977 in their 'science fiction and fantasy' category), there was a section asking her to list her previous publications. Angela wrote simply '7 novels', without giving even the titles.

Some time before this, she wrote to me from Albert Road, Sheffield, about Virago, and her great friend and fan Carmen Callil's plans to *re*publish women. She was thinking hard about 'the woman writer', and meeting a pissed Elizabeth Smart at a party at Emma Tennant's had given her bitter food for thought:

> 'It is hard for women,' she slurred. Actually it was a very peculiar experience because she clearly wanted to talk in polished gnomic epigrams about anguish and death and boredom and I honestly couldn't think of anything to say. Except, I understand why men hate women and they are right, yes, right. Because we should set good examples to the poor things. (Was surprised to find Mary Wollstonecraft making exactly the same point, in a way.) . . . It was all very odd. I don't mean to sound hard. I mean, I'm sure her life has been astoundingly tragic. And I began to plot a study of the Jean Rhys/E. Smart/E. O'Brien woman titled 'Self-inflicted wounds', which kind of brings me to the point, or anyway, a point.
>
> I'm on the editorial committee of this publishing firm, VIRAGO . . .

From her point of view, Virago was meant – among many, many other things – to make money out of and for women's writing and to rescue it from the slough of passive suffering:

The whole idea is very tentative at the moment, obviously. I suppose I am moved towards it by the desire that no daughter of mine should ever be in a position to be able to write BY GRAND CENTRAL STATION I SAT DOWN AND WEPT, exquisite prose though it might contain. (BY GRAND CENTRAL STATION I TORE OFF HIS BALLS would be more like it, I should hope.)

She herself was working on the Sade book at the time, and her ideas for Virago included some books by men (Sade's *Justine*, Richardson's *Clarissa*) which got at the roots of female 'pathology'. She feared and loathed and found hilarious the spectacle of the suffering woman. The Sade book was an exorcism of sorts, too. She needed to *theorize* in order to feel in charge and to cheer herself up, and that has left its mark marvellously on the fiction too, which is full of ideas, *armed* with them. (Desiderio in *The Infernal Desire Machines of Doctor Hoffman*, 1972, avoids being eaten by a tribe of river Indians, who are hoping magically to absorb his literacy, because he's a good enough anthropologist to rumble their plans. Like Angela, he's read his Lévi-Strauss. Much more recently, in *Nights at the Circus*, Fevvers escapes a murderous Rosicrucian by the same ploy, having this time read Frances Yates, I'd imagine.)

Anyway, with the Sade book and *The Bloody Chamber* in 1979, she rounded off the decade triumphantly. The fairy tale idea was a real breakthrough and enabled her to *read* with a new appropriateness and panache, as though she was *telling* these stories. She took to teaching creative writing too. In 1980 she went to the United States, to Brown University, where she substituted for John Hawkes: no one had read her, she said, but she enjoyed it enormously and had the company of her friends Robert and Pili Coover. Bit by bit, her earlier work would be republished (in Picador and King Penguin, as well as Virago); she would acquire a solid relation with Chatto & Windus, when Carmen Callil moved there; she would become a delighting globe-trotter, a visiting writer/teacher/performer; and her work would be translated into all the major European languages. In 1984 she was still broke enough to be tempted to come and teach on the creative writing programme at my university, East Anglia. I acted – apprehensively –

as the go-between on this deal, well aware that she didn't see eye to eye with Malcolm Bradbury, who ran the course. Since he wasn't there when she was, this arrangement survived precariously until 1987, with the two of them alternating like the man and woman who forecast the weather. She chucked it in with relief, though students as different as Kazuo Ishiguro and Glenn Patterson had been rewards in themselves. I suppose the point to make about these years is this: she had to struggle hard to sustain her confidence, in the face of frequent indifference, condescension and type-casting. She was not, either, able to repose securely in the bosom of the sisterhood, since her insistence on reclaiming the territory of the pornographers – just for example – set her against feminist puritans and separatists. And of course she was in general an offence to the modest, inward, realist version of the woman writer. John Bayley, lately, in the *New York Review of Books*, contrived to imply that she had an almost cosy 'place' from the start: a magical realist, a post-modernist. This couldn't be further from the truth. Her work was unclassifiable in terms of British fiction, except as 'Gothic' or 'fantasy', throughout the whole difficult middle period of her career. If that situation has changed, it is largely because she refused to write 'fantasy' as (merely) alternative, 'in opposition', and because she made large demands on her readers.

Bad-tempered footnotes department:

Exhibit One: a letter undated, 'Tuesday':

> *Very* bland place. At least, Toronto is . . . The son and his father didn't miss me. But they seem glad to see me back. It seems we might well be going to Texas next spring; am awaiting letter. Am planning to write novel about sensitive, fine-grained art historian whose
> PTO
> life is totally changed by winning large, vulgar cash prize, she dies [sic] her hair green and wears leather trousers etc. Sniffs glue and turns into Kathy Acker . . .

Exhibit Two: a postcard from the States:

> Have just heard about the Booker. I hope he drinks himself to death on the prize money (you know me, ever fair and compassionate). Will

telephone soon – I keep meaning to write you the kind of letter people write in biographies, but there ain't time.

Ending

Because I simply could not have existed, as I am, in any other preceding time or place . . . I could have been a professional writer at any period since the seventeenth century in Britain or in France. But I could *not* have combined this latter with a life as a sexually active woman until the introduction of contraception . . . A 'new kind of being,' unburdened with a past. The voluntarily sterile yet sexually active being, existing in more than a few numbers, *is* a being without precedent . . .

Angela Carter, 'Notes from the Front Line', 1983

Angela made parenthood her theme in her last novel, *Wise Children* – parenthood of all sorts, literary, literal and lateral (twins as mirrors to each other). She'd also had her son, Alexander, at the last minute in 1983. Alex was perhaps partly responsible for the long gap between this novel and its predecessor (seven years), but it had always taken her a long time to 'gestate' the next because she *was* original, always moving on and changing. She didn't think there was anything Mytho-logical about that: *Wise Children* in fact is all about coming from the wrong side of the tracks to claim kin with Shakespeare, traditionally one of the favourite examples of mythic fatherhood.

She had long before used pregnancy as a plot device, a way of ending a novel: first in *Heroes and Villains* (1969) and then in *New Eve* very elaborately indeed, so that it turns into an evolutionary re-run, with branches of the family tree for archaeopteryx and other intermedi-ate beings missed out first time round. She had trouble with endings once she had taken to using the picaresque format of allegorical travels, and wanted them to stay 'open'. And it wasn't too different with her life. She and Mark Pearce had 'settled down' over the years, but in a most vagrant fashion. She travelled all over the place for jobs, residencies, tours; the Clapham house was always being changed around (her friend Christine moved out quite shortly), and was never finished. 'At home' they cooked, decorated, gardened, collected cats, kites, prints, paintings, gadgets, all piecemeal. The house became filled with the jetsam of their enthusiasms. Mark worked as a potter for a while and made plates that were beautiful but also enormous, so that they hardly fitted on the makeshift kitchen table and you felt like a guest at a giants' feast. The two of them took to wearing identical military surplus greatcoats outdoors, announcing their unanimity and accentuating their height. Domestically they communed in silence, which was very much Mark's speciality, though she was pretty good at it too. They conspired to present their relationship as somehow *sui generis*, like a relation between creatures of different species who both happened to be tall. They had nothing much conventionally 'in common' except that they were both eccentric, stubborn, intransigent, wordlessly intimate.

She didn't, I'm sure, study to conceive, but simply found herself pregnant and decided to go ahead with it. An aged *primagravida*, she joked, but obviously her condition underlined the difference in their ages and made her granny disguise all the more outrageous. That November, in her last weeks of pregnancy and on the day after she had helped to judge the Booker Prize (which went to J. M. Coetzee), she developed high blood pressure and was hospitalized. From hospital she wrote me a furious letter:

My blood pressure rating has not been improved by my second run-in with the consultant obstetrician. Every time I remember what she said, I feel raptly incredulous and racked by impotent fury. Although at the time I said nothing, because I could not believe my ears.

So she says: 'How are you feeling?'

'Fine but apprehensive,' I say, 'not of the birth itself but of the next 20 years.'

'How is your husband feeling?' she asked.

I paused to think of the right way of putting it and she said quickly: 'I know he's only your common-law husband.'

While I was digesting this, she pressed down on my belly so I couldn't move and said:

'Of course you've done absolutely the right thing by *not* having an abortion but now is the time to contemplate adoption and I urge you to think about it very seriously.'

That is *exactly* what she said! Each time I think about it, the adrenalin surges through my veins. I want to *kill* this woman. I want the BMA to crucify her. I want to rip out her insides.

Anyway, then she said: 'Its [sic] policy of the hospital to put older women into hospital for the last two weeks of pregnancy and I'll be generous, you can go home to collect your nightie & be back in an hour.'

Nobody had told me about this policy before & I feel she may have made it up on the spur of the moment. Needless to say, she then buggered off back to her private practice. Was she being punitive? Why didn't I kick her in the crotch, you may ask. Why didn't I cry, shreik [sic] & kick my heels on the ground, demanding she be forthwith stripped of her degrees & set to cleaning out the latrines. Why did I *come in*, after all that! Everybody else in this hospital is so nice & kind & sensible & sympathetic. There would have been a round of *applause* if I'd kicked her in the crotch. But, anyway, it turns out that I'm not in here for nothing—this ward is full of women with high blood pressure, swollen feet & the thing they make you collect your piss for, the dreaded protein in the urine. The doctor who looked at me today said they all spent a lot of time patching things up after my consultant, who is evidently famed for making strong women break down. Evidently I can agitate to go home again on Monday if my blood pressure has gone down.

'What about the consultant's weekly clinic?' I said, because I'm supposed to go to it.

'Dodge her,' the doctor said. The doctor is a slip of a right-on sister young enough to be my daughter. The consultant is a Thatcher-clone – evidently a Catholic, I'm told – old enough to be my mother. I am the uneasy filling in this sandwich.

A good example, this, of the way motherhood is used as a means of denying a woman's own meanings, taking away her choices, extruding her from normality's roster. Actually, the birth went all right, and despite the seemingly inevitable hospital infection, Angela was able to rejoice from the beginning in Alex's Caravaggiesque beauty. But you can see how hard it was for her, at times, to make up her life as she went along. The writing in this letter belongs to a genre she disliked – the low mimetic, the language that reproduces the world. Small wonder she preferred surreal transformations, nothing to do with autobiography or confession or testament. But that seeming impersonality was, I'm arguing, entirely personal at base – a refusal to be placed or characterized or *saved* from oneself. One of the last things she wrote, *The Holy Family Album* (1992) for television, attacked God the Father for the tortures inflicted on His Son in the name of Love, but in the cause of Power: a piece of deliberate blasphemy against the Almighty Author. And a plea for mortality. *Flesh comes to us out of history*. Nothing stays, endings are final, which is why they are also beginnings.

The man they mistook for Marcel Proust

Obituary of Terry Kilmartin

TERENCE KILMARTIN, *DOYEN* OF literary editors, Proust's brilliant and meticulous re-translator, died yesterday, at the age of 69.

He was the most self-deprecating of men – a quality rare among men of letters who tend to be a vain lot – and I can see now the humorous wince with which he would greet any personal tribute.

It is impossible, though, to separate his professional and personal qualities. His intelligence was many-sided, his balance and wit were not confined to his dealings with the world of books. He was something of a mentor to both colleagues and friends: his good opinion mattered. This was the central paradox about him, in fact, that his dislike of self-assertion and his penchant for irony gave him an extraordinary authority.

As genial as he was exigent, Terry was splendid company, a man always alive to the interest in any situation, whether it tended towards pathos or hilarity. Hilarity won often, which was maybe an aspect of his Irishness, though mostly his Irish origins were obscured by the impeccably English accent which was part of his protective coloration. None the less, that background explains a lot about his independence of mind. He was not turned out by the usual educational mill. I once accused him of sounding 'Oxbridge'. This provoked a rare outburst: not only was he not Oxbridge, he had never been to university at all. MI5 during the war had been his university.

Terry was born into the Catholic middle classes in the Republic, the seventh of eight children. His father died when he was tiny, there was suddenly no money, and the family was farmed out and split up.

When he was 16, his mother saw an advertisement for a tutor to teach English to the children of a French family; with the aid of a photograph of an elder brother he landed the job, Frenchless and far too young – and learned the language and grew up, very fast.

With the war he came to England, ineligible for military service because he had lost a kidney in a childhood illness, and was 'recruited' by his sister who was a typist at MI5. He worked for SOE, the Special Operations Executive, which specialised in subversion and sabotage. And it was on a mission in France during the invasion in 1944 (most of the agents were French) that he got to know David Astor, son of *The Observer's* proprietor, who was with Mountbatten's headquarters.

After the war, Terry worked for a while for a station broadcasting from Cyprus to the Middle East, then joined the paper as a journalist, before taking over the books section in January, 1952. David Astor says, with very Kilmartin understatement: 'I didn't want to have the ordinary sort of literary editor.' For him, what was striking was Terry's integrity: 'No flattery would move him, in fact it had the opposite effect; it was dangerous to advocate anything. Even Ken Tynan wouldn't cross Terry, he adored writing for *The Observer*. Terry stood by Anthony Burgess when he reviewed his own book, published under another name, but then he didn't give it a very good review.'

Working mostly behind the scenes, Terry celebrated literature in the widest sense, not cut off from politics or personalities, but not absorbed into them either. Under his aegis, *The Observer* awarded its short-story prize to a newcomer called Muriel Spark, and printed Angus Wilson's reviews. Terry's reviewers relied on him to 'see the point' (a favourite Terry phrase) of an argument, an issue, a book, an anecdote, your 'piece' for the week even. Not that he went in for lavish praise: 'That wasn't bad, by the way,' was about as enthusiastic as he got. He was the embodiment of the reader over your shoulder, the one you trusted to help you make sense.

His revision of Scott Moncrieff's translation of Proust's *A la recherche du temps perdu*, along with his selection and translation of the Proust letters, have confirmed him as a literary figure in his own right. This large enterprise had modest beginnings. At the start, in the mid-1970s, anticipating the moment when Scott Moncrieff's famous and much-loved translation would come out of copyright, Chatto & Windus asked Terry (already a well-known translator) to revise it, by incorporating changes made in the French text in the 1954 Pléiade edition. All that was envisaged, according to Terry's editor D. J. Enright, was that he would 'find the right bits and plonk them in'.

But as he worked, he began to identify numerous errors and misunderstandings, and the result (in 1981) was a significant modification of the English Proust. Dennis Enright says that at Chatto they almost expected the admirers of Scott Moncrieff to up and storm the building.

In the event, however, Terry's version was seen to retain the best of Moncrieff. John Charlton of Chatto points to the balance and fluency of the translations, their sensitivity to nuance – in short, Terry's 'natural' way with Proust's language. 'He has changed Proust in an evolutionary way, a healthy way: his revised version will stand the test of time.'

Though Terry quietly deplored Moncrieff's tendency towards the purple and precious, it was characteristic of him not to want to efface the quality of the earlier version, but to work to make it more faithful to the original. At Chatto, Terry became so identified with *A la recherche* that they made out one of his royalty cheques to 'Marcel Proust' by mistake.

His work on Proust's fiction and letters went on uninterrupted, with the help of his wife Joanna, throughout his illness. He had retired from *The Observer* in 1986 when he and Joanna cashed in their Chelsea house for a flat in Clapham and a house near Eygalieres in Provence.

Sadly, they did not have very long to enjoy this double Anglo-French life that so exactly reflected their shared affections. Terry's courage and resilience, however, helped win him many remissions from the cancer that finally killed him. I recall his wit, warmth and sheer civilised intelligence with gratitude and a sense of irreplaceable loss.

Boy in a box springs forth

Daphne du Maurier

MARGARET FORSTER

ALL LADY ROMANCE-WRITERS claim kin with the Brontës. Usually it's Charlotte or Emily, though; Daphne du Maurier's distinction was that *her* secret affinity was with Branwell. In fact, she published a biography – *The Internal World of Branwell Brontë* – in 1960. Her fans could not have known, however, that one of the reasons for her interest in this lost boy and failed genius, overshadowed by his sisters, was that she saw her own innermost self in him. Daphne, the distinguished, best-selling authoress of *Rebecca* and *Jamaica Inn*, had long thought of herself as a boy in disguise.

Margaret Forster's clever, searching and subtle biography uncovers this hidden life in such a way that you sense something of its true strangeness. It's not – in other words – yet another gay 'outing' (they're becoming glum and routine enough these days, God knows) but a study in human oddity.

British middle-class mores, nursery double-speak and family codes all played a vital part in training up a girl who could keep herself secret from herself. Her identification with actor-father Gerald – a charmer, and womaniser, who encouraged her to think of herself as boyishly superior to her sisters – helped to set the pattern. In childhood photos, Daphne gangles apart, looking defiantly 'different' as best she can, although her conventional cool, blonde prettiness is against her.

At finishing school in France she had her first fling with a rather louche-looking woman teacher nicknamed 'Ferdy'; and in 1929, aged 22 and back in England, she had her first affair with a man, film-director-to-be Carol Reed, who was only six months older than she. He wanted to get married, she not. 'What she liked best', according to Margaret Forster, 'was not the love-making, but the talking and the listening and the hanging around cafés, speculating about strangers.'

In fact, she was fumbling her way towards becoming a writer, developing the taste for solitude, the habits of concealment, and the strategies for living with contradictions that fed into her fiction. In 1931 she married Major 'Boy' Browning, and disappointedly produced two daughters, Tessa and Flavia, before giving birth in 1940 to the son Christian ('Kits') she openly and violently desired.

By this time she'd also produced six books, including, in 1938, *Rebecca*. In later years she would say things like: 'I think one has to choose, you know. Either to create after one's own fashion, or be a woman and breed.' Or again: 'I mean, really, women should not have careers. It's people like me who have careers who really have bitched up the old relationship between men and women ... Disembodied spirits like myself are all *wrong*.'

And that seems to be her secret: a talent for contradiction so intense, and so carefully-nurtured, that it created the special atmospheric uncanniness that Hitchcock got so well in the *Rebecca* movie (and, of course, in *The Birds*, whose germ was a du Maurier short story).

Disembodied spirits felt wrong: the one time in her life she seems to have felt *almost* right was when, in 1949–50, she was involved in a kind of double love-affair with two different women – the wife of her American publisher, Ellen Doubleday, and the actress Gertrude Lawrence, who played the character based on Ellen in Daphne's play *September Tide*.

As Margaret Forster ingeniously points out, it's as though Daphne was making love with one of her own fictions, crossing a magic boundary between the real and unreal. Ellen was 'straight' and untouchable, and brought Daphne out (in letters) in ecstasies of gallantry:

> . . . a boy of 18 all over again with nervous hands and a beating heart, incurably romantic and wanting to throw a cloak before his lady's feet.

Gertie was physical, a lover in body ('I couldn't talk to her, you know'). Despite the snobbism of this remark, Gertie's sudden death devastated her – 'Yet there was a mutual language. Something all mixed up with theatre and writing.'

So perhaps it was precisely the absence of 'talk' that created the freedom and space for love? At each turn in this strange story you come back to the importance of inarticulacy – not having the words, not naming the acts, is what preserves her sense of selfhood and uniqueness.

Her closet code ('the boy in the box') enables her to be perfectly rudely superior, convinced she's one of a kind – 'Nobody could be more bored with all the "L" people than I am.' She liked to think, she said, 'my Jack-in-the-box was, and is, unique'. And certainly, the implicit lie she lived seems to have given her fiction its edge, and its macabre bite. To put it very crudely (which this book doesn't) you can see why the second Mrs de Winter is shy and strange and not-at-home in the role when you work out that she's really a boy.

Margaret Forster doesn't go in for speculation. She has a reticence of her own in this book that is very effective indeed, and very suggestive. There is a whole sub-plot about houses and places, marvellously handled and her evocation of the anger of du Maurier's old age, and of the way she starved herself to death, wilful to the last, is both moving and appropriately cool.

Altogether a model biography – human sympathy tempered with honesty and spiced with real intelligence.

The secret sharer

What Remains and Other Stories
The Writer's Dimension: Selected Essays

CHRISTA WOLF

CHRISTA WOLF WAS A runner-up for the Nobel prize in 1988. Nowadays, though, it's not her stories but the stories about her that command attention. From being East Germany's literary conscience, the very voice (it seemed) of painful honesty, the one who spoke for the individual from inside the walls, she has become for the new Germany a symbol of duplicity.

There were two stages to this process. First, in 1989, she published the novella *What Remains*, written (she said) 10 years earlier, about being harassed by the Stasi, the secret police of the German Democratic Republic, and spied on by fellow intellectuals. Many readers' responses were sceptical and sour. Why hadn't she published it in 1979, when to do so would have been dangerous? Wasn't she retrospectively justifying herself as a victim? Wasn't she also claiming a kind of outsider-status she didn't really have? All of this was fuelled by the fact that her best writing had always been based in autobiography – now there was a gap between that 'secret' self and another one, seemingly even more secret. However, the discovery of a whole bank of Stasi files on Wolf and her husband, compiled between 1968 and 1980, lent credibility to the story of the story.

Except that there was another Stasi file lurking – its existence first hinted at last summer in the German press. This was not a file on Wolf, but one to which she had contributed as an 'informal collaborator' of the Stasi, long before. It turned out that in the heyday of her infatuation with the regime – between 1959 and 1962 – she'd chatted to the thought-police. She broke the story eventually (when it was about to break anyway, said her enemies) in January of this year. By this time, ironically enough, she was on a Getty grant in California, working on a book about classical myth (Medea and guilt). By this time, too, the GDR, the country she'd defined herself for, and against, had been erased from the map.

Now her own words turn against her, on every side. It's impossible to read *What Remains* without reversing the roles, hard to remember her brilliant study of a girl (herself?) contriving to forget the Nazi past in *A Model Childhood* without reflecting on the feat of amnesia she's more recently managed. She said to the *New York Times Book Review* earlier this month that she must obviously have been 'a case for Dr Freud . . . a classic case of repression', since she'd really forgotten most of her informal collaborating – the codename out of Goethe (Margarete), the details she furnished, and so on. Her 'I' no longer includes 'the person I was at that time: a believer in ideology, a good comrade', with all the ideologue's 'pigheadedness'. Getting out my old paperback copies of her books I discover, on one blurb, this from the *Guardian*: 'A writer of scrupulous, "touchstone" honesty.'

And there it is. She was one of those writers shaped by repression, who represented in the indifferently 'free' world a value for writing, and for realism, and for truth-telling, which we revered. It was our bad faith she reminded us of, the playful emptiness we all too often detected in our literary versions of liberty. What we forgot was that the state that defined her was also a state she'd helped define. Her East German generation congratulated itself on rooting-out and rejecting fascism: 'We in our part of Germany confronted German Fascism uncompromisingly and thoroughly,' she wrote in 1989. 'Today many of us see that at first we were in danger of just substituting one doctrine of salvation for another.'

This piece is reprinted in *The Writer's Dimension* and, along with some pieces from 20 or 25 years earlier, it does begin to sketch out the collective psychological mechanism whereby the rejection of fascism made way for the new regime. This next quotation comes from a piece on her generation – she was born in 1929, so was 16 when the war ended – written in 1965:

Our situation was unique in that our path into adulthood, our search for our appropriate place in life, coincided with the rise of a new society, with its quest for forms of existence, with its growth, its mistakes, its consolidation. Since we learned to move around freely and securely in this society, to identify with it and at the same time stay critical as one can be only towards one's own work – since that time we have turned 30 or 35 and our books have become more vivid, more truthful, and filled with reality.

Fascinating to read this now. It explains in its own way the quality of almost Victorian density and depth that Christa Wolf's kind of fiction managed – the 'realism' of writers who *also* see themselves as creating the reality they record and resent ('reality is created by common effort', the young Raymond Williams used to say, nostalgic for those days). The last section of *The Writer's Dimension*, headed 'The End of the German Democratic Republic (1989–90)', mostly comprises the texts of speeches. She was pleading in these speeches for the preservation of the 'real' country of her imagination, while helping to dismantle the shell of dead GDR institutions.

As it turned out, the extra 'dimension' she believed in simply vanished. In her Sixties' days of hope she had triumphantly contrasted 'our language, the accurate, serviceable language of reason' with 'the abracadabra' of the consumer culture next door in West Germany ('Talking German', 1965). Now, she had lost her place. In her most famous novel, *The Quest for Christa T*, Wolf wrote about 'the new world that we were making and making unassailable – even if it meant building ourselves into its foundations'. Well yes, with hindsight, that's what she did. And now the walls are down, and the 'sacrifices' have come unglamorously to light.

There's one story in *What Remains* in which Wolf revisits the lost world of moral idealism at the end of the war. In this atmosphere, she remembers trucksful of waste paper, soldiers 'throwing it out of *Wehrmacht* vehicles . . . forms . . . files . . . documents'. At every turn her writing acquires ambiguities, suggestions, self-references she didn't mean. It is as if she is being written by the words, being written out and exposed by a language she's always despised. In another long quotation, from *Cassandra* (1983), she talks about her hatred of precisely the kind of public exposure she's now writhing under:

> About reality. The insane fact that in all the 'civilised', industrialised nations, literature, if it is realistic, speaks a completely different language from any and all public disclosures. As if every country existed twice over. As if every resident existed twice over: once as himself and as the potential perceiver of an artistic presentation; second, as an object of statistics, publicity, agitation, advertisement, political propaganda ... Vital, contradictory people ... have rigidified into ready-made parts and stage scenery ...

These two worlds have – for the moment at least – collapsed into one another for her and her readers. Her 'realism' looks indistinguishable from lies and propaganda, her 'writer's dimension' looks like a sleight of hand, a way of constructing an apologia, a space to hide in.

The last point she makes, though, about the grossness of publicity's simplifications, is also true. Germany's unification may have demolished the space she lived in, may have revealed her claim to dissenting authority as mired and mirrored in the authority of the dead state, but it has also encouraged a cynical purity-crusade that enables the bad faith of the right to disappear again behind attacks on her kind.

Will she be able to write about this? Live, on the page, with her new inheritance of shame, and share it out? In her best-selling book on Chernobyl, *The Accident*, published in 1987, she wrote: 'Once again ... our age had created a Before and After for itself. I realised that I could describe my life as a series of just such incisions, a gradual clouding over produced by ever thickening shadows. Or, on the contrary, as a continuous acclimatisation to ever harsher lighting ...' Or again (in the same book): 'We are more and more obliged to act the part of writer and, by falling out of character, to pull off our masks ...' Perhaps she will be overwhelmed by the hideously prophetic force of her own words – 'growing older means: all that one would never have thought possible comes true'. Truth has overtaken her realism, and has given the very hacks whom she despised a carnival. The more playful

pieces in *What Remains* – a Flann O'Brienish tale about what happens to
left-over fictional characters, a speculative whimsy about a sex-change –
do not begin to cope with what happens if you really take on literature-
as-lies. But then that was Before.

Writers who never lay claim to her kind of responsibility for their
worlds are forgiven for their duplicities and dark secrets in a way that
Wolf can't and won't be. In 1965, for instance, Marguerite Duras published *La Douleur*, which purported to be mostly old manuscripts
belonging to the moral no-man's-land at the end of the war: 'I found
this diary . . . I have no recollection of having written it. I know I did.'
One of the stories is about a resistance group, and particularly a
character called Thérèse, torturing to death an informer. 'Thérèse,'
Duras said in an introductory note, 'is me. The person who tortures
the informer is me.' And yet, partly because of Duras's habitual insistence on the murkiness of *écriture*, and the way words spread obscurity
and ambivalence rather than enlightenment – not to mention her claim
that this is the special territory of the *woman* writer, who's a subversive
in the cause of anarchy – one is enabled to side-step the real implication
of this 'confession'. Whereas Wolf, having identified herself with the
cause of naming and mapping and remembering, is exposed. Wolf,
moreover, never fancied or allowed herself the womanly get-out; in the
sex-change story she writes with jokey contempt about 'that division
of labour which leaves the right to sadness, hysteria and the majority
of neuroses to women'.

No post-modern escape hatch, then. Just the dystopian mess that
has replaced her Utopian project. For Wolf's kind of realism, you now
can see, *was* Utopian, news from nowhere, a vanished country where
public and private life, intellectuals and the rest, past and present
generations, were supposed to be able to find common ground. One
of the things that hurt her most in 1989 was the exodus of the young
to the West – 'did a bonding ever take place, a dialogue?' she asked
herself dismally. Her own experience of suppressed memories now helps
to explain why her communist generation – like her parents' fascist
generation – failed to make links. She tried to write a literature which,
however private-sounding, had ties with public history. And it's that

prospect – 'that's what writing means, to furnish examples' – which, for the moment at least, has vanished along with her reputation for integrity.

In full spate

Obituary of Anthony Burgess

THE MOST TELLING MEMORIAL to Anthony Burgess would have been to leave a big white gap on the pages of the *Observer* or the *Independent* or whatever – the space his words would have filled. His death must surely supply work for a good handful of aspiring literary journalists, job opportunities galore. And that's just in the Grub Street corner of the literary A to Z. But did his many roles and his polyphonous *oeuvre* – novelist, librettist, composer, scriptwriter, reviewer, teacher – add up? Even if you concentrate on the prose, and leave out the lyrics and the music (which, being tone-deaf, I'm obliged to), it's still hard to decide whether his work is as much as the sum of its parts.

It's the kind of question he had deliberately posed, to himself as well as to his readers, at least from the 1970s on, when instead of settling down and producing books that were densely layered and epically difficult and despairing *and very far apart* in the manner of (say) Pynchon or Gaddis he started throwing off playful, complex novels – *MF* (1971), *Napoleon Symphony* (1974), *Beard's Roman Women* (1976), *ABBA ABBA* (1971), – at such indecently close intervals that they somehow disqualified themselves as canonical texts. Burgess didn't strike people as *post* anything because he wasn't troubled enough. He was too blithely at home with the promiscuous tricks of language. He throve on epistemological anxiety, took it in his stride, and so seemed to contradict the founding hypothesis about a crisis of signification. Authorship for him was a way of life in more senses than one, and when he took on the fashionable paradoxes – writing as dissemination in *Earthly Powers*, for instance (paper Onanism, recklessly spending words, echoes of Derrida) – then too his very enjoyment of his task, his ingenuity and irreverence and fluency, told against him.

Joyce was his great hero and mentor, but it's characteristic that in the second part of his autobiography, *You've Had Your Time* in 1990, thinking about what the life of letters really meant to him, he questioned even that allegiance, and bracketed Joyce with Woolf (very much not his favourite modernist). 'Here I lay myself open to charges of middlebrowism. But probably the novel is a middlebrow form and both Joyce and Virginia Woolf were on the wrong track.' Word-play, self-consciousness, polyglot punning AB enjoyed beyond measure, but at the same time he liked to combine these signs of Literature with a capital L, literature squared, with a no-nonsense approach derived from Grub Street mores. He disapproved of Joyce for being a scrounger, he thought you could and should produce great art for money, in the style of Herman Wouk or – let's not be modest – Shakespeare, or Mozart. He admired Mozart for being 'prolific', 'a serious craftsman and a breadwinner', as he said in his bicentennial tribute-cum-travesty, *Mozart and the Wolf Gang*, Bloomsbury gentility and 'costiveness' (Forster was the prize example) could be relied on to provoke his scorn for several reasons at once therefore: mystificatory reverence for Art, snobbish resentment of one's audience, and a kind of stinginess with one's talent which he seems Freudianly to have associated with anal retentiveness.

By contrast – though retaining the same metaphor – he was unashamed of his own logorrhoea. Pressed to explain why he wrote so much, he developed over time a number of motives. The first and most famous is the diagnosis of an inoperable brain tumour in 1959, when John Wilson was given a year to live at the most, and as a result became Anthony Burgess full-time in order to earn royalties for his prospective widow, as he put it – 'I was not able to achieve more than five and a half novels of very moderate size in the pseudo-terminal year. Still, it was very nearly E. M. Forster's long life's output'. It's a chillingly good story, and seems to be true, though it doesn't explain why he went on going on at such a lick once the misdiagnosis was discovered.

In fact, the reprieve hardly slowed him down at all, whereupon he produced a second strand of explanation which had to do with the childlessness of his first marriage to Lynne. Perhaps it was, he suggested, a matter of books substituting for babies – 'I had converted what I termed paternity lust into art.' This may sound an implausibly Platonic theory, but George Steiner gave it a convincing run for its money not long ago in *Real Presences*, and Burgess himself in *Earthly Powers* had lent it an extra colour of likelihood by making his compulsive writer-hero homosexual. Except that by the date of *Earthly Powers* (1980) he wasn't childless any longer. When Lynne died in 1968, there was a new wife-to-be, Liana, plus their son (of whose birth he'd been unaware) waiting in the wings. But this meant, of course, that now he had a wife and child to support . . .

All of which suggests that he didn't quite know why his writing was so compulsive. It was as though the words wrote him. While other literary folk were addicted to alcohol, or sex, or drugs, he was innocently fixated on his profession. Here the book-reviewing came in handy – to fill the gaps between books – and also the script-writing. Gore Vidal recalls that he more than once passed on to Burgess lucrative jobs in that line, which were snapped up and dispatched with alacrity. The relationship between the two of them is perhaps more of a clue to 'placing' Burgess than this venal tie suggests. For though Vidal exercises more quality control, and separates out his different kinds of writing more – so that, for instance, the histories are done in lucid, ironic, discursive style, while the satires are *lusciously* vile, masterpieces of inverted decorum – they both belong to the tradition of carnivalesque adventurers, the breed of writer who (according to the school of Bakhtin) follows on from Petronius, Apuleius, Rabelais and Sterne. This kind of serio-comic writing is made up of parodies of the straight kinds. It was (says Bakhtin) 'the "journalistic" genre of antiquity . . . full of overt and hidden polemics with various philosophical, religious, ideological and scientific schools . . . seeking to unravel and evaluate the general spirit and direction of evolving contemporary life.' This comes from the book on *Dostoevsky's Poetics*, so it has to be slightly edited to fit, but it does fit rather well, since it gets the sense of epic ambition, along with mock-epic tactics like (another good phrase) 'slum naturalism'.

*

So a ragbag of a book like *The End of the World News* in 1982 – a
tripartite travesty, made up of a drama-doc about Freud, a libretto for
a musical about Trotsky, and a sci-fi 'or futfic' story about the end of
culture as we know it – does have a *genre* after all. Burgess suggests as
much when he complains in the autobiography that 'That term "ragbag"
is always turning up, usually when my work is at its most structured.'
He wasn't thinking of Bakhtin, but of structuralism and Lévi-Strauss,
but in a general way the notion of programmed mayhem, or self-
conscious surface disorder with an underlying pattern, can be accommo-
dated to the carnival idea. Music, he liked to say, can aspire to
universality ('Music is the Armagnac of the saved. The musician alone
has access to God'), whereas the arts of words, by contrast, are local,
referential, impure: 'to deal in pure structure is a huge relief from
peddling those impure structures called linguistic statements'. Literature
is in league with imperfection, and even within the Babel-world of
literature, there are those who understand that comedy has the last
word (like Cervantes) and those who (like Shakespeare) hanker after
the glamour of tragedy. Just as he loved Joyce this side idolatry, so he
adored Shakespeare but found him less myriad-minded than he's
cracked up to be. That Shakespeare is the national bard had something
to do with it: Burgess was all for crossing frontiers and cross-breeding
cultures, an Esperantist of the spirit.

Burgess does, then, 'make sense', he has a poetics. And yet there
remains something resistant and idiosyncratic about his work which
even the right anti-tradition can't quite accommodate. You can line
him up with the correct contemporary attitudes, but there's something
left over, something anachronistic about his postmodern-seeming stress
on the arbitrary, shifting and ephemeral nature of words. It's as though
he is trying to turn writing back into the condition of speech and set
up a dialogue with his readers, a running commentary almost as continuous as breathing. This means that he doesn't go in for the double-
think which finds a surreptitious sublimity in the very recognition that
Literature is discredited. By the sheer quantity and continuity of his
writing, he produced a real sense of the limits of what words can do.
He lived that wry comedy (not a tragedy at all) and acted it out.

This involves a very special kind of modesty which almost amounts to the opposite (the devil's mode, he called it in one book) – a modesty which despises those who take themselves too seriously. Look, he's saying, I can do it just as well as you if not better, any old time, week in week out, without trying to set it in stone. This in the end, I'm sure, was why he liked literary journalism so much: the proud debasement of Grub Street, the place where you know exactly what your words are worth. So he wrote all the hours God gave. He hoped, perhaps, that if in this curious way he kept his head down, the Almighty might look the other way, and Art would creep in at the back door. If you identify writing with living so closely, you don't want to produce something too finished – after all, time will do that for you.

Secret agonies and allergies

Elizabeth Bishop, One Art:
Selected Letters

EDITED BY ROBERT GIROUX

THIS MARVELLOUS, OVERWEIGHT VOLUME of letters traces Elizabeth Bishop's life all the way from her brilliant teens, on the verge of Vassar, through her years in Brazil with the love of her life, Lota Soares, to her death in Boston in 1979, at 68. As editor Robert Giroux says, it forms a kind of autobiography – the kind, in fact, she would never have allowed into her poetry.

'In general, I deplore the "confessional"' she wrote to her ex-mentor and permanent friend Robert Lowell in 1972, when he'd committed the ultimate deliberate indiscretion of incorporating passages from his ex-wife Hardwick's letters into the poems of *The Dolphin*. She referred scathingly to 'the anguish-school that Cal [Lowell] seems innocently to have inspired – the self-pitiers' (that is, Anne Sexton, and Sylvia Plath) and did her gallant and stoic best ('*art just isn't worth that much*', she wrote to Lowell) to keep her pages pure.

And even in the letters – though there are the seismic side-effects of life's mess, Lota's illness and suicide, other lovers' breakdowns, Cal's manic and depressive disaster, anxieties galore – she is always able to look *outwards*, to pay attention to the world around her, its colours and voices and shapes.

One can only speculate about the influence on her of her extraordinarily orphaned state: her father's death in her infancy, her mother's terminal disappearance into a mental institution when she was five. Like her Vassar contemporary Mary McCarthy (orphaned by the flu epidemic of 1918), she seems to have become preternaturally self-reliant and ambitious – though unlike McCarthy she was not all conscious intelligence. That her great life-long epistolary friendships were with Moore and Lowell tells you that her predilections were for the stranger shores of consciousness, even if she didn't map them out herself.

She sometimes comes close, particularly in letters to Marianne Moore, where she describes the life she leads behind the writing eye:

> I have that continuous uncomfortable feeling of 'things' in the head, like icebergs or rocks or awkwardly placed pieces of furniture ... And I can't help having the theory that if they are joggled around hard enough and long enough some kind of electricity will occur, just by friction.

But obviously, even here, she's set on avoiding the language of self-analysis, all the picturesque Freudian maps of the inner landscape. Her intimacy with Moore, in fact, was established on quite different terms, all to do with animals and zoos and circuses. No wonder living in Brazil, in a 'Rousseau jungle', she was in her element. Weather and plants and creatures are the central features of her descriptions of the happiest part of her life. One sample – the toucan, called uncle Sam:

> He has brilliant, electric-blue eyes, gray-blue legs and feet. Most of him is black, except the base of the enormous bill is green and yellow and he has a bright gold bib and bunches of red feathers on his stomach and under his tail. He eats six bananas a day. I must say they seem to go right through him & come out practically as good as new ... They sleep with their tails straight up over their heads, and their heads under a wing, so the silhouette is just like an inverted comma.

She plunged into this sort of writing when she was in danger of getting too intensely literary or personal. When a probably manic Lowell proposed marriage to her (on the analogy of Virginia Woolf and Lytton Strachey, he said) she delayed for months before replying, and then wrote a letter full of diversionary local colour, without directly saying a thing.

Much as she loved animals, she was asthmatically allergic to them, and you get the story of her allergies here, too, in letters to her doctor full of wheezing and adrenaline. She suffered from eczema as well, and was thin-skinned, over-sensitive, prone to swell up with odd 'reactions'.

Perhaps this was where the suppressions came out (a sheepskin coat in someone's car nearly finished her off, on one occasion); certainly she and her beloved Lota seem in the end to have driven each other up the wall, each becoming convinced the other was the sick one. As she wrote to poet Frank Biddart, 'being so fearfully, automatically "observant" can be a "Calvary"' – though as usual the quotation marks are disowning this confessional stuff. Not long before he died, she was ticking Lowell off for talking so much about illness and decay – 'Please, *please*, don't talk about old age so much . . . I just *won't* feel ancient – I wish Auden hadn't gone on about it so in his last years, and I hope you won't.'

She didn't. But then, much as she loved the natural world, she always suspected the passive 'philosophy' of the traditional nature poet. Among many of the delights here is a savage comment (to Randall Jarrell) about Robert Frost – 'there's something still *unturned* about Robert Frost – something slightly unpleasant under that lichen-covered stone'. No wonder so many of her correspondents became epistolary intimates for life: she made letters into a living landscape, with the humans only one item in the menagerie.

Home is where the art is, south of the psyche

The Still Moment: Eudora Welty, Portrait of a Writer

PAUL BINDING

EUDORA WELTY WAS ACCLAIMED as 'the high priestess of oral tradition' by Cleanth Brooks, high priest of the New Criticism. Both hailed from the American South, and it is Welty's embodiment of that double-sided Southern tradition – facing towards modernism and complexity, and at the same time towards rootedness and rural stillness – that has given her work such weight. Paul Binding celebrates her eighty-fifth year with a 'critical portrait' that's critical only in the admiring and expository sense. No biographical revelations, and not a lot of 'close reading' either, it turns out.

The effect is to highlight something more diffuse – Welty's 'world', a country of the mind, part-invented, part-recorded, where continuity is the keynote. We're reminded at the outset that she's lived in the same house, more or less, since she was 16, and the same Mississippi always except for a spell at college in New York. Once upon a time this wouldn't have seemed odd, but now (Binding is right) it does.

The reason is the one spelled out by a very different kind of writer, Doris Lessing, when she recently revisited her childhood home in what is now Zimbabwe. The most traditional societies, the oral cultures, are everywhere riven with change: 'There are more and more people who have had to leave, been driven from, a country, the valley, the city . . . there are gaps and holes or a thinning of the substance, as if a light that suffused the loved street or valley has drained away.'

If you are the Lessing-style of writer you become an un-settler, a representative consciousness by virtue of your displacement. Eudora Welty, on the other hand, contrives to recreate a sense of dense, ineluctable inter-relatedness, a sort of vital claustrophobia, as though you're trapped in a tiny community: the sort of feeling people only get now inside families, and often not even there. Binding quotes a 1981 interview in which she came close to describing her territory:

> I think – this is probably no longer true in the South or anywhere –
> in the days when no-one moved around very much and you and every-
> body else in town lived in the same place for a long time, you followed
> the generations. You had a wonderful sense of the continuity of life . . .
> It gives you a narrative sense without knowing it. Cause and effect. And
> the surprises of life and the unpredictability of life. I do think that's
> important.

The world she started to write about in the 1930s was in any case a fertile breeding ground for atavistic impulses, and over the productive years until the 1960s she practised the art of translating this into humane and subtle myth. From this South of the psyche, as Binding points out, she derives a pattern, registering the nightmare of racism, but disowning its substance by virtue of the implicit propaganda for complexity in her tales.

This is the importance of the oral connection – the voices on the page. Binding rightly pays homage, *à propos Losing Battles*, to the way in which 'Eudora Welty loses herself almost as thoroughly as any author could, with virtually no authorial comment, and only the similes and metaphors to indicate the cast of her mind'. In *The Optimist's Daughter* there is more of a narrative voice at work, but it's one that stands back to make room for 'the great interrelated family of those who never know the meaning of what has happened to them'.

You can see from this line that Welty doesn't mind whether she sounds democratic on the surface or not, but trusts to the energies she sets going to absolve her from the charge of pastoral condescension. It seems appropriate that she liked to echo W. B. Yeats, and that perhaps her closest literary friendship was with Elizabeth Bowen, since Irishness (for the British reader) has something of the same connection back to the idea of art as spilling out in people's speech.

It's surely a myth, though: a grand illusion, the idea of art as a homeland, which comes about precisely when the ordinary reality of such a thing is disintegrating. You can see this, for instance, in the novels of one of Welty's great admirers in a younger generation, Anne Tyler, with their stylised realism, and their last-ditch appeal to the extended family.

Binding praises Welty, in a fine phrase, as 'the rapt mystic of the layered moment'. It has to be said, though, that at this level she has no convincing literary inheritors – not Tyler, nor Richard Ford, whose intensities are narrower and more studied, as though they know the 'ineluctable' world is actually full of gaps, and you have to paper over the cracks in order to convince yourself you are shut in.

Surviving in the wrong

The Silent Woman: Sylvia Plath and Ted Hughes

JANET MALCOLM

BIOGRAPHY HAS LONG ESCAPED the reflexiveness that afflicts serious fiction, and makes realistic writing look irresponsibly innocent. Theorists may demonstrate with ease how compromised the biographer's project is, but this awareness has scarcely invaded the world of biography, which has stayed remarkably, confidently intact. Because, Janet Malcolm would say, we collude: this is why we put up with crude and clumsy writing we would scorn in a novel. We sacrifice taste and better judgment for the illicit pleasures of 'voyeurism and busybodyism'. With consummate bad faith, we accept the popular picture of the biographer – 'He is seen as sacrificing years of his life to his task ... tirelessly sitting in archives and libraries ... and the more his book reflects his industry the more the reader believes that he is having an elevating literary experience, rather than simply listening to back stairs gossip and reading other people's mail.' Well, Malcolm is here to hold the mirror up to human nature, and paint an unflattering portrait of the biographer and biography-addict.

She has found a vocation as a fifth-columnist in the archive of lives, a meta-biographer tracing out the after-life of people who've been cruelly and meanly reduced to 'characters in bad novels'. Her special training and qualification for the role, ironically enough, is that she is a journalist (parts of this book first appeared in the *New Yorker*, her home territory), and journalists share the biographer's burglarious proclivities, 'breaking into a house, rifling through certain drawers ... tiptoeing down the corridor ... to stand in front of the bedroom door and try to peep through the keyhole'. Eavesdropping on the peeping toms means that she stands there accused herself, but *knowingly*, of course, making the transgressive nature of biography her theme, turning its cluttered, realistic stage-sets into a hall of mirrors. She has been, is still being, sued herself, in fact, for her portrait of rogue analyst Jeffrey Masson in *The Freud Archives* ten years ago, so you can tell that her assault on the genre that pretends to the whole truth is a hands-on affair. This is a world of writing in which everyone has an axe to grind, in which there are always sides – 'writing cannot be done in a state of desirelessness. The pose of fairmindedness, the charade of evenhandedness, the striking of an attitude of detachment can never be more than rhetorical ruses . . .'

Her new book on Sylvia Plath and Ted Hughes – or rather, on the books of Sylvia Plath and Ted Hughes – came, she says, out of a partisan impulse. She had always admired the work of the poet, Anne Stevenson, and when Stevenson's 1989 biography of Plath, *Bitter Fame*, was so comprehensively savaged by reviewers, she recognised the symptoms of the 'bacillus of bad faith' that is the special subject of her researches and her love-hate: 'I began to feel the . . . familiar stirrings of repertorial desire'. Or in another metaphor – Malcolm's metaphors are strikingly deliberate, offered with a kind of sanitizing self-consciousness – 'When *Bitter Fame* appeared, and raised the stakes of the game, I decided to become a player.' This gambling image is particularly appropriate, because the whole succession of Plath exhumations and *post mortems* was begun once upon a time back in the 1960s by that notable poker-player and friend of Plath and Hughes, A. Alvarez.

In *The Savage God*, Alvarez told the story of Plath's last days, and linked her suicide inextricably with her rare powers as a *woman* poet. 'Once the plot of the suicidal poetess and her abandonment by the man with the witty mouth was released into the world, there would be no end to the variations played on it', writes Malcolm:

> The world likes to hold on to its fantasy . . . and ghoulish gossip, not dispel them, and nobody wanted to hear that it was Hughes who was good and Plath who was bad. The pleasure of hearing ill of the dead is not a negligible one, but it pales before the pleasure of hearing ill of the living.

Stevenson's book had the temerity to suggest that perhaps in the break-up of the grandly ambitious marriage of true minds Plath had made with Hughes, '*both* partners – and their children – were truly victims'. It was the book's moral atmosphere, not its narrative, that offended.

There is no significant disagreement these days about the basic outline of Plath's life. Her father Otto was a martinet, and she took his death when she was eight as a betrayal and a desertion; she grew up an over-achiever, impersonating the model scholarship-girl her mother Aurelia wanted (and had wanted to be herself), while nurturing the poisonous insecurity and resentment chronicled in *The Bell Jar* and her journals. She attempted suicide by an overdose in 1953, as in the novel, was put back together again, and resumed her studies at Smith. In photographs, she looks like the young women in advertisements – a bleached blonde with a pageboy hairdo, lots of 'grooming', understated preppy clothes. Unlike most of her peer-group, though, she took her sexual adventures 'all the way', losing her virginity in a bloody haemorrhage chronicled by her Smith room-mate Nancy Hunter Steiner in *A Closer Look at Ariel* – which also records her demandingness and the intensities that in the end repelled many of the people who got close to her.

Not Ted Hughes, though, whom she met at Cambridge (where she went on a Fulbright) in February 1956, and married four months later. Or not for quite a while. *The Bell Jar* describes the contradictory wants and ambitions she had stored up by now–

> I saw my life branching out before me like the green fig tree in the story. From the tip of every branch, like a fat purple fig, a wonderful future beckoned and winked. One fig was a husband and a happy home and children, and another fig was a famous poet . . . I wanted each and every one of them . . .

Their daughter Frieda was born in 1960, their son Nicholas in 1962. By the end of that year Hughes was having an affair, and they had separated. Early in 1963, she killed herself in the London flat where she was living with the children. The last eighteen months of her life were agonized but enormously productive: she came into her voice, let her hair grow dark and shaggy, turned herself into the stuff of legend.

Sevenson measured out her sympathy, counted the cost of Plath's apotheosis. She gave space to hostile witnesses – most memorably Dido Merwin, who had become estranged from Plath before the end, and recalled her as a monster of selfishness. This, combined with signs of sympathy with Hughes, says Malcolm, earned Stevenson her critical roasting. She threatened to spoil the biography game.

In showing sensitivity to the plight of Sylvia's survivors, in particular by attending to Hughes via his fiercely protective sister, Olwyn, long cast as the suppressors of the whole truth, she interjected 'the sound of doubt, the sound of a crack opening in the wall of the biographer's self-assurance'. And she was soundly punished for letting the side down. Alvarez, for one, 'raked over *Bitter Fame*, and when he was finished there were three bad guys where previously only one had stood: to Ted Hughes were now added Anne Stevenson and Olwyn Hughes. An ancillary narrative was born . . . the narrative of the corrupt biographer and the evil sister.' Stevenson had tried to do justice to the dead and the living, but got recruited to the wax museum for her pains.

When Malcolm interviews Alvarez, he is unrepentant, indeed has nailed Stevenson to his satisfaction: 'I thought there was a huge element of unconscious envy in *Bitter Fame* . . . A minor poet's envy of a major poet.' Not that he's read much of her work, 'but I just feel she's a kind of pale figure . . .' Alvarez preserves his own writerly innocence, in Malcolm's account, by acts of strategic non-attention: not reading Stevenson's poetry, not really looking too hard at the outraged letters Hughes sent him about *Savage God*. He is her favourite kind of interviewee, one would guess, the kind who convicts himself: 'My impression of those [Hughes] letters, which I don't remember much of – I kind of skimmed them before giving them to the British Library – was that he'd gone kind of barmy . . . The death had kind of put her into the public domain, do you see what I mean?'

For her part, Malcolm diagnoses Stevenson rather differently. She should have been the right person to write about Plath because she was the right American generation, also German-American, lived in

England too, a woman poet who used her own life in her work . . .
And she *was* the right person – *Bitter Fame* is a good revisionist account
of Plath – except that she was altogether too susceptible to self-doubt,
and thus to Olwyn Hughes's eager performance in the role of anti-Muse,
the critical, demanding voice that turned the book into an agony for
its author. Malcolm dives into Stevenson's own writings, and surfaces
with a line of her own: 'I pondered her many inevitably troubled
relationships with men . . . began to obscurely make out a pattern . . .
with a literary project that was new and full of uncertainty, [Stevenson]
once again drifted into a relationship of dependency, a sort of marriage
of literary convenience [with Olwyn] . . . The unconscious is no respecter
of gender.' Ironic, this, of course – since it is precisely the mutual
dependency of Plath and Hughes that's at stake in all the biographical
rows. In Malcolm's hall-of-mirrors scenario, Stevenson's problems
become a reflection of her subject-matter.

Yet she is right that *Bitter Fame* is a good book. Stevenson makes
sense, particularly about death and the public domain. She quoted
Sylvia's mother, writing in 1978, on the topic of the bad magic of that
eloquent suicide, its power to pull the living into the realms of the
dead:

> [Sylvia] often transmuted gold into lead . . . emotions . . . ineradicable as
> an epitaph engraved on a tombstone . . . She has posthumous fame – at
> what price to her children, to those of us who loved her so dearly and
> whom she has trapped into her past . . . There is no escape for us.

This chilling view, in which Mrs Plath for once reneged on what her
daughter cruelly called the 'smarmy matriarchy of togetherness' the
two of them shared on the surface, is the one Malcolm subscribes to.
Hence her title. Plath, she notes, would in life express her fears and
resentments by giving those who had offended her the silent treatment.
A tiff with Olwyn, for example, stayed unresolved; Sylvia whisked Ted
away early the next morning, refusing to make it up. 'Plath' says
Malcolm, drawing the moral, 'as we know, "left at dawn" on another
day, in 1963. The suicide "goes away", and the survivors are forever in
the wrong. They are like the damned, who can never make amends . . .'

In fact, to the biographers and hagiographers, the living often seem more dead than Plath is, as though they have fewer rights. Hughes has written about what this feels like:

> the most interesting and dramatic part of S. P.'s life is only 1/2 S. P. – the other 1/2 is *me* . . . I'm still here, to check, and . . . I've no intention of feeding myself to their digestions and submitting myself to their reconstitution, if I can help it.

Buried alive in some cannibalistic gullet. Gothic imagery doesn't even seem particularly exaggerated. The banal truism, that life goes on, doesn't obtain here – or rather only obtains for those who are growing older and more exasperated: 'Sylvia Plath will always be young and in a rage over Hughes's unfaithfulness.' And, of course, the case is darkened – the claustrophobic feeling heightened – by the fact that Plath felt she had to wrest her real writing out of that anger; it was generated out of the death of the ideal of the creative marriage. As she said succinctly, 'The Muse has come to live here, now Ted has gone'.

She had complained she couldn't get outside herself, but she did it by going *in*, as Joyce Carol Oates wrote in a splendid 1970s essay on Plath wrestling with the 'Death Throes of Romanticism': 'tragedy is cultural, mysteriously enlarging the individual so that what he has experienced is both what we have experienced and what we need not experience – because of his, or her, private agony'. Malcolm is perhaps putting the same point more dryly when she says: 'the awful mixture of self-loathing, loathing and envy that Plath expresses . . . is a central concern, perhaps *the* central concern, of contemporary feminism. But [in the 1950s] relations between men and women were at a nadir of helpless transferential misprision.' This is one of the few points where Malcolm abandons an otherwise vigilant and scrupulous policy of banishing jargon, and it's probably there, that 'transferential mis-prision', to signal the embarrassment of the question of where exactly she stands herself. Is 'envy' really the central concern of contemporary feminism? Is it still the case that to make room for the woman writer you have to metaphorically enter the kind of horrible imprisoning space she imagines as the setting for the 'game' of Plath biography?

It is being played in a room so dark and gloomy that one has a hard
time seeing one's hand . . . The air in the room is bad . . . Through a
door one sees an open coffin . . .

Is there really no space for one's own writing? In a way, Malcolm
obviously thinks not – or at least she is a connoisseur of claustrophobia,
making her way through the interstices of others' stories, leafing through
their accounts of others' accounts of long-dead enemies and friends.

She is at the same time a most ambitious writer, calling up the
ghost of Borges to help her with an image of another of these rooms
where lives get lost, dismembered, put together again: 'a cellar, where
he has the experience of encountering everything in the world . . .
"tigers, pistons, bison, tides, and armies . . . all the ants on the planet"'.
She too, Malcolm confesses, has spent days 'hanging around the door
to that forbidden cellar', trying to get everything on to the page. 'How
can one see all the ants on the planet when one is wearing the blinders
of narrative?' This is why, you realize, she goes out of her way to
confess that she too – a mere journalist, a mere meta-biographer – is
in bad faith: because it is a kind of cover for the desire to really write.
She is not only impatient with the more inept biographers of Plath,
but with smart post-structuralist Jacqueline Rose, precisely because Rose
refuses to admit this *desire*: 'Writing cannot be done in a state of
desirelessness.' When she effaces herself, interviewing people, listening,
seeming to empathize, she is at the same time looking for the fault-line
or crack that will give her her own space to work in. Her very scepticism
and fastidiousness have almost an elation about them, perversely
enough – others' eager slips are the grist to her fine mill.

So no wonder she confesses to bad faith. The very qualities of
discrimination, ingenuity, all that studied use of imagery, are ultimately
devoted not – as you might initially expect – to exposing myth-making
for what it is, highlighting falsification, but to making a space for her
own kind of writing, her own claim to a corner of our contemporary
Parnassus. God knows what genre this writing belongs to. Certainly it
is liminal, stuck on the threshold of that cellar – writing about writing.
When she's able to describe one of the unselfconsciously selfish troglo-

dytes – such as Trevor Thomas, who was probably the last person to see Plath alive, since he lived in the flat underneath the one where she gassed herself – she is almost hugging herself. She saves Thomas till last. He has written a memoir complaining that people aren't interested enough (Plath wasn't interested enough, back then, either) in his own creative projects. He lives in a house that is 'a depository of bizarre clutter . . . on every surface hundreds, perhaps thousands, of objects were piled . . . and over everything there was a film of dust: not ordinary transient dust but dust that itself was overlaid with dust . . .' This marvellous vision of infinite regress is, for her, infinite riches in a little room: 'Later . . . it appeared to me as a kind of monstrous allegory of truth . . .' In Thomas's bad faith and self-absorption, in other words, she finds a mirror of her own obsessions. It's this ruthless return on herself that gives a special coldness and edge to the writing; in the end, there's no empathy, no sympathy to spare, only a love–hate affair with writing, conducted from the sidelines.

Alone in the middle of it all

Angus Wilson: A Biography

MARGARET DRABBLE

WRITERS' LIFE-STORIES ALWAYS seemed to Angus Wilson to secrete the springs of their creativity. He enjoyed himself, back in the heyday of the Intentional Fallacy, preaching this heretical doctrine to literature students as a general truth. However, the life-stories that work best this way have a particular plot: about childhood, the child as father of the man, the visionary terrors of separating out your own self. His books on Dickens and Kipling have this kind of plot (the boy abandoned in the blacking factory, the lost boy at boarding-school), and so did the stories he told about his own life. Childhood is the key, and insecurity is the keynote of childhood. You glimpse what it's like to be orphaned, and the thrill of terror inspires you to invent yourself, and so you're launched on a lifetime of making it up as you go along – or something along those lines.

Perhaps this is what Rebecca West meant when she said nastily that Angus Wilson reminded her of Jane Eyre. Sex aside, though, the Brontë connection suggests something too romantically asocial: a blacking-factory nightmare involves losing caste, losing your social place, and its convincingness comes from acknowledging that a self is a social fiction. All of which means that Margaret Drabble can start off her biography fairly straightforwardly, following in Wilson's own footsteps, opening with a solid, colourful social-historical pageant complete with grotesques and eccentrics from the Wilson family background ('characters' all), and Angus's early years. It's when we leave childhood and youth behind, and come to the years at the heart of his creative career (the 1950s and 60s, his own forties and fifties), that the hero of her story is revealed as a kind of addict of the insecurity he has supposedly escaped, his writing a brilliantly precarious performance or balancing act.

This is the *writer* as a social fiction. The most striking thing about the biography is the manic pace and scale of Wilson's social life, a crowding-in of names and places that becomes quite pathological, for all the world as though he was terrified ever to be alone. This made writing very difficult, yet at the same time it seems to have been what fed his writing. He was needy, and as a consequence enormously generous – he sang for his supper and, more often than not, laid on the supper too. To some readers, the lists of people and engagements and menus will doubtless seem trivial or appalling or both. Where is this man's inner life? But that is the point, I think: his inner life was lived on the outside to a quite extraordinary degree. Not for nothing did he become, by reluctant but seemingly inevitable stages, a great admirer of Virginia Woolf. He was singularly thin-skinned, and he acted his own part as both a protection and a dare. And this is where narrative gets harder – indeed, it got harder for Wilson himself, in the ambitious novels he wrote on the run and in the interstices of his impossibly populated life. If Margaret Drabble has trouble finding a clear path through this human jungle, you can see why. Another kind of plot has taken over, one in which the moves are sideways and self-conscious, and where the 'world' gets wider and wider all the time, so that any structure you find is infinitely questionable and frangible.

He had reacted against his scrounging 'playacting' family by upping the stakes, rather than turning into a realist. The awful Johnstone-Wilsons, with their so-called independent means, lived increasingly on shifts and tall tales. Father was a Scots *rentier*, mother second-generation South African, and they had led a vagrant life in a sequence of lodgings and private hotels for many years before Angus arrived, in Bexhill-on-Sea, in 1913. He was the youngest of six sons (the youngest by thirteen years, his mother was forty-five when he was born) and grew up petted, neglected and precocious. In 1922, he was taken to South Africa to visit his mother's family for an idyllic sun-soaked year and a half which – as Margaret Drabble points out, 'expanded in his memory to occupy great tracts of his childhood'. His parents had been hoping for a haven from the insecurities of England, but had to return to 'settle' in Kensington hotels, retreating ahead of their debts. (Years later, he would dream about his parents walking down the street and falling into the coal-holes.)

No one had much respect for schooling in this sporty-seedy world, and he acquired his conventionally privileged Westminster-and-Oxford education rather against the family grain (his mother left money in trust for him). He wasn't, however, insulated from the diverse destinies of his brothers – Fred, farmed out to fleece grandparents, Winn who was a war hero and started a prep school, Captain Clive who flourished a bit shadily in business, and Colin and Pat who camped it up and peddled their charms in Piccadilly before finding the Catholic Church. Wounded Winn, who was the only one with a home and children of his own, found himself bled dry by the rest. The odds were stacked against respectability in this clan. You could, it seemed, 'be' anything at all:

> Towards the end of the war Colin joined the Black and Tans and went to Ireland where he was seduced by a sergeant, who gave him a make-up box and encouraged him to paint his face.

A 'Firbankian character', Colin. But as often there's no documentary evidence to be found for this story, though Colin certainly used make-up, as did Pat, and took an otherwise unexplained and rather proprietorial interest in Irish affairs. When Angus wrote up the family saga in the 1960s, in *No Laughing Matter*, he made them into three boys and three girls, in tribute in part perhaps to the dressing-up games he shared once upon a time with Colin and Pat, featuring the execution of Mary Queen of Scots or Marie Antoinette. He himself 'belonged to no generation', though he never doubted he was 'queer'. He became very much the daughter of the house after his mother's death in 1929, taking her place with doddering but indefatigable Dad, who lasted until 1938.

By this time, Angus was working as a temporary assistant cataloguer at the British Museum, slowly entering in the General Catalogue the 'literature' that arrived by the barrowload. Soon he was escorting Museum stock to safety in Wales, and, soon after that, salvaging and evacuating bomb-damaged books in the Blitz. From the Museum, like several other cataloguers, he removed to war work at the decoding centre at Bletchley Park, which was tense, inbred and claustrophobic. Some enjoyed the camaraderie. Angus threw tantrums, had a nervous breakdown and visited a refugee analyst called Kosterlitz, who got him to write down his dreams, and also suggested in passing that he join a writers' group. Nothing came of this at the time. Instead of discovering his vocation, he fell in love, with a radiant young man (judging from his photograph) called Ian Calder, whom he shared with his long-time friend Bentley Bridgewater. It wasn't until after the war, when he was back at the Museum, that he wrote, in a burst, the stories that would make up *The Wrong Set*. He was thirty-six when the book came out, and he became instantly famous. Suddenly everything had fallen into place: the dream-diary horrors about vulnerability (his first story was the torture-tale 'Raspberry Jam'); the family anecdotes he'd regaled friends with, ever since his schooldays at Westminster; and the bookishness that until now had been displaced on to codes and catalogues.

The stories were luminous, mocking and intensely sensitive to all the itchy symptoms of bad faith. He observed and described the processes of social life with daunting accuracy, and at the same time with collusive inwardness: social intercourse charged with the sexiness of – well, sex. In short, he wrote under the sign of Camp. Not only or mainly in the obvious sense of bringing in gay characters, nor in the sense of gross comic travesty, but in the more subtle style Susan Sontag described in 'Notes on Camp' in 1964 – 'the love of the exaggerated, the "off", of things-being-what-they-are-not'; seeing everything 'in quotation marks'; the glorification of 'character', 'the unity, the force of the person'. In short, 'the theatricalization of experience', a Sontag phrase which very exactly fits the Wilson world. Angus was to be much involved with homosexual law reform, and – in his first novel, *Hemlock and After* (1952) – explored the corrupting effects of living a closeted life. However, it's obviously arguable that the most potent effect of his gayness on his writing was the edge he acquired from this 'alternative' sensibility. The worlds of the British Museum and of Bletchley had another side – as did the whole of respectable middle-class culture. One of his colleagues at the Museum was Willie King (Ceramics), whose wife Viva (Queen of queens) ran a notable salon in Thurloe Square, frequented by Sitwells, Norman Douglas, Somerset Maugham, Ivy Compton-Burnett and Margaret Jourdain, Beverley Nichols, Ernest Thesiger, Nina Hamnett and Mrs Frances Watson, 'whose withered brown Egyptian visage betrayed decades of cat-worship'. Angus had been a lively member of this and other similar 'sets' since the 1930s, and his début as a writer in 1949 – 'the nicest nasty writer after the war', according to the *Daily Telegraph* – fed their style into the mainstream. C. P. Snow (not a friend of Mrs King) described the effect when reviewing a later collection of stories. They were, he said, 'part-savage and part-maudlin': 'It is rather as though a man of acute sensibility felt left out of the human party . . . and was surveying it from the corner of the room . . .' Possibly a smear was intended, but minus the malice, this aptly characterizes Wilson's angle on the human zoo.

Of course, he took to the role of Man of Letters like a duck to water. He was a connoisseur of insecurity, after all, so no novice at this game. The success of *The Wrong Set* came just before a Museum promotion that might have kept him in his profession, and pensionable. As it turned out, he would earn his living from journalism, radio talks, public appearances and (shortly) television and teaching. The fiction never earned enough, however grand his reputation. For years, though, this didn't matter. He loved the vagrant life of ambassadorial British Council tours and conferences and reviewing and literary lunches and dinners and general book-chat so much, he hardly bothered to join in the profession's ritual complaints about it – though he did work hard on behalf of Public Lending Right, to improve the lot of writers much borrowed but less bought. And there was one constant person in his life, who turned up almost at the same time as the stories – Tony Garrett. During the 1950s, they set up house together, metaphorically speaking, and acquired in 1955 an actual house, the flint cottage at Felsham Woodside near Bury St Edmunds which they bought in 1962. That same year, Angus agreed to teach at the brand-new University of

East Anglia, and had an exciting time at the Edinburgh Festival, where – along with Henry Miller, Norman Mailer, Rebecca West, Alexander Trocchi, Muriel Spark and a host of others – he took part in a set of noisy seminars about homosexuality, drugs and Scottish nationalism.

Maybe the idea of the Suffolk cottage was that, off the beaten track, there would be peace and quiet, but it certainly didn't work out that way. Endless people came to visit, and to stay, and there were famous parties. There was also local scandal, which forced Tony out of his job as a probation officer, and into the role of Angus's full-time minder. Yukio Mishima, who came to stay, wrote a splendid thank-you letter describing Tony as 'a seldom man who knows penetratively how a lonely traveller feels'. Travelling (the United States, India, Australia, Russia, Japan) was vital – travelling and people. And Angus had to get away, and wander yet more, in order to work – he wrote in hot countries, composing 'amidst flapping laundry in Morocco and on the Nile, and in the banana groves of Jericho . . .' Wherever they went, he acquired new people: in Sri Lanka, for instance, there was Arthur C. Clarke, who fed him toad-in-the-hole. From India, graduate researchers followed him back to Suffolk, and trudged through the mud to the cottage. Former students like Ian McEwan stayed around as friends. This was the picaresque life. 'There was no stasis to be found', says Drabble (herself a friend by this stage), admiring and appalled.

It's a story that has to end in tears, and so it does. The generous improvidence, the carnival appetite for more (and more), the faith in invention, came to grief in the late 1970s and 80s, when the cultural climate changed. The sun went in, the reviews were mixed at best, his 1980 knighthood had been greeted in some quarters with homophobic malice, he suddenly aged, and became ill and depressed. He looked around and there were only 'endless changing faces and meaningless names', and in 1985 he decided to turn his back on Thatcher's kingdom, and live in France. He had spent all he earned, lived hand-to-mouth, and now the money started to run out, along with his powers of improvisation. This part of the story is sombre, but – as Drabble says – it's 'not a story of compromise or failure'. He died in 1991, back in a

Suffolk nursing home, confined to a small room at the last. One almost feels (and there's a touch of black humour in this) a kind of relief as a reader; at last the breathless lists have stopped, the people have thinned out into a trickle of visitors, and the life surviving in the books is what's left. Margaret Drabble doesn't go in for critical post-mortems. She does, however, stress the bravery and vulnerability of the books and the man alike – as well as the wit and worldliness. You can catch perhaps a sense of what his example meant in her remark that 'If some men weren't really "men", then, thank God, maybe women didn't have to be women.' For other writers he was, like his character Marcus in *No Laughing Matter*, a 'matriarch-patriarch' – writers as different as Paul Bailey and Drabble herself and Jonathan Raban. You can see affinities with his work in writers who figure in the life (Rose Tremain), and those who don't (Alan Hollinghurst). V. S. Pritchett once said that Angus was like an anthropologist at work among the remnants of the middle class. This catches something of his sense of human strangeness, but makes him sound too cool, perhaps. He was the life and soul of the party, and yet at the same time – as he wrote once to Drabble herself, apologizing for a fit of paranoia that ruined a dinner-party she gave – alone in the middle of it all. The public life was in a sense as much his invention as the books. So this is a life-story that gets less solid as it goes on, almost as though the characters were 'characters' indeed, proliferating on all sides, but just a bit transparent, not quite plausible. Thin-skinned, he thinned out the boundary between realities and unrealities, with zest and – it turns out – a touch of terror.

Living like a poet, or, Hello to all that

Robert Graves: Life on the Edge

MIRANDA SEYMOUR

Robert Graves: His Life and Work

MARTIN SEYMOUR-SMITH

Collected Writings on Poetry

ROBERT GRAVES

THIS YEAR MARKS THE centenary of Robert Graves's birth. It is also the moment when he truly crosses over to the other side where the subjects of literary biography live eternally. Miranda Seymour's portrait is balanced, convincing, rounded, done from a strategic, but also inevitable distance. By contrast, Martin Seymour-Smith's 1982 book, now revised and reissued, bears all the stigmata of actual intimacy with its subject. It is edgy, defensive, angry and intimate, the author smarting from his hero's betrayals, yet still loyal to the generous Great Man who answered his letters when he was a schoolboy.

Seymour-Smith thinks *The White Goddess* was a mistake, and deplores the late love-affairs with 'Muses' with names like Cindy, when Graves, acting out his own mythology, coincided so conveniently with Sixties mores. For Miranda Seymour it's all a history, a story. Her Graves is less of a mess, he makes more sense.

Graves himself started the job, in *Goodbye to all That* in 1929. There his puritanical mother Amy (born von Ranke) and his horrible time at philistine Charterhouse form an emotional backdrop to the chaste intensity, the 'wet bond of blood', that united him with his comrades in the trenches. He was so badly wounded he officially died on the Somme in 1916, and when he found himself alive, as Miranda Seymour says, it would have been hard not to feel a touch mythic, 'as if he had been born again'.

His shell-shocked marriage to tomboyish Bohemian Nancy Nicholson didn't solve his problems with sex in general, and heterosexual sex in particular ('loutish he/And sluttish she' he wrote in a prissy verse about what other ranks got up to). They did make babies, though, four, too close together; and contrived to live the kind of pastoral life, cold, damp houses, home-made furniture and clothes, holidays in caravans, that reduced them quite shortly to mutual despair. (In the Fifties Ted Hughes regarded Graves as a mentor, and introduced Sylvia Plath to his work. Hughes and Plath wore themselves down with jam-making, wet nappies, arts and crafts in the same sort of way.) Graves and Nicholson took to importing people to share their marriage, and it was one of these, Sam Harries, who drew their attention to the work of poet Laura Riding. Sam went off to Nepal in pursuit of a guru he and Graves both briefly fancied, and died there. Laura (after unpromising adventures, including sharing a bed with Hart Crane) was persuaded to leave the States to join them and the children and the nanny, on their departure for Egypt, where Graves had taken a job at the university of Cairo. In that exotic setting, which they were all too emotionally fixated to notice, they formed a trio. This became a foursome with an obliging Irishman on their return to London, and then split up, bloodily.

The great event of this time was Riding's suicidal leap from a fourth-floor window, when Geoffrey Phibbs (the Irishman) refused to go on with the game. She survived her horrible injuries, and she and Graves took off into a mythic realm of their own, and 'seemingly at Gertrude Stein's suggestion' went to live in Majorca, leaving Nancy and the children behind. Laura Riding is the Other in Graves's life, and while Miranda Seymour tries to be cool about her, as Graves's invention, someone who fitted into the ready-made Bardic scheme, she still emerges as memorably crazy and sometimes wicked, a painted, hieratic figure, with a mean genius of her own.

In Majorca Graves lost and found himself, became the 'dedicated poet' who, as he said, 'sees history as a dangerous deviation from the true course of human life, an attempt to deny women their age-old moral ascendancy'. This goddess-worship is the perverse flowering of Graves's inability to see women as people. But since Laura was historical enough to be expensive to keep, he was, luckily for posterity, forced to write the *Claudius* books for cash, as well as the poems from out of time the Muse inspired.

The myth survived Laura's 1939 defection (she went to oust another wife, and four more children, and live with a 'farmer-poet' and fan back in America). Graves had already found his second wife Beryl, for whom he wrote some genuinely loving poems, and who saw him through the swinging Muses, flirtations with Sufi gurus, magic mushrooms, the Oxford Professorship of Poetry, American tours, and his long leathery senility (he died in 1985).

He'd become a post-war celebrity, and gathered children and grandchildren around him back in Majorca, but stayed embarrassing, intransigent, gullible and guilty. He believed you had to live like a poet, and so he did. He spoke with an Outsider's edgy authority, as you can see in *Collected Writings on Poetry*, the first volume of a Graves reprint from Carcanet. A pity that it omits his most original early project, *A Survey of Modernist Poetry*, which anticipated brilliantly the close-reading techniques of *New Critics*. But that was a collaboration with Riding, and even from the grave she's able to make a goddess-shaped hole over copyright.

None the less, there's lots of interesting stuff. 'I would always rather be a Court Fool than a Laureate', he said, and even the centenary fuss won't erase his folly, since it's bound together inextricably with the last-ditch romanticism that made his best work so moving.

The culture hero's vision of sameness

F. R. Leavis: A Life in Criticism

IAN MACKILLOP

F. R. LEAVIS IN THE STREETS of Cambridge looked, said one observer, 'like a gas-fitter who read Bunyan'. It's an image that conjures up the Leavis of heroic tradition, a champion of non-conformity, an outsider who recalled the cultural establishment to the values they 'professed' so slackly.

He was a 'Cambridge man', born in the city. Father Harry was a cultivated tradesman, a generation away from the rural Fens, and Frank Raymond brought with him an exigent sensibility (sharpened by war service with a Quaker ambulance unit) when he crossed the town–gown divide to begin a career as a literature teacher. He never became a Cambridge Professor, despite the authority he acquired as a spokesman for English Studies. Ian MacKillop's *Life* is the story of why.

It's a blow-by-blow account of the in-fighting that established Leavis and his students as, in his own words, 'the essential Cam-bridge, in spite of Cambridge . . .' MacKillop, who was a student in the late Fifties, after the great days of the Leavis house-journal *Scrutiny*, when outrage had become almost orthodoxy, writes as an insider, with a judicious air of impersonality, but also protectively, and intimately.

He adopts the Leavis perspective, Cambridge as the world, and he casts serious doubts on the picture of the heroical outsider. His Leavis couldn't be more at home, he forms himself in opposition, thrives on suspicion, back-stabbing and cliques. He does it all in the name of 'organic unity', the quality he feels great works of literature embody. His marriage in 1929 to Queenie embodied unity: she was disowned by her Orthodox Jewish family for marrying 'out' and this consolidated their dialogue of one. If F. R. occasionally flagged in his rebarbative stance, Q. D. stiffened his resolve. Over the years his focus of attention converged with hers. He moved from criticism of poetry to the novel. *The Great Tradition* in 1948, celebrating George Eliot, James and Conrad as the core of English writing, she described as 'my husband's or rather our book on the novel'. The last major work, on Dickens (1970), was openly and officially a collaborative effort.

He had begun in *New Bearings in English Poetry* (1932) by sharing the style of analysis invented by the two earliest heroes of Cambridge criticism, I. A. Richards and William Empson, but he quickly found their understanding of modernity too promiscuous. Richards, says MacKillop, 'had shown the modern world to be a bazaar of beliefs'; Empson's *Seven Types of Ambiguity* celebrated the multiplication of meaning, at the expense of unity, and they both had an unacceptable readiness to embrace hybrid contemporary culture.

MacKillop does his best to make Leavis look daringly modern because he ordered a banned copy of Joyce's *Ulysses*. Actually, he went on to detest Joyce: the way he made sex hilarious, his verbal promiscuity. His contemporary hero was the Eliot of *The Waste Land*: 'the poem exactly fitted Leavis's conviction that modernity meant alienation from an older unified world . . .' His unrequited passion for Eliot is one of the more tragi-comic strands in the narrative, where it's entwined with Leavis's growing sense of persecution. In 1950, he read that Geoffrey Grigson would be giving a series of talks on the English novel, and demanded (in advance) that his publishers take legal action since Grigson was certain to plagiarise *The Great Tradition*.

The English novel was Leavis territory, his proprietorial sense growing ever more acute. Even patient MacKillop says that no reasonable person could attribute his failure to be promoted in Cambridge to 'spite or conspiracy', Leavis 'so frankly ran a system within the system'. Ex-pupils in schools and teacher-training colleges, publishing, British Council posts, 'the crème de la crème that I work with' as he described them, sounding like Miss Jean Brodie, whom he rather came to resemble.

His Cambridge power-base was disintegrating. He couldn't find an heir he could stand, and suspected his disciples of rewriting the 'line' in anticipation of his going. In a cloud of sulphur, he went, to the new University of York, a culture-hero in his own time, speaking out against the technocrats who were hi-jacking university expansion.

MacKillop doesn't question that he was 'English' in his day. But Leavis wasn't so magnanimous. He banished any serious respect for diversity and difference. His modernism is monological, inturned and authoritarian. After Leavis the values of heterogeneity had to be reimported from Europe via structuralism and semiotics: if Richards and Empson had set the agenda, we might have had a more home-grown version. There's an ideal Leavis who stands for literary values, he was invoked in these very pages by John Naughton (on Leavis versus C. P. Snow) only last week. The actual man could only love a very little, and only when he'd read into it a visionary sameness.

Landlocked

Romancing: The Life and Work of Henry Green

JEREMY TREGLOWN

H ENRY GREEN PUT IN an incongruous cameo appearance in
Jeremy Treglown's 1994 biography of Roald Dahl. When an interviewer from the Houston *Post* asked the bestselling author of the low-life
and hilarious 'adult' short-story collection *Someone like You* who his
favourite British writer was, he answered loftily: 'Henry Green'. Treglown thought the reason might have been that Dahl (who anyway loved
a put-down) shared a friend with Green, the painter Matthew Smith,
whose work he *did* know and like. For surely Dahl could have had
little time for an avant-garde writer like Green? Besides, Green was just
the kind of Eton-and-Oxford Englishman who had made him feel so
alien and unappreciated in the London literary world when he first
tried to set up as a writer after the war.

The truth, as it turns out, is that by the 1950s Green was in his
way as much of an outsider as Dahl. His literary friends and fans, too,
were un-English – the Americans Eudora Welty and Terry Southern
(author of *The Magic Christian* and the famously dirty book *Candy*); or
the French New Novelist Nathalie Satraute, who singled out Green and
Ivy Compton-Burnett as (after the demise of Woolf) the most original
and distinctive voices in British writing. Southern managed to coax out
of Green, who was notoriously inarticulate (and not just from the booze),
a 1958 *Paris Review* interview in which he confessed to admiring Céline,
Joyce and Kafka: but they were 'like cats which have licked the plate clean.
You've got to dream up another dish if you're to be a writer.'

By now Green was pretty hopelessly blocked. Sarraute, who thought
this a perfectly natural and logical state for any real writer to find

himself in in the later 20th century, praised him for making the deadly conventionality of British life into a kind of brilliant metafiction. Writer's block was a starting point, a theme, an inspiration for writing about writing. Her description of the contemporary character fiction should be focusing on – 'a being devoid of outline, indefinable, intangible and invisible', an avatar of the author – fits Green's writing very exactly. Except that for Sarraute this was contemporary fiction's game, whereas for Green, it seems, it had become an authentic, personal mess. By the time he was being regularly praised as an original he truly hadn't two ideas to rub together.

It's this double alienation – being without definition, being so much the outsider to your own vocation that you can't work any longer – that Treglown's book explores in Green. It's partly the story of the relations between his family identity as Henry Yorke, upper-class inheritor of the family firm, and his character as Green the writer; but it's also an exploration of the fatal attraction of anonymity, the love affair with society's nobodies that's at the centre of Green's best writing. The title, *Romancing: The Life and Work of Henry Green*, sounds thoroughly traditional, but signals a provocative intent. The puzzles of Green's texts are, Treglown wants to argue, intimately connected with his singularly centreless personality: 'his fiction is an oblique form of self-portrait', and readers 'who have not swallowed the critical dogma that tries to exclude authors from their works' should find the life-story illuminating. Which it is. Green's Modernist textual density and his authorial absenteeism are here inextricably entangled with the way he set about the business of living and working.

So we're not going to reread Green and understand how he ended up imaginatively bankrupt unless we have a Life. This sounds like an echo of Treglown's protracted negotiations with the Yorke family – first this biography was authorised, then authorisation was withdrawn, though there's no blow by blow account of the process. Nor, in the book itself, of any seriously scandalous revelations people might have wanted to suppress. But then that's not necessarily why survivors and family feel so equivocal about biographers. Another reason, and a good one, is the fear that the subject will join the wax museum of 'characters' on display in accounts of 'Bloomsbury', or of the Waughs and Spenders and Actons and Nicolsons and . . . Lives too often deny their subjects' particularity, the banal but precious fact of everyone's uniqueness, which is just what they're cracked up to celebrate. Indeed, it's often the juiciest biographical subjects, Vita Sackville-West, say, or Kingsley Amis, who anticipate the process, and turn themselves into caricatures and stereotypes in life. There's a touch of this about Green's long years of decline, when he drank himself silly, and retreated into an especially British style of polite, slurred anecdotage. But earlier on he was one of the few real anti-novelists whose books explored the dissolution of the old social and sexual plots that kept – still keep – the heritage show on the road.

Green's masterpieces, like *Party Going* (1939) and *Loving* (1945), are devoted to demonstrating the hollowness of traditional loyalties and roles, for all the world as if he were a fictional anthropologist looking at the last days of an alien culture, except that, uniquely uncomfortably, he's doing it from the inside, almost as trapped and confused as his characters. Treglown quotes V. S. Pritchett finely describing Green's special subject as 'the injury done to certain English minds by the main, conventional emphases of English life'. Hence his New-Novelish expertise in 'the blurred, the lethargic, inarticulate part of human beings'.

One of the things *Romancing* brings out with great vividness is the tragicomic character of Green's disaffection – less traumatic than bathetic. His parents belonged to the previous century, and lived on a larger, altogether more picturesque and energetic scale: Vincent Yorke was a classically rounded character, a scholar, a huntsman, a shrewd and autocratic businessman; his mother, Maud, lived for dogs and horses, and seems to have exhausted her interest in her sons with her monumental grief over the death of the eldest, Philip, while still a schoolboy at Eton. She turned his bedroom into a shrine, where nothing could be changed or moved, and then – this is the really revealing bit of the story – moved her maid Mabel in there for convenience's sake, so that Mabel had to sleep among the relics. But then Mabel could sleep among the relics without dispelling the magic of mourning, because she didn't occupy space in the same way at all.

And nor did Henry. He sided with the help. *Loving*, for instance, reverses the Maud/Mabel set-up, with Anglo-Irish nobs Mrs Tennant and her careless, adulterous daughter-in-law Mrs Jack playing bit parts in the lives of their servants. The plot stages an ingenious double-take: Mrs Jack is caught in flagrante by the maid bringing in her breakfast, because what the servants see doesn't count much, for her. But in fact what Mrs Jack gets up to doesn't matter that much to Edith, because Edith has a perfectly absorbing life of her own, with quite enough excitement and confusion and loose ends to be going on with. Evelyn Waugh, revealingly, found this book infuriating; prewar he'd praised Green, but while he confined himself to complaining fussily to his face about some of the social detail in *Loving* – surely if these were really gentry they wouldn't be renting the house, and so forth – to others he declared it 'obscene'. Perhaps he was thinking of scenes like this one between Edith and her friend Kate, in the afternoon, in their bedroom:

'Kate I'm getting too hot.'
'Take off some of your clothes then silly. Come on with you I'll help.'
'Quiet. There's Mrs Jack's stockings I've got to go over.'
'If you lie on your buttons I can't undo 'em at the back can I?' Kate said. Then she tickled Edith to make her shift.
'Mercy stop it,' Edith screamed . . . But she made it easier for Kate by moving her body here and there as was required.
'It's only your old uniform,' Kate said and soon Edith was lying almost naked.
'I'll stroke you if you like,' Kate said. 'Shut your eyes now.'
'I ought to be going over those silk stockings.'
'If you don't take good care I'll run over you like you was an old pair Edie and darn you in all sorts of places you wouldn't think.'
They giggled in shrieks again at this and then quietened down.

Perhaps the most disturbing thing about the writing here is that it's *not* voyeuristic, but one of those moments of (textual) bliss when Green seems to lose himself – his gender, his class, his authorial voice – in his characters. 'It's only your old uniform . . .' He longs to be 'demobbed', liberated into a state of indeterminacy and ambiguity. Not that it's possible to sustain it for long. Edie and Kate will go their separate, conventional ways; the children of the house, allowed to run wild and play with the cook's nephew, will be safely accounted for as they grow up, the world will restabilise itself, more's the pity.

You can hardly imagine a scene more at odds with the sensibility of the author of *Brideshead Revisited*. And to add insult to injury, the whole thing has no camp allusion to metaphysics, either. Emma Tennant, who was briefly Green's daughter-in-law, thinks that his scepticism is one of the keys to his elusive character as a writer and as a man:

> He was too clear-sighted to have any religion. He wasn't going to have any Communism or Fascism or any God or anything at all. That was a cruel fate for him. But if he hadn't had that complete lack of belief in things he wouldn't have been able to write those books with their extraordinary poetic distance, because something sentimental would have got into the writing. It's because he didn't that the writing lives.

Thus his 1929 novel, *Living*, the book that established his reputation at the age of 24, dealt with the lives of factory-workers, based on those he'd met when he dropped out of Oxford and went to work on the shop-floor of the family foundry in Birmingham, entirely without benefit of 'collective' political language or conviction. And this is of a piece with his particular vision, if you can call it that.

One sign that he knew what he was up to is the fact that in *Living* Mr Craigan, who belongs to the older generation, reads Dickens and asks his granddaughter Lily when she runs off with Bert to Liverpool whether they spent the night together. He expects a full-blooded Victorian plot. But that's not at all what has happened: Lily and Bert simply run out of steam in Liverpool, en route to Canada – they cannot, when it comes to it, plunge into the unknown, they're defeated by the amorphousness of their personalities, being products of the present time. Landlocked, they panic at the smell of the sea: Lily has the horrors as the searchlight from a lighthouse sweeps the sky: 'She would not look up again . . . She was blank, blank. Again it came along the sky.' She returns home, to settle for the old prospects.

Green himself, in his life as Henry Yorke, did something rather similar. During his two-year stint in the Farringdon Works he never lost touch with his family or friends, he kept one foot on their ground always, and if he was – as everyone who knew him thought – happy for once, it seems to have been because he was liberated as an observer, able to store up for himself other people's voices, hobbies (racing pigeons, football), awful Sundays ('worst day in the world'), and look at his own class from the outside, too. The year *Living* was published he married Dig Biddulph, the daughter of his parents' neighbours at Ledbury Park, though he was rather in love with her sister Mary, too, and they both seem to have been very fond of him – the kind of eminently suitable, vaguely incestuous marriage that typified his world. The line of least resistance for all concerned. They had a son, Sebastian, and entertained and partied, and he went to work at head office in London, and fell in love from time to time with other women, some of them – like Rosamond Lehmann – formidably wilful and attractive, though there was never any question of leaving his wife. His girlfriends usually stayed friends once the affairs were over; and Dig usually stayed friends with them too, and no one ever knew whether she 'knew' or not – certainly no one ever spoke about it.

There were no domestic scenes, no 'words'. And never a question either of affairs with women outside his class (or at least outside London's bohemia): he wanted to be those girls, write them, not make love to them. Indeed the Yorkes seem to have been rather inept with their 'help', always losing cooks and having to eat out. And though he wrote children so well, he wasn't by the sound of things a better than conventional father, a bit distant. The only other real digression was the war, when he joined the London Auxiliary Fire Service, and once again was working alongside strangers, and this period seems to have acted – as did the foundry – as a source of energy and inspiration. Otherwise he more and more listened to other people's voices in the pub, or in the bus on his way to the office, where he also drank, and gradually lost heart. He seems to have wanted quite badly to think of his writing as honest toil, 'work': but the main result of *that* was interfering unhelpfully in his publisher's sales of foreign rights, or wisely deciding that paperbacks were a bad idea.

His last book was *Doting* in 1952. Its characters, as Treglown points out, come close to home: 'Arthur's mid-life crisis, Diana's reiterations of the doctor's warnings against his drinking . . . her unhappiness, yet her unflagging dedication to her in every sense hopeless husband'. The novel's last sentence is: 'The next day they all went on very much the same.' And so they did, for twenty more years, except that he wrote nothing more, though he went through the motions. He was only in his forties, but redundant, out of work, unemployed. The last chapters recounting Green's achingly slow disintegration are the best and most original. Treglown has taken a leaf out of his subject's books in describing the surreally inarticulate life Henry and Dig lived – she saying to dismayed visitors that poor Henry has a chill, when he's insensible, or even, sometimes, in hospital.

Michael Holroyd, working on his book on Lytton Strachey, went to interview Green about Ottoline Morrell, whom he'd known well, of course, like most of those more flamboyant contemporaries who were figuring in new Lives: 'Dig received him politely, picking her way gracefully over a disheveled, sleeping figure on the stairs whom Holroyd took to be a tramp. It was Henry. Dig mildly instructed him to tidy himself up and he soon reappeared neatly shaved and well dressed, and sat down to talk helpfully to the interviewer.' Almost to the end Henry could on occasion get back into uniform, though apparently he usually wore his bedroom slippers with his suit. Asked for his opinions on the world, he'd tell people one should sit as still as possible, try not to go out. He didn't actually talk helpfully to interviewers, almost ever, he simply adopted a parody of the correct language. His very emptiness – that weird domestic space he shared with Dig, his true other half in this, a genius of 'denial' – becomes memorably real. Treglown, who has had a thing about anonymity ever since editing the *TLS* (and is currently plotting to 'out' all those past generations of anonymous reviewers), clearly takes a perverse pleasure in Green's end. Now you see him, and now you don't. *Romancing* is a hidden polemic on behalf of the much maligned craft of literary biography. Like his subject, though, Treglown can't quite bring himself to come out and say so.

III

The Women's Camp

The old girl network

Literary Women

ELLEN MOERS

THIS IS THE FIRST really good general book on women's writing to emerge from the broody hum and cackle of the past decade. There have been many fighting revaluations of respectable women writers, and a few genuine rediscoveries, but no one has managed to combine partisanship with criticism at all consistently. Ellen Moers does: for once there is no necessity to respond with mental reservations ('all in a good cause', 'women's studies is in its infancy' and so forth). Her sophistication, style and density of information make the notion of a distinct tradition of women's writing (complete with anti-traditions, contradictory turnings, dead-ends and wild offshoots) into a critical reality. And the edifice she assembles is entertaining enough, with its gothic nurseries and epic salons, to banish decisively the memory of her predecessors and their plodding progress from Fanny Burney to Margaret Drabble, which all too often came out as a short distance indeed, a mere shuffle across the carpet.

The women who set the pace for Ellen Moers are, as the subtitle says, 'the great writers', showy, extravagant and plentifully endowed with imagination. French and American women, often who point up the signs of passion and ambition in their quieter sisters. Her opening chapter ('my tale is one of triumph, not a quest for failure') focuses on two of the luckiest and most successful writers of the nineteenth century, George Sand and Elizabeth Barrett Browning. They ate their cake and had it too – lived their fantasy lives in fact. And they represented for their contemporaries the incarnation of the woman of genius. ' 'Tis pretty, to remark', says a rueful fellow in Mrs Browning's *Aurora Leigh*,

How women can love women of your sort,
And tie their hearts with love-knots to your feet,
Grown insolent about you against men
And put us down by putting up the lip. . . .

That last phrase is presumably a potted Jacobeanism about scorn, but like so much in Mrs Browning it is a prophetic approximation to modern slang – the sort of thing that made her seem both sublime and approachable, splendid and vulgar (as was George Sand, in a different way). They stand at the beginning here for that reason: their confident, prolific and self-delighting assertion of the public power of the writer.

Ms Moers wrote another very good book, *The Dandy* (1960), and it is that sense of style – a compound of attitudes, postures and personal myths as well as a matter of language – that works so well here on the women. Brummel, Count D'Orsay and Disraeli were artists of appearances, not essences, and they seem to have provided her with a wonderfully effective precedent for getting away from the introspective, bluestocking version of literary ladies. She starts with their outsides, their famous, not quite empty gestures ('Let us try to take *Corinne* seriously . . . the novel that Mme de Staël had the brilliance but not the talent to write'), and so contrives to capture her subjects whole. The book also has twenty-four pages of portraits and photographs to exemplify the fascination of surfaces: prize grotesques like late Colette, or Isak Dinesen wearing her ancient skin as if it were New Look drapery; Harriet Martineau (by Daniel Maclise) toasting a muffin, or more likely a chop, and rubbing noses with a prickly cat; bold Mary Wollstonecraft face to face with her sadder, more Victorian (if more exposed) daughter Mary Shelley; and Mme de Staël at thirteen, a bewigged and bright Lolita. Ms Moers assumes (surely rightly) that the language of looks is something women have studied in greater 'depth' than men (except dandies), and she ticks off George Eliot for being so lyingly censorious about pretty women. She writes with relish about the images of themselves writers project. For example, on the giants of the early twentieth century, Cather, Stein, Woolf, Colette:

There is something imposing, even alarming, about the four of them. As a company, I can't help visualizing them blocked out together in stone as a sort of Henry Moore grouping – massive sculptural forms, sombre, solid and remote, with heavy shoulders, strongly modelled skulls, and perhaps a hole – in the Moore style – where the heart is.

This is fun, but there is a straightforward critical point: an awareness of the importance of imitation, of how literature is made out of other literature, by borrowings and appropriations, one writer finding 'her' voice in another. She has little time for the weary idea that what characterizes women's writing is artlessness, spontaneity – it was Richardson who invented that coy manner, and tutored his female correspondents in it. Although the web of influence crosses sexual boundaries, she argues convincingly that women, to whom much of the 'personal give-and-take of the literary life was closed . . . studied with a special closeness the works written by their own sex'. Through reading, and often through letters, they part-created, part-stole their own idioms, so that critics are not going to be able to assess, say, *Aurora Leigh* (a 'kaleidoscopic view of nineteenth-century fiction, mainly by women') until they come to terms with this enthusiastic mutual plunder. Women writers are engaged in 'refashioning' a language largely fabricated 'before the days of widespread female literacy'. (There is an obvious analogy with the problems of dealing with 'popular' literature, where it's also no good looking for 'authenticity' – working-class writers in the nineteenth century all pinched their language and made defiant fictions out of hand-me-downs.) Not that Ms Moers takes issue very directly with the routine critical assumptions about originality; perhaps wisely (certainly tactfully) she relies on quotation and analysis to show that these shared myths and borrowed plumes produced a various, vital – and occasionally great – tradition.

The networks of influence, rejection and cunning borrowing she uncovers are utterly absorbing: George Eliot's irritatingly saintly Dina Morris in *Adam Bede*, preaching on the village green, becomes a lot more intriguing as a descendant of Mme de Staël's scandalously romantic *improvisatrice*, strumming her lyre at a Roman carnival; and even Adam acquires some interest if you entertain Ms Moers's suggestion that he's really Robert Martin from *Emma* turned inside out. Jane Austen's reading list in turn (except for Shakespeare, Cowper and Dr Johnson, mostly a collection of baddish women novelists) demonstrates how the individual feeds off the pioneering, provincial ruck; though she did, interestingly, make good use of Mme de Genlis's moral tales as well. The literary incest that went on between Emily Dickinson and Mrs Browning (and Mrs Browning and *Jane Eyre*) is her most extreme example, but there are wildly improbable conjunctions too, such as Mme de Staël and Hannah More. They could all pillage each other because, despite the cultural differences and furious arguments dividing them, they shared the chosen vocation of writing, and the more or less unwilling vocation of their sex. George Sand reviewed *Uncle Tom's Cabin*, Gertrude Stein found her 'red deeps' in George Eliot. Ms Moers is particularly good on the special angle sex gave them on topics as diverse as literacy, travel and monsters. And she confronts without embarrassment the likely fact that the most passionate poets (Emily Brontë, Emily Dickinson; Christina Rossetti) were virgins – 'we now can say, with both assurance and relief, that it was not some pawky, consumptive Yorkshire curate [but] ... Julius Brenzaida, Prince of Agora ...'. In short, one more thing they shared was an elaborate, shameless and highly satisfying fantasy life. Except that Ms Moers would want to add that 'fantasy' is indistinguishable from imagination, and that the sneers it has provoked are merely impertinent.

Her best energies are devoted to explicating the generous, large-scale myth-makers of the nineteenth century. The book's one systematic foray into literary history deals with this 'epic age', and more recent literature has a (comparatively) thin time, not only because it is impossible to do everything at once; but also because by implication she finds less to admire in it. Precisely why, it is hard to tell: though among the few gaps it is possible to detect in her narrative is one called masochism (her piece on Ann Radcliffe, stressing how sensible suffering Emily is, seems entirely unconvincing); and another I cannot put a name to, where Simone de Beauvoir should come in. It seems to me, if I interpret her omissions correctly, that she is censoring the dry and weepy poles of women's writings (the ones most about men) and so misses out on some of the choicest pleasures of the sex war.

But since her focus on the collective epic produces so many insights, it would be ungracious to complain. After all, she is almost certainly right that segregating women's writing, and concentrating on their interrelations, is for the moment necessary and exhilarating. Some readers may be irritated by her bibliographical apparatus (where Wordsworth, William appears under Wordsworth, Dorothy, and Ted Hughes seems to have become a bad dream invented by Sylvia Plath), although on the whole the gesture seems fair enough in an unfair world. More seriously, what she has achieved in *Literary Women* is the all-important critical feat of bringing attention (clever, sympathetic attention) to a range of literary issues that until recently were almost invisible. It may take time for judgments about the quality of some of her material to settle down – she admits that until she thought of them as women, she could not stand Mary Shelley or Mrs Browning. Without reading them fully in the first place, however, judgments are impossible. Which is why this book has enriched the practice of criticism.

The heroine as hero

Elizabeth Barrett Browning: Aurora Leigh and Other Poems

INTRODUCED BY CORA KAPLAN

*A*URORA LEIGH IS THE most interesting test-case so far for a feminist revaluation of literary history. On its publication in 1856, and for a generation afterwards, it was both hugely popular and intensely admired (by, for example, Paskin, George Eliot, Landor); it seemed to break the male monopoly on epic and on comprehensiveness of soul – that rather confused tradition in which the mantle of Shakespeare was held to have fallen on Scott, or Dickens – and to rescue the image of the woman artist from chivalrous contempt. In the event, however, its reputation slumped, and Elizabeth Barrett Browning with her spaniel ringlets, opium-bright eyes and romantic elopement became, with a little help from Hollywood, almost the archetype of the powerless, fey poetess. Having surfaced briefly from the throng of women writers whose work could be regarded more or less as a side-effect of frustration (or, in the difficult case of George Eliot, as an extension of the womanly duty of mediation) she sank without trace. Or was submerged.

Either way, *Aurora Leigh* remains a problematic monument to what Ellen Moers, in *Literary Women*, called the 'epic age' of women's literature: that is, the period between the 1780s and the 1860s when women again and again appropriated the grand style to themselves (mostly in France and America, which is why Elizabeth Barrett Browning stands out) only finally to lose it. Cora Kaplan takes up the point in her introduction to this new edition. *Aurora Leigh*, she says, is a collage of allusions to and borrowings from heroic predecessors. The heroine is Mme de Staël's Corinne unsubtly modified: 'The most significant alteration made by Barrett Browning is the most vulgar one. Corinne dies of disappointed love; Barrett Browning makes damned sure that Aurora, her modern Corinne, survives'. She is given George Sand's real name, as a signal that nice Mrs Browning had not only gleefully read but inwardly digested the novels of that 'large-brained woman and large-hearted man'. And Romney Leigh, the unfortunate hero, has to live through a condensed version of *Jane Eyre*, in which he suffers the fates of both St John Rivers and Rochester before he's fit to be married. There was no shortage of sources for an epic of modern life: Elizabeth Barrett Browning, partly by dint of a determined programme of subversive reading ('I read Mary Wollstonecraft when I was thirteen – no, twelve!'), had a whole range of fictional types and incidents she could make over into poetic shorthand. The problem of reassessment is, as a result, twofold: first, you need to recover her context pretty thoroughly before you can make up your mind how intelligently and creatively she uses all her borrowings; and secondly, since her style of epic collage spawned no later tradition, there's a more general critical embarrassment about its status and meaning. Is it after all merely derivative? Or is her art of re-creation (as Ellen Moers suggested and as Cora Kaplan reasserts here) to be understood as a most inventive response to the fact that she needed to avoid or upturn 'a metaphorical tradition and political perspective formed and dominated by the male voice'?

Certainly, she both intensified her female predecessors' self-centredness, and systematically undermined male claims to objectivity and social action. Romney Leigh, as well as getting the benefit of Charlotte Brontë's meditations on heroes, has to stand for Charles Kingsley's Christian Socialist aspirations: he is pure, chilly, selfless and dedicated (via statistics, blue books and resettlement schemes) to cleaning up the slums and rehabilitating the degraded poor. Aurora, like her creator, attacks him for his lack of poetry, his flouting of metaphysics (some people are just *evil*) and his preoccupation with mankind in general, as opposed to passionate involvement with individuals in particular (in particular, herself). His philanthropic schemes, she argues (and of course the plot proves her right), are doomed because he's trying to restore a sense of spiritual identity to people without having it himself (rather like J. S. Mill working for the greatest happiness of the greatest number in a state of suicidal depression). Unfairly, but very effectively, Elizabeth Barrett Browning, who had seen almost nothing of outcast London, borrows from the earnest descriptions of poverty in Kingsley's *Alton Locke* to score against Romney (and Kingsley too). She selects and condenses her material until she arrives at a picture of the poor that is so grotesque it makes Romney's solemn schemes look absurd.

Not that she was indifferent to suffering, exactly. She knew very well that her individualist-spiritualist line on these things was suspect – 'many at this hour are ... dying from want. Can we tell them to think of their souls?' – and she spoke up eloquently for factory children, slaves and prostitutes. However, in *Aurora Leigh* the priority is to find yourself, and that means turning down the invitation to be Romney's 'helpmate', because 'He might cut/My body into coins to give away/Among his other paupers'. As she pointed out elsewhere, apropos of Florence Nightingale, women had been binding wounds since the siege of Troy, and it hadn't got them, or their men, very far. For her the truly radical act was to write, to claim an individual vocation and, unlike any of her English predecessors, to make her heroine Aurora a writer too. As Cora Kaplan says, in doing this she 'breaks a very specific silence, almost a gentleman's agreement between women authors and the arbiters of high culture in Victorian England, that allowed women to write if only they would shut up about it'. Far from shutting up, of course, the poem boasts and exults about its heroine's and its author's pleasure in writing, and contrasts the inwardness and genuineness of Aurora's work ('Transfixing with a special, central power/The flat experience of the common man') with the hollowness of Romney's.

The writing about writing produces some of the best lines, where Elizabeth Barrett Browning's long invalid experience of living through books feeds into her verbal excitement. She nowhere apologizes for calling it 'work', and indeed conducts a provocative campaign against the usual use of that word where genteel women are concerned – i.e., needlework. Perhaps she remembered Mary Wollstonecraft's withering analysis of sewing as part of society's conspiracy to keep middle-class women (literally and politically) short-sighted, and to deprive working-class women of employment. Anyway, she has Aurora loathe needlework quite as much as, according to letters, she did herself, and obviously makes a connection between such approved accomplishments and the detailed, prosaic vision other women writers were praised for. Her borrowed plumes, symbolical shorthand and defiant literariness were designed to cut out that patient, domestic labour, as well as the more public versions of service ('Come, sweep my barns and keep my hospitals'), and provide a direct route to separate self-fulfilment.

The costs in terms of social realism are clear – compared with Mrs Gaskell, for instance, she's insensitive, bizarre, self-indulgent. However, her hybrid, aggressive novel-poem does reveal a mental geography altogether more challenging than anything to be found in such even-tempered and observant contemporaries, precisely because she is more selfish. She was surely not entirely wrong to suggest that philanthropy based on self-ignorance was a characteristic disease of her age, and that middle-class men had better take account of the oppression of their wives before expecting them to look after the other paupers. In a poem on the grand scale, she could say things about herself and her sex by way of metaphor ('My multitudinous mountains, sitting in/The magic circle with the mutual touch/ Electric panting from their full deep hearts') which were a great deal coarser and more narcissistic than the vulgarities Charlotte Brontë's reviewers flayed her for. The very unevenness of the texture of her verse, overlapping with colloquial prose at one extreme and *Paradise Lost* at the other allows her extraordinary escapes from Victorianism: lines incongruously anticipating Wallace Stevens ('All actual heroes are essential men'); horrors from Jacobean tragedy ('cheek to cheek/With him who stinks since Friday'); cheerful pastoral ('cows push out/ Impatient horns and tolerant churning mouths'); and *Waste Land* cadences ('let us clear the tubes/And wait for rains'). Altogether, The Women's Press and Cora Kaplan are to be congratulated for rescuing a poem so well-equipped for time-travel out of the *Collected Works* buried in secondhand bookshops, though I wish they had not themselves gone in for the sublime slapdash of transposing pp. 79/80, 83/4 and 171/2. Despite that, *Aurora Leigh* will now take its place in the history of

Victorian fiction, elbowing a few altruists aside; it should also, given its author's recalcitrant and ruthless individualism, provide a sharp focus for feminist debate.

A contrary Muse

Lawrence and Women

EDITED BY ANNE SMITH

THERE IS A PHOTOGRAPH, reproduced a few years back in Robert Lucas's biography of Frieda Lawrence, which the title *Lawrence and Women* instantly conjures up. It shows from left to right, Mabel Dodge Luhan, Frieda and Dorothy Brett in a grinning huddle (presumably at the ranch in Taos, New Mexico): Frieda, large, flowered, frilled, tough and frowsy has her big mouth derisively stretched, with a fag hanging from one corner. They would look like the witches from *Macbeth*, except that they are a bit too jolly. The picture has no date, so one does not know whether it belongs to the period when aggressive millionaire Mabel and stubborn, devoted Brett were each trying to take Lawrence off Frieda's hands, or to the later time when Frieda returned to the ranch to squabble over his ashes with them, and mind his shrine. Either way, it is a daunting reminder of Lawrence's women. Looking at that picture, you have to admit: he didn't pick the easy ones.

Or as Anne Smith puts it in her opening essay in *Lawrence and Women*, 'at least the battle of the sexes was still a valid one for Lawrence, and we should probably be grateful to Frieda for the fact that it was . . .'. And even before their momentous meeting in 1912, the women he experimented with were almost all 'challenges', trying for various forms of emancipation. Anne Smith deals mainly with the biographical angle and reassembles what is now a fairly well-established but still nastily fascinating story: his doomed, stifling love for his mother and her jealous possession of him; his confusion about sex-roles as an ailing, 'sensitive' child ('Dicky Dicky Denches plays with the wenches'); his frigid teasing friendship with Jessie Chambers, and the battle between

Jessie and Mrs Lawrence for his love (Frieda: 'the best horse won'). This phase culminated in *Sons and Lovers* in which Jessie (whom he asked to read the proofs) is cruelly done over as 'Miriam', and Alice Dax and Louie Burrows, his fleshlier loves, are unconvincingly compressed into 'Clara': the novel reveals him as a suffering, sex-crucified and so very dangerous man. His sense that his very survival was at stake enabled him to make ruthless use of his women while seeing himself as humiliatingly passive.

Frieda claimed she did not think much of *Sons and Lovers* (which he finally rewrote with her) but also admitted that at the time she was probably busy punishing him for having had to leave her children behind, and for his jealousy of them. But though she was a rather slap-happy literary critic, one of her comments on the novel does suggest she early understood the special relation between life and literature in Lawrence's work. Writing to Edward Garnett about 'L's formlessness', she says – '"form" . . . Why are you English so keen on it? Their own form wants smashing in almost any direction, but they can't come out of their snail house.' She seems to have associated the anxiety about aesthetic distance with 'good form', and she may have a point. While the others (Jessie Chambers most sadly) felt violated and betrayed by Lawrence's fictional use of them, Frieda from the beginning barged her way into his creative processes ('I hate art, it seems like grammar') and fought him at every stage. One result of this – it's surely as much to do with Frieda as the First World War – is the painfully disintegrated and fluid 'form' of *Women in Love*. Mark Kinkead-Weekes in his essay 'Eros and Metaphor' in this anthology describes it this way: 'the belief that conflict is the condition of growth encouraged Lawrence to dramatize conflicting readings of life and relationship in his characters, so that they subject one another's insights, and his, to a continuous crossfire of criticism, intenser than ever before.' In short Frieda not only got into the novels as a character (adored, loathed, caricatured, 'mastered') but radically altered their shape and style. The very English plot about growing up and putting yourself together (*Sons and Lovers*, but also on a larger scale the first two generations of *The Rainbow*) falls violently apart, as Lawrence did.

It seems worthwhile to emphasize the untidiness and virulence of the relation between the fiction and the life, since most of the contributors to this volume rather take it for granted, and so leave themselves open to attack for importing irrelevant and trendy 'Women's Studies' notions into an essentially literary problem. But when Lawrence becomes 'literary' (Frieda watched it beginning to happen with incredulity towards the end of her long life) he will also have failed in the most decisive way. The number of books written about him by his 'friends' is not just evidence of their idolatry and resentment, but of the nature of his writing. Even the awful psychic acrobatics of Mabel Dodge Luhan – 'I drew myself all in to the core of my being where there is a live, plangent force lying passive . . . becoming entirely that . . . I leaped through space joining myself to the central core of Lawrence' – get uncomfortably close to the frantic inanities of his worst fiction. The question is not whether you can usefully talk about the topic of women, but how to do it. Anne Smith's biographical piece is for the most part tactful and shrewd: of the elopement and marriage with Frieda, for instance, she writes, 'she did not release him from his oedipal compulsions, she only cured him of the uncomfortable guilt which attached to them', which seems right. However, there is an occasional tone of diagnostic common sense that makes me uneasy – 'over a long period, he lacked a healthy sense of the "otherness" of women, and for the whole of his life he could not reconcile an intimate knowledge of a woman's mind with sexual attraction towards her'. I can't work out here what a 'healthy sense' would be. In one way, it sounds like a wild understatement: Lawrence's transgressions against normalcy are much more glaring and lurid than that, surely? And isn't it his capacity *not* to reconcile things that makes him impressive?

Something of the same worry attaches to Faith Pullin's essay on 'Lawrence's Treatment of Women'; it is the most waspish piece in the book, but misfires because what it is saying ('infantile', 'regressive', 'unable to relate to women as people') is in a sense obviously true, and yet unilluminating. Again it is a question of norms (Paul's desolation at the end of *Sons and Lovers* is 'infinitely greater than that that should attend the death of a parent, however beloved') and what emerges is a rather shallow sense of how enlightened we all are now. Perhaps demonstrating how unhealthy and maladjusted Lawrence was still matters, as an antidote to Leavis's version, and to his monotonously respectable presence on A-level syllabuses. If so, well and good – anything that helps stamp out the college-of-education pieties about organic wisdom is useful. But assuming that Lawrence is unlikely to be rehabilitated as the 'vitally whole' writer of the great tradition, the priority is to redefine for ourselves his *particular* meaning and place, the more exact nature of his formlessness. Frieda gets quoted a bit too often as though she was a neutral observer, and as though she did not horribly relish their conflicts, whereas if you go back to her letters and memoirs you begin to wonder whether Lawrence may not have had good reason to think of women as something other than people.

For example, one of Frieda's most telling observations was that 'In his heart of hearts I think he always dreaded women, felt that they were in the end more powerful than men' (*Not I, But the Wind . . .*, 1935). The passage goes on 'Woman is so absolute and undeniable. Man moves, this spirit flies here and there but you can't go beyond a woman . . .' And so on. Lawrence was not alone in his world of mythic conflict. Frieda had her own titanic abstractions to pit against his, partly derived no doubt from the 'erotic movement' in Germany which (as Martin Green showed in *The von Richthofen Sisters*) spawned a dire matriarchal mutant of the 'new woman'. Frieda seems to have taken to the role of Muse, too: Otto Gross, Freudian apostate and prophet of eroticism, wrote to her in about 1907, 'I need you because you make me sure and good'; and in the 1940s Karl von Marbahr, a sweetheart she hadn't seen for more than forty years, wrote, 'Now I know if I had resigned my commission and started something else, together with you, I would have amounted to something as a writer or a journalist'. She had her own powerful 'aura' that predated Lawrence, and survived him, though he was of course its main beneficiary, willing and unwilling. Her accounts of their famous battles make sad reading, but there is still the implication that, in several senses, he has met his match:

I was many times frightened but never the last bit of me. Once, I
remember, he had worked himself up and his hands were on my throat
and he was pressing me against the wall and ground out: 'I am the
master. I am the master.' I said: 'Is that all? You may be master as
much as you like. I don't care.' His hands dropped away, he looked at
me in astonishment and was all right.

'Never the last bit of me' – generous, reckless and committed as
she was, Frieda retained a private corner of herself from which to
condescend. One doubts very much whether Lawrence was 'all right';
in fact, it's clear she deeply damaged him, tit for tat. 'She may give
her life for me', says the Marchese in *Aaron's Rod*. 'But why? Only
because I am *here*.'

The novels of hatred, misogyny and male togetherness – *Aaron's
Rod*, *Kangaroo*, *The Plumed Serpent* – bear Frieda's imprint most unmistakably. 'Don't swank' says Harriet in *Kangaroo*, 'you don't live alone
. . . I know how much alone you are with me always there keeping you
together.' And even when Kate in *The Plumed Serpent* swoons before
the newly risen Mexican god-man, we are told:

> At the same time, as is so often the case with any spell, it did not bind
> her completely. She was spellbound, but not utterly acquiescent. In one
> corner of her soul was revulsion and a touch of nausea.

In these books Lawrence invents the most elaborate psychological
machinery for producing awe, but can never be satisfied, because even
submission can mean contempt. 'If I remember rightly', Frieda wrote
to one scholarly inquirer, 'I did not oppose his colony plan; my reason:
I never believed in it.' And to another, less bluntly, 'I don't think
"respect" matters to women. I didn't apply "principles" to him . . .'
Someone in *Aaron's Rod* suggests 'a balancing of wills'; someone else
says spitefully, 'My dear boy, the balance lies in that, that when one
goes up, the other goes down'. It doesn't do to treat this as counter-
revolutionary chauvinism merely. If Lawrence sometimes behaved mon-
strously, so did Frieda; 'of course I am an anarchist and a beastly
"aristo",' she wrote jokily in a letter – and she was.

This is not meant exactly as an apologia for Lawrence; only to suggest that fairness, justice, balance, niceness and so on may not have been (may not be now) plausible terms to apply to his treatment of sexual relations and marriage. T. E. Apter, herself a wilfully individual novelist, makes a similar point in her essay here, 'Let's Hear What the Male Chauvinist is Saying'. She takes the notorious scene in *The Plumed Serpent* where Cipriano deliberately denies Kate her usual orgasm ('the beak-line friction of Aphrodite of the foam') and she settles, after a moment's disappointment, for passive 'untellable' satisfaction 'from the volcanic deeps'. Though it is implausibly and infuriatingly described, Ms Apter argues, Lawrence does here have a point about the difference between the enlightened therapists' view of sex and its 'more elemental and untamable aspects' – 'it is not pleasure alone that makes sex so deeply rooted in our lives'. *The Hite Report* would, I imagine, confirm all Lawrence's most evil suspicions about women's unnatural nature, in its deliberate drift towards a vision of the lone, liberated, masturbatory female, who may or may not use a man for her pleasure. He would have recognized at once the attraction of the nunnery, since he himself, in his blood-brotherhood phases, felt the same pull towards the monastery, the same wearily angry revolution against the 'terrible passive games of fixed tension' between the sexes.

But what of *Lady Chatterley*? In truth, the writers of this volume seem a bit embarrassed about it. Mark Kinkead-Weekes detects an 'absence of conflict and opposition', an 'imaginative process based on exclusion'. Mark Spilka in the book's concluding piece on 'Lawrence's Hostility in Wilful Women' argues humorously and expertly that its theme is the final wisdom of weariness – 'if you wait long enough, the world will do it for you', that is, time and failure will efface self-will in the dread woman, allow a kind of lapse into the past and into biological identity (so that Lawrence can at long last identify with his father, in Mellors). 'His maleness, if not his potency, was finally secure . . .' despite the burst of aggression and the sodomy, which Professor Spilka sees Connie as accepting rather in the Frieda spirit of all-embracing love ('Don't you think', Frieda says in a letter, 'one wants to be loved with one's littleness, one's everything of shame and all'). It is an argument that makes for a mellow ending – but still a far cry from Lady C's reputation in the 1950s and 1960s, and in the heady days of the trial. Lawrence simply no longer looks like a liberator of sexual energies, a source of strength, or even a pillar of cloud. Feminist re-readings have something to do with this, but so have the 'straighter' academic critics, who have started stressing the gaps and conflicts Frieda relished. We have returned, in many ways, to the Lawrence Middleton Murry agonized over in 1931 – 'not the forerunner of the integration of a new man, but the perfect paradigm of the disintegration of an old one'.

Lawrence and Women does not really live up to the interest of its topic, partly because the writers are selfconscious about trying to be fair, and partly because, I think, they feel a bit defensive about all this mythic heterosexuality, as though they are not sure it has much future, on the grand scale. Anne Smith's sentence sticks in the mind – 'at least the battle of the sexes was still a valid one for Lawrence'. Certainly in much contemporary fiction, it is not: being alone provides the goal, the horror and the excitement. There are women writers with the battle-animus and the furious unfairness of Lawrence, though the one that fits the bill best – Christina Stead – really belongs to the 1940s, and was out of print until very recently. The fight goes on in other modes, however, in Angela Carter's Gothic sex-change operations for example. And surely it must, unless (like Kate Millett) you contemplate with glee some sort of Amazonian imaginative community – or unless you feel confident that the old bugbear of sexual smothering (and the old vision of an erotic paradise regained) have vanished away, changed out of recognition. In that case Lawrence becomes a museum piece, an interesting fetish(ist). And the novel of the solitary 'I' surrounded by unreachable or unresisting 'others' becomes the right metaphor. It sounds unlikely, and drab. 'Without contraries is no progression' as we all know. But it's not easy, since *with* them there's not much progression either – especially if your contrary Muse is as stubbornly, intimately alien as Frieda.

Practical ecstasies

St Teresa of Avila

STEPHEN CLISSOLD

THANKS TO THE BAROQUE imaginations of Bernini and Crashaw, St Teresa of Avila has survived a lot better in sceptical times than other God-ravished Counter-Reformation saints. Other little girls doubtless played at convents and longed for martyrdom; other nuns experienced mystic marriages out of their Song of Songs, but she wrote out her life with a fervour and literalness that made her ecstasy contagious. And not only to artists; according to Stephen Clissold in this new biography, General Franco carried her left hand around with him for 40 years.

This macabre snippet of information is not entirely besides the point. It was her exploration of the intimate relations between soul and sense – her power in her writings and her life, to give the soul a body – that sainted her. She's a very *solid* figure: however consumed by holy passion, she always survived her raptures to encounter the world with renewed determination; the reformed Carmelite convents she founded, the unwilling bishops and nunciates and grandees who helped her, all bear witness to her personal toughness.

Despite her masochistic-sounding stress on absolute obedience, she joined with awesome efficiency in the political power struggles over reform, and got her own way (largely a matter, seemingly, of finding spiritual advisers who agreed with her, and 'obeying' them). It was obviously dangerous to grant her a personal interview, so confident was she, and so tirelessly eloquent in her demands for 'guidance'. Even the devils she sometimes saw in visions didn't daunt her – 'indeed', as she observed in her *Life*, 'they seemed to be afraid of me'.

The more totally she submitted her will to God's, the more expert and assured she became in her dealings with others. In a sense, her capacity to persuade other people of her voices and visions (to translate possession into self-possession) really is more remarkable than the spiritual jerks themselves. As Mr Clissold points out, there was no lack of visionaries in sixteenth-century Spain, rather the reverse – *alumbrados* ('illuminated ones') sprang up everywhere, and often struck the Inquisition 'as a sect suspiciously akin to those spawned by Luther in Northern Europe'. For this reason (and perhaps because her grandfather, a converted Jew, had been hounded by the Holy Office) Teresa had to work very hard at acquiring and passing on her certainty of divine inspiration. Some of the symptoms she dealt with in private:

> '. . . for 20 years I suffered from morning sickness . . . Now that I go oftener to Communion, I have to bring on the sickness at night, with feathers or in some other way . . .'

Others, like levitation, presented more of a problem:

> '. . . when I have felt that the Lord was going to enrapture me (once it happened during a sermon, on our Patronal festival, when some great ladies were present), I have lain on the ground and the sisters have come and held me down . . .'

This may sound like an extreme of fake modesty, but it wasn't: not only did people naturally resent 'holier than thou' manifestations, but such acrobatics were likely to be adulated one day, excommunicated the next. At best, they often evaporated in convent gossip.

Her most famous and orgasmic mystical experience, quaintly known as the 'transverberation', happened in 1559 when she was in her forties: a small and smiling angel pierced her heart repeatedly with a golden spear. By then, though, she had become adept at absorbing and describing such things, and converting them into personal magnetism. Instead of basking in temporary notoriety, or having a breakdown, or any of the other more usual responses, she built on her visions, both figuratively in her books (*The Way of Perfection*, *The Interior Castle*) and literally, in the houses of the reformed Carmelite Order. The very fact that she was canonised in 1622 so soon after her death (1582) is yet another proof of her efficiency in taking on the Church bureaucracy. Her body (which began to be messily dismembered almost as soon as she was supposedly buried) exuded perfume, and was miraculously uncorrupted; likewise the character she left behind.

Understandably, Stephen Clissold spends much of the book paraphrasing the saint herself, and other contemporary witnesses. Still, the result is rather disappointing – less vivid than her account, and without the analytic energy to really interpret her from the outside. When Mr Clissold is moved, he lapses into limp lay piety, and when he tries for a more panoramic view (despite calling on a supporting cast that includes St John of the Cross and the Princess of Eboli, an hysterical beauty with a black eye-patch) he is inclined to be cautious and drab. The full story of how she managed to invent her soul and persuade other people to respect it remains to be told.

Hearts of stone

Monuments and Maidens: The Allegory of the Female Form

MARINA WARNER

W HY SHOULD TRUTH BE a woman? or Nature? or Justice? or Liberty? Not, certainly, because women have been more free, just, truthful, nor even (though this one has a double edge) more natural. Marina Warner sets out to breathe some life into the army of petrified personages that litters western cityscapes, and to pose some questions people have been too bored with allegory (not to mention civic sculpture) to ask for a long time. As her book shows, these stony ladies can be persuaded to yield surprisingly interesting answers.

Before that, though, they have to become truly visible. Ms Warner's mini-tours of New York (seen from the Statue of Liberty), Paris and London are marvellously done: she looks at Muses, Victories, Virtues and such with a fresh eye, and describes them crisply, appreciatively and learnedly. Liberty's obvious struts and props and colossally dumb nobility move her to ironic sympathy. Paris is – with the right focus – 'the city of Ladies':

> Public statements have their roots in private dreams ... Walking through Paris, you can see the caryatids speak; if you can unlock the silence of the stone, you can begin to see why they take the form they do, and what effect they might have.

London becomes a museum of imperial motifs, Britannias and Boadiceas complete with corselets versus nameless nymphs, with the Prime Minister and the Greenham women acting as real-life understudies to the statuary stars. There's also a disquisition on Mrs Thatcher's 'hardness' which, quite by coincidence, has acquired an extra quirk of meaning –

Ms Warner argues, surely rightly, that changing one's public image is very difficult, Dominion and Charity won't mix.

Some of the reasons why emerge in the middle section, which traces back the (female) allegory of (male) ideas of virtue to the mythic origins of the goddess Athena. She may have been resourceful and protean in the *Odyssey*, but in the *Iliad* she becomes rigid, warlike and marriage-minded, the true daughter of Zeus. She sprang from his head without a mother, and to make her meaning even clearer she wears on her breastplate the severed head of Medusa, who represents the mothers' line.

Athena dominates the tradition of allegories of the female form; indeed (going back even further) women in myth were, like Pandora or Pygmalion's marble mistress, often thought of as male artefacts anyway.

> At the heart of this web of symbols, where woman as *fons et origo* and woman as a manufactured maiden are assimilated, where woman as original matter and woman as artefact become interchangeable terms in the discussion of the creative act in life and art, we can find the source of the tradition of ascribing meaning more readily to the female form than the male. The female was perceived to be a vehicle of attributed meaning at the beginning of the world . . .

The argument isn't entirely new, but the wealth of detail (backed up by illustrations) is. One by one the familiar forms come to life, from the winged victories Queen Victoria was named for to the many metamorphoses of Minerva, and the various wise virgins who stand helplessly and hopefully around in public places. However, it's the woman armed and impervious who is the central symbol. Ms Warner recalls the strange story of Tuccia the Vestal Virgin of Rome, who 'proved' she was still chaste by miraculously carrying water from the Tiber in a sieve, and suggests that we think of it as a further clue – the allegorical figure is a 'sealed container of the meaning she conveys', her armour makes her 'watertight', the weaker vessel stoppered to carry patriarchal platitudes.

Perhaps most ingenious is the final twist to the tale, where nature is called in question, along with naked Truth. Nothing, Ms Warner argues, could be more paradoxical and (sadly) predictable than seeing a woman trapped in stone as the sign of what's most wild, free, 'other'. We're back where we started, in a sense, with the Statue of Liberty. This time, though, we're really inside her head, looking out.

Ms Warner dallies with revolutionary and iconoclastic thoughts – abolish the images altogether, opt for formlessness as the sign of the female – but, characteristically, she ends with a plea for *occupying* them, dwelling in them imaginatively until we can persuade them to step from their plinths, or even learn to fly . . . Though one needs to be patient, she wryly admits. Patience on a monument, perhaps, with a sympathetic stiffness in the joints, but smiling.

Sisters of Sisyphus

Beyond Power: Women, Men and Morals

MARILYN FRENCH

THE NEW FEMINISM COMES of age around now, and Marilyn French is taking stock. Her title might sound as though she was heralding that 'post-feminist' era lots of people (including some weary, guilty feminists) would like to believe in; but no. Nearly everything is still to do: most of the women who've penetrated the public world have been, are being, ritually assimilated. What the feminists turn out to want, says Ms French, is a moral revolution: 'Although they want access for women to decision-making posts . . . *they do not want women to assimilate to society as it presently exists, but to change it.*'

There's an obvious catch here, and the sheer size of this book (640 pages) is, among other things, a kind of advance warning sign of the amount of slog and hard labour even thinking about that eventuality entails. 'Boulder-pushing' Doris Lessing called it at the end of *The Golden Notebook*, boulder-pushing Sisyphus-style up the hill. The hill here consists in Patriarchy, traced back to its early origins and exhaustively documented in its current institutionalised forms. And the boulder is Sisterhood.

One part of Marilyn French's dilemma is that the boulder itself has to be continuously redefined too: feminism plus Greens plus Greenham women plus women in the Third World . . . and, of course, closer to home, women whose lives and interests circle back into the 'private' sphere always, having never really left it – like the three woman in a recent *Times* feature, triumphantly offered as examples of marriage chosen over a career. One gave up being an ambassador's social secretary to be a junior minister's wife, another a career as a probation officer to marry a vicar, and the third gave up acting to marry an actor. In short, whether 'working' officially or not, most women are still close to their traditional roles, and Ms French wants to recruit them too.

The result is a good deal of (deliberate) fudging about 'feminine' values we can all agree on – the importance of nurturing, fostering, community feeling, continuity, care for the environment, the survival of the species. Like Germaine Greer, she has come round to the view that motherhood is the political point, and the basis for a renewed polemic. 'Feminine' values, on this view, aren't so much the product of repression, stereotyping, or 'castration' (as in *The Female Eunuch*) as survivals from the period of human origins, and the recipe for future survival. The way Ms French tells the story, it goes as follows:

'In the beginning was the Word, and the Word was a lie . . .' The Old Testament, like other cultures' stories about beginning, is a monument to a patriarchal takeover that happened when men became aware of the part they played in reproduction, and when population growth (thanks to all that nurturing) generated the need for more elaborate social organisation than the mother-centred groups of the real beginning. Ironically enough, it may have been the relative 'marginality' of men in pre-cultures that enabled them to go off and invent a role for themselves which distinguished them from animals (and women) and allied them to gods.

So men discovered 'transcendence' (good anthropological items like the one about the Chaga men 'who pretend they no longer defecate once they are initiated'), and set about the long haul of defining themselves as human. 'Rather like women meeting in consciousness-raising groups in the 1960s, men may have spoken together secretly at cult meetings . . .' For a while – thousands of years – it may not have been too bad:

> In many cultures men and women seem to have made a bargain: women agree to call men more important, and allow them to monopolise public authority and prestige, while they, running the household, the farm, or small shop, possess most of the real power in village life.

But the stage was set for the Juggernaut of Western civilisation, technology and science, the Gospels merging with the ambitions of avatars of alienation like Bacon – 'I am come in very truth leading you to Nature with all her children to bind her to your service and make her your slave.' The book piles example on example, to arrive at a glumly eloquent portrait of modern institutional man and his perverse and polluted world with its squandered resources, where there are no longer – except for the deliberately blinkered – 'secure corners' in which to hide.

It's an argument that proceeds by accretion, trailing hundreds of footnotes, and Ms French is obviously aware of the danger that if she convinces her readers too thoroughly, 'the projection of a matricentric world based on fragmentary evidence' will hardly be enough to persuade them that the present sickness isn't indeed terminal, that change is possible. She's engaged in a very difficult balancing act – all the more so because she's convinced that power-worship is so contagious that women can't infiltrate the inner sanctums without becoming denatured. There's a lot of miserable material on the way revolutionary govern-ments have chewed women up and spat them out: in fact, one of the side-effects of all the work that's been done on women's history is to undermine the cause, by documenting the obstacles.

Which is where 'Morals' come in. Only by what used to be called a 'change of heart' can the book envisage a future. What Ms French has in mind is a kind of 'privatisation' of public life. She quotes (more than once) Simone Weil – 'the common run of moralists complain that man is moved by his private interests: would to heaven it were so!' Except of course that heaven is part of the problem. We must realise our own transience, be more modest, think small:

> The end of life is the continuation of life . . . We are like soldier ants . . . We have encountered a river that separates us from sight of the future; we have a choice only to die where we stand, or to enter it.

With an incongruous echo of the heady days of the 1960s Ms French calls this the pursuit of the pleasure principle, but it sounds a lot more like pain. And in general a book less dedicated to the pleasure principle would be hard to envisage. The hunting-and-gathering society it looks back to has taken over in the writing too: ant-like, patient, laborious, in a word, boulder-pushing.

Staying outside the skin

Intercourse

ANDREA DWORKIN

Women

NAIM ATTALLAH

By the time Swift's Gulliver paddles away from Houyhnhnm-land in his Yahoo-skin canoe, he is so consumed with self-disgust and self-hatred (Yahoo-hatred) that it seems he has only two alternatives – to skin himself, to jump out of his skin, or (the one he chooses) to loathe everyone else, and particularly (when he gets home) his nearest and dearest, from whose foul closeness he escapes to the stable to inhale the horses. Andrea Dworkin's *Intercourse* is a book that belongs in a similar landscape of extremity. It's about skinlessness, about coming home to revulsion:

> In Amerika, there is the nearly universal conviction – or so it appears – that sex (fucking) is good and that liking it is right: morally right; a sign of human health; nearly a standard of citizenship. Even those who believe in original sin and have a theology of hellfire and damnation express the Amerikan creed, an optimism that glows in the dark: sex is good, healthy, wholesome, pleasant, fun; we like it, we enjoy it, we want it, we are cheerful about it; it is as simple as we are, the citizens of this strange country with no memory and no mind.

This Amerika, though (think of Donne, 'O my America! my new-found-land, /My kingdome, safeliest when with one man mann'd'), is somewhere we all live, or rather, that lives in us. You discover it – ironically enough – as a result of consciousness-raising, rather as Gulliver did.

Dworkin's position assumes an impasse in feminist thinking. The reformist strain is wearing itself out (this is almost a definition, in any case: it's about wearing itself out) in conflict with both consumerism (which makes use of 'liberation' for its own purpose) and the various forms of fundamentalist backlash. At the same time, there is a retreat, a green retreat, into separatism, with the stress on feminine, nurturing qualities. All of these things keep women busy, patching and mending. Dworkin, however, is interested in picking off the cultural patina that persuades people of the naturalness of their 'nature', and disputing over again the category of the human.

The literary examples from which she starts (Tolstoy on chastity, or Tennessee Williams on intimacy with strangers, or James Baldwin on 'communion') aren't the kind that would make up a 'women's studies' reading-list. Those work usually by cumulative comfort, the building of traditions, the argument of quantity, but this argument is opposite, and works (or wants to work) by way of quality, and stripping down, through the persuasiveness of images and metaphors. Here she is, improvising on the central metaphor of *The Face of Another* by Kobo Abe:

> The skin is a line of demarcation, a periphery, the fence, the form, the shape . . . The skin is separation, individuality, the basis for corporeal privacy . . . Especially, it is both identity and sex, what one is and what one feels in the realm of the sensual, being and passion, where the self meets the world – intercourse being, ultimately, the self in the act of meeting the world.

Woman's privacy (and hence her individuality, her integrity, her significance) is never real or complete – Dworkin cannot, any more than Milton, praise a cloistered virtue, virgin ignorance – because her meeting with the world is an invasion. She is not the owner or sole inhabitant (her privates we) of her own skin, 'her insides are worn away over time, and she, possessed, becomes weak, depleted, usurped . . .'

Dworkin has been accused of misunderstanding and/or being led astray by metaphors of penetration and possession. Certainly, the book develops and sustains its momentum on metaphor, and metaphor's powers of provoking recognition, of outwitting the rational desire to take things apart *only in such a way that they can be put together again*. Metaphors redraw the map, and put the boundaries in different places; *these* metaphors, in particular, make women into territory that has had a boundary drawn not round its edge, but on the inside, in the name of nature. It is an argument *ad feminam*, with all the unfairness that implies: if you can't recognize what I'm saying you're in thrall; if you can, you're in thrall too, but you've been rescued from banality, and can say, with all bitterness and bleakness, 'we': 'this elegant blood-letting of sex is a so-called freedom exercised in alienation, cruelty and despair. Trivial and decadent; proud; foolish; liars; we are free.' This climax to Chapter Six ('Virginity', and Bram Stoker's *Dracula*) perhaps conveys something of the sublimity of the preacher's style that sells so bleak a sermon, and avoids (like the plague) any suggestion of patching and mending reasonableness. It's worth looking at what the book has to say about the production of meaning:

> It is human to experience these differences whether or not one cares to bring them into consciousness. Humans, including women, construct meaning. Humans find meaning in poverty and tyranny and the atrocities of history; those who have suffered most still construct meaning . . . we can understand some things if we try hard to learn empathy; we can seek freedom and honour and dignity; that we care about meaning gives us a human pride that has the fragility of a butterfly and the strength of tempered steel. The measure of women's oppression is that we do not take intercourse – entry, penetration, occupation – and ask or say what it means . . .

'Ask or say' are synonyms here: asking the questions, you supply the answers. The argument is weakened by this tactic, though not as much as might appear. It *is* cheap to ask, on page 128, 'Is intercourse itself then a basis of or a key to women's continuing social and sexual inequality?' It is less so to ask, 'To what extent does intercourse depend on the inferiority of women?' On this, the book suggests, for once, fewer answers than questions. The notion of the 'real privacy of the body' ('There is never a real privacy of the body that can coexist with intercourse') is for Dworkin inseparable from full selfhood, from freedom, from integrity, from the 'discrete' individual. 'Liberal' is for her a term of abuse ('A false sympathy of abstract self-indulgence'), but it's from that background that her sense of the human is derived. Or at least, it's on that sense of the self – as choosing, willing, meaning – that her map of women's possession is based. She is in this sense as much an 'enlightenment' figure as Mary Wollstonecraft, who argued that she didn't want women to have power over men, but over themselves.

There remains the question, then, of human closeness under any circumstances – the Yahoo problem. And here the book is eloquent by its silence on lesbianism. By the logic of its own metaphors it should be saying that women's sense of their own sex is invaded by the 'natural' and cultural climate, that they are no less 'objectified' in relations with each other. But by the message of its silence it produces an unthought, unarticulated alternative, which does more than any of its rhetorical excesses to undermine it. Do women stay outside each other's skins? To ask the question is to flounder on a technicality. It's clear from the whole tenor of the argument that Dworkin will have no truck with tender, sentimental same-sex notions about peace and merging, but at the same time it's impossible not to suspect that this is also a question to which she feels she knows the answer. Either that, or there's the prospect of a kind of 'existential' pathos, a celebration of the alienation caused by boundaries that's not so different from what Simone de Beauvoir grappled with in (with?) Sartre.

The voice, in fact, is very much that of the heroic polemics of the late 1960s. Dworkin describes (surely) herself when she bitterly praises those who refuse to submit to 'the indignity of inferiority' – 'the lone, crazy resisters, the organized resistance'. *Intercourse* embarrasses not only by its visceral imagery, but by its refusal to speak any of the conciliatory public languages of feminism. The contrast with the tone of (say) Germaine Greer's preface to her collected essays and occasional pieces (*The Madwoman's Underclothes*, 1986) is instructive. Greer writes:

> The quality of daily life is what matters, the taste of the food on the table, the light in the room, the peace and wholeness of the moment. Perfect love casteth out fear. The only perfect love to be found on earth

is not sexual love, but the wordless commitment of families, which takes as its model mother-love.

Dworkin's preoccupation is precisely the obscenity of the ordinary, a gross metaphysical joke played on women. None the less, there is a marked continuity with the tone of Greer's earliest pieces – 'Morality is essentially connected with choice, with the exercise of will itself.' And this same piece (1972, on abortion) provides a name for Dworkin's special quality: 'spiritual muscle'.

The days have (probably) gone when this metaphor could be put down to penis envy. Now it is merely unfashionably harsh and individualistic. Now we have Naim Attallah's cheerful gossipy compendium, *Women*, which goes to show, if nothing else, that women are almost pathologically patient. Attallah's strategy was to ask the questions, then excise them (together with large parts of the answers). As a result the women (289 of them in over 1,000 pages) are reduced to presenting themselves as eagerly interested in the after-dinner topics that intrigue him. It's a method as old as social documentary: Henry Mayhew in *London Labour and the London Poor*, interviewing the underclass of Victorian England, did the same, and teased the bourgeoisie with the spectre of street urchins aggressively denying all the pieties. No, they said, seemingly without being asked, I never go to church. No, I don't know who my father is. The results, with this technique, depend, however, on the quality and motives of the questions.

Here, the women – the privileged class of their sex, whatever that means (and we're not going to find out) – almost all say yes. Or possibly the nay-sayers have been eliminated from the miles of tape, having nothing positive to contribute. They are for the most part public women, public figures even, but what the questions are after is their privacy – on the assumption that that is where they exist *as women*. The questions not asked are those about the wide world. God hardly comes into it (reasonably perhaps) but nor does the work of these women who 'have all, in some way, made their mark in the world'. Here, they might as well sign themselves with a cross. Would they have chosen to talk about Mrs Thatcher (under the heading of 'Feminism') or (under

'Creativity') about babies and Beethoven? Impossible to say. Very few contributions call the book's bluff. Jenny Agutter comes close:

> You suddenly find yourself realizing, talking with people, that you are an alien animal. You are not being talked to as any sort of equal . . . Sometimes you feel there is this wonderful respect; actually it's not respect: It's just enjoyment of something, that you are terrific, but you're still an alien animal.

Some contributors sound like collaborationists (or is the association between rolling your own, woolly jumpers, hairy armpits and feminism spontaneous?). Some are resigned – 'We've got to get on with one another to reproduce' – and a very few have their own metaphors. This is Mary Quant:

> The worrying thing about sex is that the design of it is disturbing. It does tend to encourage the male to overwhelm the female, and the female reaction tends to be to want that to happen. The actual design has a flaw in that it brings on, at its worst, violence . . .

Women is a non-book, but that will not interfere with its success. What it does is take the interests of the tabloid press and the chat-show up-market. What it reveals is the poverty of 'dialogue', never mind 'intercourse'. No wonder Andrea Dworkin talks to herself.

Woman's whole existence

Women and Love: The New Hite Report

SHERE HITE

THE FIRST HITE REPORT, back in 1976, broke the news that women had orgasms more often and more satisfactorily by themselves. The second, on male sexuality (1981), caused a stir by suggesting that men had something missing, an organ for 'caring' perhaps. This one, completing the trilogy, has 4,500 women talking about 'love'. So what's new? A great deal, is Shere Hite's answer: 'a cultural revolution in progress'.

Her method hasn't really changed, though clearly this is not a topic that lends itself so readily to the kind of questionnaire (how often? how? how *exactly*?) that divorced orgasm from intercourse. Here the hard statistics derive from public sources. 70 per cent of women now work outside the home; 50 per cent of marriages end in divorce; 90 per cent of divorces are initiated by women (most of whom become a lot poorer as a result).

What Hite is after ('Are you "in love" now? How can you tell?') is the emotional economy behind the figures, and – as before – the answers she elicits, though carefully matched to US female population statistics (83 per cent white, 12 per cent black; 44 per cent Democrats, 30 per cent Republican, and so forth), come from women who welcomed the opportunity to spill the beans, and spent an estimated 40,000 woman-hours doing so. One of the effects of this is to make her findings uncheckable. But it does have the undeniable advantage that the anonymous respondents are very eloquent indeed.

We plunge in at the deep end with woman after woman writing about being taught to love and nurture men – 'when I was three or four, my mother was already teaching me to *see* dust and other people's feelings' – and growing up to find their caring little ways treated with contempt:

> When we were first in love, I used to talk to him about so many things, and he would listen – or I thought he listened . . . later I noticed when I spoke, he would walk out of the room . . .

Asked: 'When were you loneliest?' they reply with startling unanimity, 'When I was married.' One woman describes herself and her husband as 'room-mates with children in common'; another says simply and bitterly: 'He fell asleep in mid-argument.'

This, according to Hite's sample, is responsible for more divorces than sexual 'problems' and extra-marital affairs put together. Extra-marital affairs seem, if anything, to be propping up the loneliness *à deux* that all these women find in marriage: after five years of not being listened to, 70 per cent of women are having 'something "strange" on the side' (as one of them memorably puts it) though they almost all 'believe in' monogamy, and say they would find the singles scene sheer hell (at least marriage is 'a private jungle'). One statistic that provides striking evidence of marital malaise is that 80 per cent of these women believe that their boring husbands are faithful, whereas 75 per cent of men report that they are having extra-marital affairs of their own.

What of the happy marriages? These are harder to describe and come to seem almost eccentric. One woman defines happiness as 'sitting around in a dark sitting room and talking about our future together'. Another enjoys the feeling of security: 'I like being able to say, "in five years let's have a baby," or "in six months, let's buy venetian blinds".' There are some surreal glimpses of family life: one much-loved husband is always asking his wife to read the encyclopaedia to him – 'how would you like to be balancing the chequebook and have someone come in and want to know if cockroaches sleep?' Many describe the delights of 'muddling along through daily life together': 'He waters the plants and feeds the fish. I feed the turtles and the frog.'

But most are discontented: 'Women are deserting marriage in droves, either through divorce, or emotionally, leaving with a large part of their hearts.' Lovers, therapists, work, best friends, children all act as cement, but still the institution totters. 'Most of the 50 per cent of women who stay married eventually use their marriage as a sort of "home base".' One obvious moral, Hite acknowledges, is perhaps that they should give up on 'love'. However, in a final, weirdly euphoric section, the book discards all the evidence of sad compromise (and even happy compromise) it has accumulated, to boldly gaze into a starry future:

> We are like astronauts now, watching the earth recede ever further into the distance, becoming smaller and smaller – seeing the 'male' ideology ever more clearly . . .

As one last woman puts it, 'I'd like to see private morality extended to the earth.' It's hard not to be sceptical – and not just because of the changes in scale involved. The 'evidence' suggests a different message about privatised emotions – that where they actually lead is further into 'verbalising' and therapy-speak, and oral and masturbatory sub-culture, of which the Hite Reports are themselves a part. This one has a new questionnaire at the end: 'With which parts of this book did you most agree? Disagree? Find most emotionally involving?' The process feeds itself; and meanwhile, the politicians fall asleep in mid-argument.

Forever black suspenders

Divine Decadence: Fascism, Female Spectacle and the
Making of Sally Bowles

LINDA MIZEJEWSKI

SALLY BOWLES, _CABARET_ CHARACTER and camp icon, has flourished for more than 50 years. Since Christopher Isherwood got her on to the page in _Goodbye to Berlin_, she has mirrored several revolutions in sexual mores – culminating in Bob Fosse's 1972 movie with Liza Minnelli – yet stayed eerily unchanged. For all the world as though the erotic imagination was compelled to wear black suspenders for eternity.

Not so, says Linda Mizejewski in this fascinating and gruesomely detailed analysis of Sally's career: the very shallowness and elusiveness of the character mean she can embody lots of different meanings without (seemingly) ever developing.

In fact, Sally's real-life original, Jean Ross, complained about her treatment. After her brief Berlin period she herself went off to marry Claud Cockburn, report the Spanish Civil War, work for a variety of liberal-left causes, raise a daughter alone. And yet journalists, she said, just 'don't want to know about the unemployment or the poverty or the Nazis marching through the streets – all they want to know ... how many men I went to bed with'.

Isherwood's narrator could not talk about his own gay sexuality back then, so Sally (who acquired her surname from handsome writer Paul Bowles, Isherwood said) had to have sex for two. And the sex had, of course, to have an equivocal edge to it – Fascism's parodic 'other' and at the same time its inner secret. By the time Ross died, in the 1970s, her shadow Sally had become a triumphant type of criminal innocence, a sado-masochistic 'performer', guilty by association with Nazism.

This association is heavily ironic: it was Nazism that closed down the cabarets and slapped pink triangles on gays. But as Mizejewski shows, Sally is on both sides at once: one of the boys, cheerfully travestying sexual pieties, and a girl who's as often as not the butt of the boys' jokes. Also, notoriously, the girl who has an abortion – in every version except the 1955 movie, when she gets her dates wrong – thus giving the game away about her biological difference. Even her sexiness, her whole point, you might think, and the most obvious thing about her, is dubious. Is she sexy, or 'sexy'? – and do those camp quotation marks make her sexier or the reverse?

Looking at the 1951 Broadway play, *I Am a Camera*, adapted from Isherwood by John Van Druten, Mizejewski argues that Julie Harris made a marvellous Sally precisely because of her tomboyish and androgynous style, 'a woman playing a boy playing a woman'.

But then Van Druten invents a wholly new character, a dreadful 'Mummy' – Mrs Watson-Courtneidge – who is the focus for all the negative feelings about women, and whose attempt to take Sally home and make her respectable is foiled. Sally has her abortion and stays a child. But is this a gesture against the furious post-war propaganda about Motherhood (women back to the home), or an instance of it?

For a scholarly book, *Divine Decadence* goes through an awful lot of hoops, brought on really by quotation marks. Are the various stage and screen versions of Sally having fun with women, or 'women', or both? Certainly it looks as though the Sally story *has* to be about cross-dressing and ambiguity. The mind boggles when you try to contemplate the thought that Elizabeth Taylor was briefly considered for the role in the 1955 film. Julie Harris did it again in the event, so that the role was saved for camp and further conundrums.

The only conventionally attractive Sally was Jill Haworth in Kander and Ebb's 1966 Broadway musical, *Cabaret* – a version which normalised the sex roles, and made 'Cliff' (Christopher) Sally's lover. (The director Hal Prince is reputed to have exclaimed, 'We gotta put balls on the guy!') But this is the exception that proves the rule, since it invents the role of the perverse emcee so memorably played by Joel Gray – 'archetypal master of ceremonies of the fantasy world where . . . genders are blurred' – who upstages Sally at her own cross-dressing game.

And then (1972) there's Liza Minnelli, herself in camp quotes as Judy Garland's daughter, playing the part with gusto as 'the American cheerleader Lola'; Sally restored to centre stage, OK, but hardly a convincing figure of *real* polymorphous pleasure?

Perhaps the clue to the dubious power of this image lies in the fact that Sally was conceived from the start as a product of the camera's eye. Jean Ross, oddly enough, had introduced Isherwood to the scriptwriting business and he was already excited by its chaotic artifice and by the seduction of the spectacle. Sally's incarnations owe more than a little to *femmes fatales* from Dietrich on, but she is the relatively belated *creature* of the medium.

Some theoreticians of film would say that this makes her a kind of promiscuous 'sign' – anybody's, in fact – rather as though she was acting one moment in a Leni Riefenstahl spectacular, at the next mixing it with the Marx Brothers. I incline to think she's funnier than Mizejew-ski makes out – but perhaps it's a sign of our own glum and rather apprehensive *fin de siècle*, that *Divine Decadence* rather downplays the carnival implications, and points up the ways in which promiscuity seems to 'invite' repression. Which is why Sally won't be hanging up her black suspenders just yet.

Right but Romantic

Romanticism and Gender

ANNE K. MELLOR

Frankenstein

MARY SHELLEY

ANNE MELLOR'S MILD-MANNERED and didactic book *Romanticism and Gender* – billed as 'the first attempt to give a broad overview of British romantic literature from a feminist perspective' – marks the end of an era. Academic feminism (if Mellor is representative, and she probably is) has now embraced the protean concept of 'difference' so comprehensively and smotheringly and sensibly that it can reconstitute the romantic period as a gender-continuum. The old Gothic models of oppression and repression, imprisonment and exclusion, have long served their turn. Now, masculine Romanticism, feminine Romanticism and cross-dressing cohabit in a complicated canon: 'gender' is everywhere a question, nowhere an answer.

Innumerable women's works still remain to be recovered, edited, 'placed' – 'It will require decades of research and hundreds of books before we fully grasp the complex intellectual and formal configurations of this *terra incognita*'. And the traditional set texts of the egotistical sublime will survive nicely as monuments to over-reaching creativity myths. The whole edifice, in fact, is eminently mentally *habitable*. That is Mellor's point, of course. For she is expanding and modernizing the kind of literary-historical space that used to belong to students of social realism and Jane Austen.

This is the matriarchal domain of good sense and cynicism in a cool new guise. It's accepted as read that in taking over the realm of the emotions, the male romantics 'stole from women their primary cultural authority as the experts in delicate, tender feelings'; or again, that the period's particular brand of sexism 'denies to women even their traditional gender roles and cultural authority as experts in feeling'. But this turns out to be a blessing in disguise, for *feminine* Romanticism, we're told, embraced

> the revolutionary idea that women just think as well as feel, that they must act with prudence, avoid the pitfalls of sexual desire, and learn from their mistakes.

This 'idea', for Mellor, unites Mary Wollstonecraft and Jane Austen. Maria Edgeworth's *Belinda* is 'a textbook example of it'. None the less (as this last phrase acknowledges), it may well seem a pious 'line' denied by what is most vital in these women's writing. A lot is made to hang on the very tenuous distinction between this focus on 'a heroine who develops in intellectual and moral stature' and an eighteenth-century tradition denigrated as 'didactic', 'tracing the development of the heroine from fallible youth to a mature acceptance of the status quo and the role of dutiful wife'. It is surely not a distinction that can sustain the claim for 'revolution'. Indeed, the very argument itself partakes in the shifts and adjustments and bad faith that characterize a good woman trying to salvage some self-respect in sad straits.

This opening position, in short, is really time-honoured *anti*-romantic domestic lore. Men are impractical dreamers, women realists – 'Women writers of the romantic period for the most part foreswore the concern of their male peers with the capacities of the creative imagination . . .' Ann Radcliffe ('Domesticating the Sublime') is also, again a bit improbably, assimilated to this 'alternative program grounded on the trope of the family-politic', via the argument that her version of sublimity is all about 'the equal value and dignity of other people', and has a 'quintessentially *democratic* dimension'. Here the abstract level of the analysis (which is conducted on the basis of the *absence* of the Oedipal anxiety critics have detected in Burke's description of the sublime in nature) entirely obscures Radcliffe's actual treatment of other people in situations of domestic conflict, in which those who are judged insensible to nature (e.g., Madame Montoni in *Udolpho*) are treated with condescension and callousness by heroines who are sensibility-snobs. Radcliffe's democratic dimension perhaps consists in making this kind of vengeful feeling of superiority readily available to young women – and in showing by example how to pastiche your grandest literary forefathers without anxiety – but this is a view that belongs to an oppositional and classist reading of female aesthetics, and so has no real place here. Mellor's Radcliffe is above all right-minded, above all correct.

Not that the book lacks its *bad* women – Letitia Elizabeth Landon and Felicia Hemans play those parts, the first because she has an 'essentialist' construction of the female, the second because she 'endorses as "natural" the maintenance of an hierarchical class system'. Both have appropriately messy and unhappy lives. On the other hand, Dorothy Wordsworth's madness seems in this account to have nothing to do with her years of slavish self-abasement before William. But that in turn is because one can detect in Dorothy's autobiographical writings 'a relational, fluid, embodied self', our author's slippery, deconstructed, home-loving ideal. The 'plot' of *Romanticism and Gender* is deeply conventional, a tribute to women's studies' – and perhaps women's – awful capacity to make the best of things as you find them. One major sign of the restriction of vision that involves is the book's refusal to talk at all seriously about religion, or about the 'priestly' role which the male writers were busily taking on – and the new problems with definitions of creativity and originality that it produced for women. Leaving the metaphysics invisible – now, as then – makes the domestic realm look a lot more spacious than it is.

Mary Shelley's *Frankenstein*, on which Anne Mellor is something of an authority, is the *locus classicus* for the clash of these worlds, and Marilyn Butler's introduction to the Pickering Women's Classics edition emphasizes just how open to opposite allegories the book is. The 'family-politic' line would stress, as Butler says, 'parental nurture or the lack of it . . . the failure of communication and mutual support', and in general the ineptitude of male intellectuals (Godwin, Percy Shelley) as helpmeets and fathers. As the Creature says to Frankenstein, to persuade him to create a female Creature:

my virtues will necessarily arise when I live in communion with an equal . . . and become linked to the chain of existence and events, from which I am now excluded.

On the other hand, what Butler wants to emphasize is the degree to which Mary Shelley's 1818 text dabbled in 'real' medical science, and aligned itself with the controversial position of the Shelleys' materialist surgeon friend William Lawrence, against a separate 'life principle' (i.e., for brain rather than soul). On this view, the book is mainly preoccupied with sloughing off superstition, a blow struck for true mind-science, as opposed to the narcissistic magus-talk of Frankenstein.

In Butler's reading, the 1818 Frankenstein is almost a comic figure, a sorcerer's apprentice who gets more than he bargained for, cannot accept the material reality of his creation, and has to mystify and demonize it. In 1831, on this view, Mary Shelley rewrote herself into conformity, by making the science vague, introducing religious values, and so enabling the book to be read as an anti-materialist allegory. (Butler quotes *Fraser's Magazine* – 'A state without religion is like a human body without a soul'.) Such radical ambivalence explains why 'difference' so readily diffuses itself everywhere in Romantic writing. It also explains why the central texts are no sooner corralled in a reading like Mellor's than they make their escape in another direction. In the case of *Frankenstein*, as Butler puts it, 'an apparently domestic drama moves through time and space . . .'

News from the revolution that never was

Sexing the Millennium

LINDA GRANT

Berkeley 1964. 'Joan Baez sang "Blowing in the Wind", the police came in and arrested 800 people.' A few memorabilia go a long way, it doesn't take much to conjure it up. For a moment *change* was the currency. And sex-for-pleasure was the common denominator, the secret solvent that would unravel all the hierarchies, and melt down the missiles. One of Linda Grant's anonymous informants recalls with cruel and comic eloquence just how this righteous magic was supposed to work:

> In the sixties you almost had to fuck for the good of the human race. It was your moral duty to keep this thing going like a transcendental chain letter, in order to improve our lot and save the planet. There was a general idea that people who controlled the world and created all the evil, did so because they couldn't fuck. . . .

'What happened?' he asks himself, and answers succinctly, 'It was bullshit. That simple.' Grant's spirited tour of the sexual mythologies of three decades plentifully exposes such utopian follies. The revolution *didn't happen*, OK. But – she wants to say – it's not that simple, either. Believing in the transforming magic of unchained female desire may be 'irredeemably un-hip', but to approach the coming millennium cocooned in privatised cynicism seems (she's right) cowardly.

For great changes have taken place in people's sexual lives. Women can be sexually active outside marriage without the threat of pregnancy or opprobrium. Hedonism is respectable, almost a duty. A whole culture of repression – which trapped sex in the realm of timeless Nature –

has given way to a consumer-cult of choice. Thanks to Alex (*Joy of Sex*) Comfort and soft-porn videos ordinary folk know things about 'technique' that once only professed libertines and whores understood. Homosexual and lesbian sex are all on the menu, on offer, equal-but-different. Ms Grant has an hilarious quotation from Peregrine Worsthorne complaining that 'what was possibly just tolerable ... when confined to a small sophisticated clique ... becomes a national scandal when adopted by the poor and ignorant.' Bloomsbury *moeurs* for all! It's still not much of a rallying cry, though. Radical ideas 'repackaged for the mass market, co-opted by the sex industry and tabloid newspapers' can become amazingly anodyne.

This is a line that the likes of Camille Paglia have pursued: no fun to fun unless you invoke the dark gods. I remember in the early 1970s visiting Amsterdam, and being presented by the tourist board with a pamphlet about the city's pleasures which told you where to go to get what you liked – here you could smoke pot with impunity, over there were the corners for same-sex sex, here transvestites, there S/M ... A canal tour took you past a listing Noah's Ark of a barge with sunflowers growing in paint tins and tie-dyed awnings. 'There,' said the guide, 'lives the King of the Hippies.' Divide and rule was the rational Dutch city fathers' motto, obviously. And on the face of things tolerance does remove the spice from ex-sins. But not when you think twice and look around you, as Linda Grant points out. It isn't merely that we're threatened with boredom and trivialisation, but also with ubiquitous violence, abuse, all the pathological variations on intimacy. Now that people's sexual characters are no longer so fixed by convention, and sexual behaviour is no longer policed in the same way, it's hard to learn tenderness and prolong passion.

One reaction is reaction: Germaine Greer gets told off for coming to the glum conclusion that pleasure has turned into a trap. Linda Grant much dislikes what she thinks of as puritan revulsion; but equally she distrusts fun for fun's sake ('Swinging was capitalism's way of co-opting the dreamers'). Her argument, based on evidence ephemeral and otherwise – brief glimpses of utopian living-experiments from the seventeenth-century on, a history of the Pill, a survey of the changing agendas of women's mags, etcetera – is that our fashionable thinking about liberation ('postmodern', 'postfeminist') has been gruesomely impoverished by the stripping away of non-sexual politics. She wants to recover a sense of 'moral adventure', speculative vistas, but by taking on the polymorphous imagery of consumerism and stepping through the mirror.

Just how difficult this is going to be is demonstrated by *Sexing the Millennium* itself, which is a book caught up in the very sense of fashionable 'change' it deplores, the sort that makes it hard to believe in real change. 'There is no doubt that by the beginning of the eighties, people were bored stiff with sex,' we're told. Or again, 'One of the most powerful women in the world is, of course, Madonna.' Or again, 'Woman are attracted to power, men to youth and beauty'. Or again (on Germaine Greer), 'Like a Fascist, she believes that only through biology can we feel, experience, live.' Rather too often Linda Grant joins the trivialising culture she's supposed to be anatomising, in short. Though this doesn't mean that the book's idea is fraudulent, of course – that's precisely the difficulty, how to discern and describe the processes of transformation now that our picture of the real is so riven with fiction. The recent history of sexual mores is a particularly tricky topic in this regard, since it shows just how malleable acts that once seemed definitive and timeless can be.

Three Steps on the Ladder of Writing

HÉLÈNE CIXOUS

TRANSLATED BY SARAH CORNELL AND SUSAN SELLERS

THE CHARM OF Hélène Cixous is that she's always trying, on the page, to do the things the theories say you can't – to embody meanings, to speak with tongues. The fact that these theories are in some sense *hers* is all part of the game. '*I* could write a thesis, but the texts I wrote were never mine.' She never just writes, but always writes about writing, and so the written-up lectures in *Three Steps on the Ladder* (the 1990 Welleck lectures at the University of California) are not, for her, somehow secondary, but more or less as primary as anything can be. This is what she does, this writing about the heroic impossibility of doing it, and when she writes as a reader she's speaking in her most creative voice.

This is familiar territory. But Cixous has stayed remarkably, almost uniquely, true to her generation's 'line' – the generation that killed off the author with Roland Barthes in 1968 ('writing is the destruction of every voice, of every point of origin . . . the negative where all identity is lost, starting with the very identity of the body writing'). This utopian, or more properly atopian, idea is in evidence here when Cixous starts with 'The School of the Dead' – 'The writer is a secret criminal . . . The writer has a foreign origin . . . as if he or she were a foreigner in his or her own country.' Writers are like the survivors *at the expense* of those who didn't. Even the most ordinary relations between generations are shadowed this way for Cixous (you kill *your author*/father/ mother) – 'We don't know we're alive as long as we haven't encountered death'. And she takes the paradigm personally:

> For a long time I lived through my father's death with the feeling of
> immense loss and childlike regret, as in an inverted fairy tale . . . until
> the day things changed colour . . . and I said to myself that I wouldn't
> have written . . . I wouldn't have had death, if my father had lived . . .
> he gave me death. To start with.

Her mother, too, had in a sense a new lease of life – 'When my father
was alive, my mother didn't work, because my father had a young,
primitive Jew's dignity . . . My mother became a midwife after my
father's death . . . conducted hundreds and hundreds of deliveries.' One
thing about the death of the author: it really meant the multiplication
of the author, of course, and his or her proliferation. Authorship, for
Cixous, is everywhere, you can 'read' its signs in the accidents of fate,
in puns and plays on words, in the most banal or baroque places.

   For instance: her 'ladder' metaphor plays on the H of her name,
and once you have 'ache', you have an axe in French, and you have
Kafka's image of taking a hatchet to 'the frozen sea inside us', and
Dostoevsky's *Notebooks* revealing that the inspiration for *The Idiot* was
a news item: 'a young sixteen-year-old girl, Umestkaia, had killed her
entire family . . . She is there throughout *The Notebooks*, she is constantly
transformed, sometimes she's a man, sometimes a woman . . .' Another
thing about the death of the author: it really meant the death of
everyone else – 'around us resounds an enormous concert of noise-and-
rumour-producing machines'. The author is a kind of high-minded
Lizzie Borden, going busily and bloodily about her work of uncreation,
giggling I like to think, since Cixous is never as serious as her fans.
Nor (certainly) is she much concerned to be 'correct' – although one
detects perhaps a certain nervousness of her American audience in her
remarks on feminism, where she explains with uncharacteristic lack of
grace that 'we are obliged to speak in feminist terms of "man" and
"woman" even though it's not the case, but 'These complexities are
not yet audible.'

   We move on to 'The School of Dreams' and 'The School of Roots'
where other differences get the same treatment – for instance,
nationalism:

Today ... people are swollen with *home-neid* (home-envy), this home-neid is not only the need for a land and roof. It is primarily a need for the proper, for a proper country, for a proper name, a need for separation and, at the same time, a rejection of the other; it is less a need of difference than a distaste for difference.

The book-jacket biography says 'Hélène Cixous emigrated from Algiers to France in 1955, where she became a professor of English'. No home-land. At moments when she loses her cool, and draws lines *against* those who mark out the borders, you can catch her out having a position after all – back in that supposed no-man's-land of the decon-structionist *avant garde*.

  Much of this book is devoted to exploring her *chosen* family, the writers who constitute her canon, 'those who play seriously with their own mortality' – Clarice Lispector, Ingeborg Bachmann, Thomas Bern-hard, Genet, Tsvetaeva, Kafka, Dostoevsky. She sees them as 'writers of *extremity*', 'the dying-clairvoyant kind', 'sleep-walking scribes'. But actually, on the death-of-the-author logic, these dead writers become her selves. 'When I write I escape myself, I uproot myself, I am a virgin ... A real reader is a writer.' Her ladder leads downwards, backwards, what used to be a vision of hell – Milton's 'in the lowest deep a lower' – is her regressive bliss, that's the *kind* of writer she is, the intransigent neo-idealist *kind*. Classifying her, you kill her, she would say. Not so, it's just that Atopia too shares the condition of regionality, no one can be anonymous enough to speak for anyone, our inability to stand for universality is also what we have in common, and so on. Cixous's gift for elusiveness – ' "I" 'am always on the run' she wrote memorably and absurdly years ago in a piece on 'The "Character" of Character' – makes her one of Atopia's most eloquent ambassadors, but ties her down too, and gives her her character.

Farewell Lady Nicotine

Cigarettes are Sublime

RICHARD KLEIN

ARE WE AT LAST alienated enough from the cigarette habit to be able to theorise about it? Or is it still too intimate and inflammatory a topic? Richard Klein, who's an ex-addict, Professor of French at Cornell University, and well-connected in the theory world (his debt to his friend Jacques Derrida, is, as he says, 'everywhere visible') thinks that the moral backlash against smoking begs a riposte, a meditation on Lady Nicotine's fatal charms.

In fact, he confesses, he himself contrived to stop in the course of writing *Cigarettes are Sublime*, and in any case, aversion-therapy doesn't seem to work. The weed has deep and subtle roots: the book itself is a case in point, since it is published (elegantly, and with a generous scatter of black and white snaps of famous *fumeurs*, from Sartre to Coco Chanel to Bogart) by the press of Duke University in North Carolina, named after James B. Duke, whose steam-powered factory first brought fags to the millions.

Klein doesn't mean to offer a social or economic or *material* history, but he can't always resist the lure of such snippets of information, illustrating as they do the many spin-offs of one of America's main export industries. That smoking is a bodily addiction, and does terrible things to your body, he has to acknowledge. He tells the story about the end of Sir Walter Raleigh, who so loved the tobacco he'd brought back from Virginia that he refused to abandon his pipe on the scaffold 'and kept it in his mouth until his head fell'. Then there's Sartre at the last gasp, warned by the doctors that unless he gave up smoking 'his toes would have to be cut off, then his feet, and then his legs . . .' Smoking and mutilation go together.

There's a missing-link image here – Aphra Behn's martyred slave-prince Oroonoko, who smokes stoically while his barbarous white tormentors lop off his privates and his limbs. Klein doesn't mention this one, but he'd see the point, of course, since one of his themes is the mystique smoking acquires *in extremis*, in wartime, from Remarque to Hemingway to Mailer. Let's be banal, though: smoking makes sense when you think you're not going to live long. If you want to explain its peace-time allure, then you have to suppose a sort of internal civil war. Cigarette-smoking itself can come to represent *both* the death-threat *and* the brief, blessed release, which feeds the death-threat in its turn, which leads to the next drag, and so on. And this is Klein's real subject, the cerebral and devious *evanescence* of cigarettes. Tobacco is the drug, cigarettes are the magic medium that makes it into a universal language.

Perhaps this sounds like sub-post-structuralist babble. In a way I rather hope it does, since it would be marvellous if the whole convoluted sophistry of smoking became unintelligible. However, I have to say that I found even Klein's more irritating specimens, like the aestheticist dandy Banville (who expatiated boringly on the sheer, superior futility of smoking), *semblables*. I too kidded myself for years that I couldn't outlive smoking – that smoking somehow *was* living, instead of the reverse. So that the book exercises a sort of baleful fascination on me. Even when I can see that it is self-indulgent ('the wavy parataxis of a smoky preface'), implausible, repetitious – if we are told once that Merimée's Carmen is the first women in literature to be offered a cigarette, we're told half-a-dozen times – I'm still hooked. For all the world as if reading about smoking still retained a ghost of the act.

As the analysts would say, it's all 'an irreducible circle of masturbatory narcissism'. One of Klein's best sections is on Italo Svevo's classic *Confessions of Zeno*, an anti-shrink self-analysis, in which he manages to give up giving up (and so gives up), one for those who've already broken their New Year's resolutions. All is not lost. Another amusing chapter is devoted to the film *Casablanca*, where Klein teases apart a vulgar Freudian analysis by a Dr Greenberg, to argue, rather convincingly, that the 'hidden' meanings are not sexual but political (devoted to changing Roosevelt's policy towards Vichy) – 'the cigarette as sexual fetish had by 1942 become such a commonplace cliché that it could be used, even by Hollywood, to conceal other more subtle themes', in this case commitment beyond the commercial cynicism of Rick's Café Americain.

But when Klein hints that *in general* cigarettes symbolise the value we put on other people's freedom, it's hard to follow him. Okay: smoking may have offered 'an exit from our boring, repetitious, confining, scared, worthless little selves', but it's also endlessly self-referring, self-obsessed, like this book. Do women smoke as a sign of freedom? 'Women today are soldiers', Klein says, in a rare moment of give-away sloganeering; a cigarette is 'both a source of visible sensual pleasure and an emblem of women's erotic life. At least that is how it appears to men . . .'

For what it's worth, looking back I reckon that my own chain-smoking (well-named) was a form of self-imposed purdah, a veil between me and the world, a way of seeming busy and preoccupied, keeping other people away. Not that this proves anything, either – it only serves to underline Klein's other main point, the truly irritating one, that cigarettes are all things to all people, the ultimately empty sign, the most efficient way of killing time we've yet invented.

The women's camp

Feminist theory is in *fin de siècle* mode: self-fashioning ('con-structivism') is winning out everywhere that's anywhere, and drag, cross-dressing, travesty are the metaphors. The result has been a vertiginous, even breath-taking renewal of theory's *effrontery*, the kind of offensive artifice seldom seen since the 1970s and the heyday of Hélène Cixous. Now, American intellectuals like Judith Butler talk of 'women' as a temporary totalization, a kind of 'necessary error' – 'the term (women) marks a dense intersection of social relations that cannot be summarized through the terms of identity'. The perverse pleasure to be extracted from even such dry formulations is what the gap between theory and practice is all about: theory is the region where common sense dies, and we can afford for a moment to recognize the life-giving properties of paradox. Women 'are' female impersonators.

So after twenty-odd years of feminist theorizing what's the big Difference? In a way it's a non-question, since that sense of returning you to the conviction of the unreality (and finality) of representations is what the whole project is *always* about. The process seems to work like a spiral or a gyre, though, so that each return is a turn of the screw – yet more self-conscious, more knowingly perverse. The 'constructivist trajectory' (the phrase comes from Eve Kosofsky Sedgwick) has arrived at the point where, under the label 'queer', it can point to its own bad faith in ripping off the history of stigmatization, and turning it around. The space in which all this is happening is the *same* space (in the campus bookshop what used to be 'feminism' has become 'gender studies'). Feminist theory is lesbian feminist theory is 'queer' theory, and so on – which is one reason why in terms of style and tone you can hear the accents of camp on every side. Mimicry, parody, travesty, appropriation are almost inevitable.

No woman, Sedgwick announces, in the course of a cheerfully anal-obsessed autobiographical piece ('A Poem is Being Written'), 'becomes less a woman through any amount of "male identification", to the extent that femaleness is always (though always differently) to be looked for in the tortuousness, in the strangeness of the figure made between the flatly gendered definition from an outside view and the always more or less crooked stiles [*sic*] to be surveyed from an inner'. (This is an unusually straight-faced sentence, except for that one give-away hiccup which is either a typo or a pun on style/stile, and that crooked man who found a crooked sixpence.) Feminist theory is gender theory is – well – theory. The whole feminist project here in a sense reaches a weird apotheosis, and vanishes for just a dizzy moment. 'How will we know the difference between the power we promote and the power we oppose?' asks Butler. And answers herself with another question: 'Is it . . . a matter of "knowing"?' This kind of knowingness merges readily into the other more familiar, camp, self-conscious kind, so that there's a striking analogy with the late-Victorian argument that female emancipation is a symptom of 'decadence' and of 'sexual anarchy' (Elaine Showalter). New women are the degenerate offspring of the decay of progress. . . .

Hence, coming full circle, the millennial euphoria-cum-gloom. For gloom there is – though before trying to account for that I want to celebrate for a moment more the 'worldliness' of the best of this theoretical writing, its refusal of separatism, the pushy and persuasive way it occupies what Edward Said calls 'the large, many-windowed house of culture as a whole'. At the same time, however, and surely not by coincidence, 'performative' feminism ('Performativity describes this relation of being implicated in that which one opposes' – Butler) has to mean the quite different styles of travesty represented by Camille Paglia and Catherine MacKinnon. A Sedgwick talking about how discourses penetrate and structure their users can make the old exploitative plots, 'brewed in the acid nuances of centuries', sound marvellous in their horrid way. But when MacKinnon refuses to separate words from acts, we're in a crude crisis of representations that threatens to banish all such subtleties. You are a victim or an oppressor or a collaborator in this scenario. Written words allow no room for shifting meanings, no place for parody or pastiche, in such a fundamentalist argument; and indeed the women themselves – MacKinnon and her inside-out travesty, Paglia – are media myths, handy types whose function is to stand in for feminism and (you might be forgiven for thinking) give it a terminally bad name. Women attack pornography and write it, sometimes even the same women. Could there be a better demonstration that feminism has joined the 'real' world to serve the powers that be? In this media-circus version of feminism there are the dandies and the inquisitors, and that's that.

And even in the academy the notion that words are acts can play a corrupting role. The language of theory gives its users the illusion that they are in charge, somehow, riding this authoritative discourse, when more of them are in truth closer to being its creatures. Talking about power becomes a kind of vicarious trip, especially when the prestige of intellectual life is so low in the world outside. Add to this the suspicion that teaching theory works out a lot cheaper than teaching even a truncated version of the history of literature – and it starts to look like a Nineties conspiracy, disseminating ignorance. A truly worldly view here would have to take into account the rivalry – for space, time, funds – between feminist theory and the women's texts – those works made available by the labours of scholars and literary and cultural historians that you can group under the relatively unglamorous heading of 'women's studies'. The recent financial troubles at Virago Press, whose back-list of reissued popular classics is, it seems, no longer profitable enough to cross-subsidize contemporary offerings, are a sobering sign of the times. The combination of burgeoning theory and the financial and imaginative poverty of recession may yet prove disastrous for the availability and reception of women's writing.

All the more ironic, then, that the smartest theoreticians are flirting so openly with 'performative' roles that involve many of them in 'creative' writing – or at least in hybrid, personalized, parodic styles which *compromise* theory in such provocative ways. If you look for the silver lining you can decide that this is a sign of real vitality which, along with the teaching of creative writing that is also growing up on every side in universities and schools, will form a springboard for a new understanding of the crafts of self-fashioning on the page. But if you focus on the cloud you see instead a triumph of rhetoric in the perfectly traditional sense. This is the banal, postmodern crisis of representation at work – which creates media feminists, confuses talk about power with power, and pictures of rape with rape. Without some separate space for words-as-words there is no room for dialogue. Stories, images, representations, can *in theory* rejoice in a bit more equality, now that theory has come out of the closet and admitted its own interested and collusive stance. Certainly we need them too, which is why we need to teach the history of literature. And the history of theory – so as to make its temporary totalizations into a narrative with characters and plots, and democratize the scene. In Utopia you wouldn't need theory, or, it would be everywhere, in between the lines. In our cloudy time, feminist theory is still too separate. Or not separate enough.

Paean to gaiety

The Apparitional Lesbian: Female Homosexuality and Modern Culture

TERRY CASTLE

IN THIS CAMP AND dashing and deliberately lightweight study of a certain strand of 'sexual ontology' Terry Castle pursues the lesbian-as-ghost from Defoe's wistful nearly-real Mrs Veal onwards. She had, she explains, been planning and researching a much heavier straight book about hauntings – on 'the waning of belief in apparitions in Western culture after the Enlightenment' – but in the end decided to come out of the closet and produce this labour of love: 'I felt scandalously energised.'

It's a fetching performance, this opening *apologia*, but also a bit of a puzzle. Hang on, you want to say: surely that particular closet disgorged its ghosts long ago? Well, no, is Castle's answer, and in a way she's right. Lesbian-feminist theoreticians may have succeeded in making the lesbian into almost the representative woman, but it's been at the cost of vanishing her, making her into a figure for absence of identity, and anti-essence. She has stood for the disembodied euphoria of a feminine gender always on the run – interstitial, liminal, betwixt. Castle takes issue here with queer theorists like Eve Sedgwick, 'lesbians who enjoy writing about male-male eros', but who seem captive to the 'privilege of unknowing' when it comes to lesbian libido. So there is a 'coming out' to be accomplished still – and along sweeps Castle like Prince Charming to rescue the lesbian heroine from liminality and carry her with a flourish over the threshold.

Another related set of arguments inhibiting literary-historical study has been the one deriving more or less lazily from Foucault: that the 'lesbian' was invented by turn-of-the-century sexologists like Havelock Ellis, a special case of the more general proposition that gender is a construct of discourse. Castle finds this line unconvincing: was it really all 'a matter of a few cuddles and "darlings" and a lot of epistemic confusion' before 1900? 'Common sense alone suggests otherwise ... For all its mystifications, literature is (still) the mirror of what is known: and Western civilisation, it seems, has always known on some level about lesbianism.'

Not that Castle wants to insist on a naively common-sense account – 'I am, I suppose, a kind of closet Wittgensteinian ... the word [lesbian] is part of a "language game" ... in which we all know the rules.' We use it as a means to an always-provisional but indispensable and living truth-in-process. So: having reconstituted the closet, and found a way out, we're launched on a quest for incarnation, putting bodies and acts and sensuous suggestiveness to the imaginative wraiths mirrored in words (mostly). And that includes the author's characterisation of her-self, via autobiographical glimpses, off-hand asides, and enthusiastic paeans to gaiety which some of her readers may find 'too rapturous and utopian'.

Some of this personalised, confessional stuff works well, some not. The brief prefatory piece coyly called 'First Ed', about a formative sighting of a ravishingly handsome gay woman in the swimming-baths at the YWCA, has its moments, mostly when it echoes *Lolita*, and Humbert Humbert: 'First, Ed – who, for all the sense of drama her name evokes, is surrounded with a certain haze, a nimbus of uncertainty. Did our encounter, the one I remember, take place in 1963 or 1964?' The idea is that this is the experience that sets one apart on enchanted ground, like H. H. the pervert and nympholept with the fancy prose style. Now you see the difference, now you don't. Of course, my spotting Nabokov's monster's traces here depends on ambivalent and fleeting signs, as do some of Castle's own readings. 'Haze' is the main clue: Lolita's surname, and the kind of caressing aura Humbert regularly placed around his love-objects. The extra gloss – 'a nimbus of uncer-tainty' – is also in his manner, studied, affected, textually pleasuring itself in its redundancy; and ditto the luxuriating self-interrogation.

This sort of tone is not the main thing Castle means when she cites Edward Said in praise of 'worldliness', but it's connected: 'gay men', she mock-complains, 'have always seemed to monopolise the wit-and-sophistication department'. Rediscovering such kitsch delights, one aspires to 'point and savoir faire' – or at least the version of those qualities represented by (say) a Violet Trefusis or a Jeanette Winterson, two Castle favourites. Common sense only gets you so far.

It's not always such fun playing along, however. The title-essay is more sentimental than pointed, and the ghostly presences she detects in work by writers ranging from Defoe and Diderot to Compton Mackenzie, Woolf and Mary Renault are not for the most part memorably haunting. There's a depressing mixture of pretension and weary piety about the argument's crowning assertion that lesbianism is 'the repressed idea at the heart of patriarchal culture'. The piece on Radclyffe Hall, however, does manage to get some amusement out of her 'infelicities of tone': despite the climactic, advertised agonies of *The Well of Loneliness*, Hall was 'not drowning but waving'. Castle is at her best when she's celebrating the powers of pastiche and parody and the sly strategies of re-writing. In essence that, for her, is how a text acquires its lesbian character: by acquiring more or less camp quotation marks. And in the absence of such self-consciousness (as with Radclyffe Hall) tragi-comic failures of feeling will do.

Still, some writers and some texts respond to this treatment splendidly. Sylvia Townsend Warner's little-known 1936 historical novel, *Summer Will Show*, forms the basis for an elaborate revision of Eve Sedgwick's 'homosocial' model for the classic novel plot (basically, women as means to male bonding). Here, argues Castle, we have a knowing 'counterplot', in which the hero's wife and mistress get together in the revolutionary Paris of 1848, parodying *L'Education sentimentale* among other things: 'What is particularly satisfying about Townsend Warner's plotting here is that it illustrates so neatly . . . what we might take to be the underlying principle of lesbian narrative itself: namely, that for female bonding to take, as it were, to metamorphose into explicit sexual desire, male bonding must be suppressed . . . Townsend Warner's Frederick has no boyhood friend, no father, no father-in-law,

no son, no gang, *no novelist on his side.*' We can extrapolate from this
the kind of generic narrative recipe that will allow space for lesbian
life – the pre- or post-marital plot. Townsend Warner's own plot, which
kills off one of the lesbian lovers (or does it?), has a more complex
savour. Plausibility is sacrificed, Castle argues, as a deliberate 'insult to
the conventional geometries of fictional eros ... an assault on the
banal'.

It's an appropriately devil-may-care argument, and one you need
an authorial dandy like Townsend Warner to sustain. Other tragedies
stay tragic. Reading Henry James's *The Bostonians* as a rewrite of Zola's
Nana doesn't cancel the cruelty of his treatment of Olive Chancellor's
love for Verena, but it does establish Olive as a specifically lesbian
tragic heroine, and so credits James, 'whether consciously or no', with
the 'opening up of ... tragic space' to women's same-sex love. Castle
is particularly proud of having been able to arrange this piece of
'intertextual pollution' for the chaste, fastidious master. It fits, too, you
realise, with a general pattern of thinking, to do with the sexual charge
associated with the old world and its pre-texts. Hence her affinities
with Humbert, of course. Her chapter on Janet Flanner emphasises just
how much all those *New Yorker* pieces from Paris went in for the
pleasure of text, the sheer 'heft and fleshliness' of the writing, and she
takes Flanner's conscientious biographer Brenda Wineapple to task for
having produced a portrait of a 'morose', 'neurotic', veiled personality:
'as long as a biographer remains imaginatively untouched by the sensual
life of his or her subject – the result will be pale and wraithlike'.

Re-enter the ghost of gaiety. The book's governing metaphor often
seems a bit forced, but there is one essay that does it proud, about
that strange book by Charlotte Moberley and Eleanor Jourdain, *An
Adventure* (1911). In it the two scholarly ladies, Principal and Vice-
Principal of St Hugh's College, Oxford, told how they had got lost in
the grounds of Versailles, strayed somehow into the past, and encountered Marie Antoinette herself. Once a famous ghost story, *An Adventure*
now takes on a new lease of life as one of a whole series of obsessive
lesbian reveries surrounding the romance-figure of the Queen – who
became, Castle is able to show, a kind of lesbian icon. Scurrilous

pamphlets published in the revolutionary period accused her of sexual liaisons with her women courtiers. These 'libels' were transposed by later hagiographers into ecstasies of sentimental friendship, and made Marie Antoinette into 'a kind of communal topos in lesbian writing of the earlier 20th century: a shared underground motif or commonplace'. For Jourdain and Moberley it was this shared vision of Marie Antoinette that made their life-long love-affair possible. She was the ghostly third who blessed them, and acted as their point of reference. It's a convincing argument, in fact, even though its links are candy-floss fine. And it combines with the book's final chapter, about Castle's own romantic adoration from a distance (a true fan) of mezzo-soprano Brigitte Fassbaender, to provide the book with a suitably kitsch set of parting images.

Fassbaender in her grandest breeches role – Octavian from *Rosenkavalier* – and Marie Antoinette from the old prints suddenly start to look terribly familiar, and eerily akin. All that silver lace, and crossdressing, the powdered wigs and panniers and buckled shoes – the whole fake 18th-century wardrobe belongs of course to the pantomime of *Cinderella*. Castle for once doesn't come out and say so, but surely that triangle at the centre of the traditional script, Cinderella, Prince Charming and Dandini, girls together, ought to figure as popular culture's testimony to her thesis? Or perhaps panto mores haven't penetrated yet to Stanford? Be that as it may, there is something saccharine about her celebration of Fassbaender, even if you assume that she has her tongue in her cheek in celebrating Brigitte–Octavian's performance of 'gynophilic rapture'. This is to push the argument about loving your subject over the top, and being knowing about it doesn't help. On the whole, though, and incongruously enough, *The Apparitional Lesbian* is doing the same job for its homoerotic tradition as a straight feminist classic like Ellen Moers's *Literary Women* did a generation ago: establishing a canon, making a common place, assembling the booklists. So the imagery of the *ancien régime* rightly prevails, you could say – deconstruction's credulous and kitsch other.

A record of honourable defeat

No Man's Land: The Place of the Woman Writer in the Twentieth Century, Volume 3, Letters from the Front

SANDRA M. GILBERT AND SUSAN GUBAR

THE QUOTATION THAT BROODED over *Sexchanges* (1989), volume two of Sandra Gilbert and Susan Gubar's history of 20th-century women's writing was Emily Dickinson's see-saw verse: 'I rose – because He sank'. After all the fun they had had with *The Madwoman* (that was back in 1979), it proved a lot harder to map out women's routes through the multiplying traditions of modernism, now that the patriarchal line was petering out in polyphonic, cross-dressed texts. You could (they did) trace the battle-lines of gender drawn across what was theoretically now no man's land – but it was a laborious business. You knew where you were in the attic, after all. And who you were. Now even the titles are running out of metaphorical steam: the 'front' in this one is the vanguard of writing, the attempt to imagine a future. The Second World War gets a chapter, but so does the self-invention of H. D. (Hilda Doolittle), done with rather more conviction. Her celebration of her own rebirth is, we are told, 'a response less to the Great War or the Second World War . . . than to the literary war between the sexes' – which takes us back to the movement of this whole, heavy volume: back to the future. The two main texts Gilbert and Gubar end on are, appropriately enough, Toni Morrison's *Beloved* and Antonia Byatt's *Possession*, novels that find a mirror for late 20th-century desires in 19th-century stories.

One reason for this is the sheer proliferation of women's writing, and the differences their work reveals. The old fairy tales about relationships between men and women have mutated in increasingly complicated ways, so that many of us – feminist critics, cultural historians – seem to be lost in a forest of stories about the future of sexuality and sex roles. Has any sense of an ending to the gender revolution emerged in recent decades?

Well, no. Or rather, Gilbert and Gubar do have a positive answer of sorts up their sleeves, but mostly they want to back all the horses, and make room for the 'complex cast of characters' the century's 'radical sociocultural disruptions' have thrown up: 'the *femme fatale*, the New Woman, the mother-woman, the woman warrior, the feminised woman, the no-woman, the female female impersonator, the goddess . . .' In fact, the last two of these get the most space, perhaps because they may be taken to represent the ends of a spectrum – the woman-as-construct and the woman born again (yet again) as myth. Edna St Vincent Millay and Marianne Moore are both interpreted as the first kind, female female impersonators, one gallantly vamping, the other playing the spinster school-marm. The woman novelists of the Harlem Renaissance, too, come in under this head, and lend cruel, paradoxical depth to the cultivation of inauthenticity and masquerade. Even the most 'savvy and spirited shape changing' runs out on you in the world of Zora Neale Hurston, letting spirituality back in.

Enter H. D. and, to stand as the very emblem of the sex war postwar, Sylvia Plath: 'Torn between her acquiescence in the decorum of the fifties and her ambition to become a boldly great artist . . . between scholarly admiration of an often misogynistic male modernist tradition and secret anxiety about that tradition, Plath seems always to have been doomed to suffer in her own person the sexual battle that marked the century in which she was born.' You can always tell when Gilbert and Gubar feel confident of their ground by the way Harold Bloom's language surfaces through theirs ('anxiety' is the key word here) and sets them up with an inspiriting sense of the enemy within. Plath, with her 'strong revision' of Lawrence, and her 'strong dialogue with literary history' (more echoes of *The Anxiety of Influence*) is the madwoman out of the attic, and it is through taking Plath as representative that the book smuggles a new-old heroine on to centre-stage: the mother-poet. At the time, in the postwar period, exorcising mother and mythology seemed the vital move. They quote a sardonic Simone de Beauvoir, listing the attributes of the eternal feminine – 'She comes down from the remoteness of ages, from Thebes, from Crete, from Chichen Itza; and she is also the totem set deep in the African jungle; she is a helicopter and she is a bird . . .' And they note, too, the parodic deconstruction of Mother in Angela Carter's *Passion of New Eve* and *The Sadeian Woman*, but their hearts are with Plath, and with Adrienne Rich, who rewrites Beauvoir into a positive vision of the coming goddess: 'I see her plunge breasted and glancing through the currents, taking the light upon her at least as beautiful as any boy or helicopter . . .'. This is the kind of answer they want to give to their central question about the future ('what would be the nature of a future in which the real world did not equal war and the difference?') Though their very attachment to the motherly notion that more means better has the odd effect of obscuring their drift. The range of reference is, as ever, catholic, generous, inclusive.

However, the argument is not, not really. Even if you believe that they are right about western women's control over their own fertility being the key to rethinking our metaphors about creativity, you may well want to take the demystificatory line, rather than theirs. There is something wrong with this book's version of magic. It is not only that the retellings of *Snow White* with which they pad out the ending are embarrassingly stiff and uninventive – a gesture towards readers-as-writers, scholars masquerading as story-tellers, that backfires badly. But that the whole assumption that the literary sex-war symbolises other wars (and so can recruit their images, as Plath does the language of fascism and concentration camps) seems wrong. The whole book seems inturned, isolationist, as a result. Writers (especially fiction writers) are enlisted in a campaign that is narrowly redefined; Doris Lessing without Africa, Angela Carter without the attack on born-again religions and so on. I stress the un-American writers to underline how wide is the Gilbert and Gubar net; the problem (which they are aware of) is how to outgrow 'the Ur-story as we interpreted it in *The Madwoman*: how is a woman to achieve personhood . . .' They sound, alas, all-too-motherly themselves. But then we all do when we try to write literary history. *Letters from the Front* is the record of an honourable defeat. How pleased the authors must be to have got that behind them, too, like veterans who can rest on their laurels now.

They lived for their work

Women on the Margins: Three Seventeenth-Century Lives

NATALIE ZEMON DAVIS

This book is in disguise. It looks like an act of pious retrieval, the kind of tradition-making that women's studies took off on a quarter of a century ago now, as old-fashioned as the space programme. But despite the title, this isn't something we've read before. Perhaps Natalie Zemon Davis, author of *The Return of Martin Guerre*, is playing a subtle game with her readers, for *Women on the Margins* is actually devoted to *hiding* its subjects, burying them and losing them in the intricacies of their stories. By insisting on seventeenth-century particularity, Davis means to render these lives unavailable to the old (or is it new?) politics of identity. So it's a less innocent enterprise than it looks, this triptych of studies. These women have nothing much in common, except for articulate careers in the century that started putting the world on one map.

Not that she dissolves her characters in broad cultural history either, though it's important that all three – matriarchal Jewish autobiographer Glikl bas Judah Leib from Hamburg, Catholic missionary to the Huron and Iroquois in Quebec, Marie de l'Incarnation who came from Tours, and Maria Sibylla Merian, born in Frankfurt, radical Protestant naturalist-artist and student of caterpillars – belonged to an age when spiritual adventures were the great springboard to expression. Urban culture, print, translations into the vernacular helped as well. Then there was global trade, which dizzyingly expanded the modest mercantile sphere these women grew up in. For Davis they are all three citizens of a European diaspora, inhabitants of a migrant, moving era that made room for new kinds of women's work.

She loves them because you can't generalise from them, though their worlds do have fugitive connections and contrasts. For instance, Glikl's society was shaken in her youth by the proclamation of the failed Messiah Sabbatai Zevi – itself arguably part of the heightened religious consciousness which in its Counter-Reformation guise inspired Marie de L'Incarnation to convert Canada's *filles sauvages* (after degreasing them and supplying them with decent French underwear, though you couldn't, she said, expect too much *politesse*). Or then again, Glikl's grandson, prospering in London in the East India trade, converted to the Church of England – its quiet Christ Messiah enough for him – which may have been the same kind of rationalist move that Maria Sibylla Merian made in middle age when she detached herself from the Last Days enthusiasm of the Labadist community in Holland, and made an expedition to study and draw the plants and insects of Suriname in 1699. Where, in fact, along with the Dutch, some left-over British, and the slaves who worked the sugar plantations, there were a handful of Jewish colonists, Sephardic Jews and Ashkenazim sharing a jungle synagogue . . . These stories are hooked onto each other by particular, idiosyncratic associations, not big overarching narrative patterns.

They *were* all widows, all had children. However even here there's a quirk of difference, for Merian declared herself a widow before she was (in fact her Lutheran husband divorced her when she joined the Labadists). They didn't exactly *choose* to be separate and strong, though Maria de l'Incarnation at least welcomed widowhood – '. . . seeing that I was free, my soul melted in thankfulness that I no longer had anyone but God in my heart' she wrote years later to the son she'd left behind when she joined the Ursuline order. He became a religious himself, and the editor of her writings, but he shouted for his mother over the convent wall as a boy. She, though, was caught up in Counter-Reformation ecstasies. She had read St Teresa of Avila in French translation (though she was literate she was only a baker's daughter), and like the heroine of some baroque fairy-tale she passed all the tests with flying colours:

> When the violence of her feelings for the sacred Incarnate Word could
> not be borne, she retired to her room for her pen. 'Ah, you are a sweet
> love. You stop our eyes, you steal our sense.' . . . She struck herself till
> she bled, then put haircloth to the wounds to intensify the pain.

Davis's moderate tone makes these excesses somehow par for the course.
What was unique was Marie's missionary vocation. She was not (like
the Jesuits) a budding ethnographer; she recorded the Amerindians'
otherness with a kind of visionary innocence. Witness the Huron woman
who harangued her people against the Christians, who came (she saw)
bearing not only their outrageous faith, but also European diseases like
smallpox that sent Indian souls to the afterworld in droves:

> 'It's the Black Robes who are making us die by their spells . . . They
> set themselves up in a village [and] . . . everyone dies . . . they have big
> pieces of wood [guns] by which they make noise and send their magic
> everywhere.'

Marie reports this in a letter, her faith undented. Davis wants us to
wonder at the way she went to the very end of the world of her own
comprehension, and peered over the edge.

Noticing what her subjects don't, putting in the other stories, is
part of the book's aim. With her first subject, Glikl, she hardly needs
to, we all know about anti-semitism – though she conveys vividly what
it was like to live in a world where complaining of a crime committed
by a Christian was itself a crime. Christians are on the margins here,
'encircling the Jews with their institutions and worldly control'. In the
centre is Glikl's family, and her Job-like argument with God:

> 'God, may his name be praised, laughed at my thoughts and plans and
> had already long decided on my doom and affliction to punish me for
> my sins in *relying on people* . . .'

Davis adds emphases to stress the quality that made Glikl a pioneer
autobiographer. Her life-narrative is interspersed with stories – folk
tales 'so troublesome, so full of surprises and reversals' that they are
just as problematic as real life. Davis saves for last the true story, told
by Glikl, of how she could not hold her dying husband because she

had her period, and ritual laws of purity kept them apart. Job's God at work again.

Each narrative has such telling moments, not always the most personally traumatic. Here is Maria Sibylla Merian on the peacock flower of Suriname:

> Indians . . . use it to abort their children so that they will not become slaves like them. The black slaves from Guinea and Angola must be treated benignly, otherwise they will produce no children at all . . . Indeed they even kill themselves . . . For they feel they will be born again . . . in a free state in their own country, as they instructed me out of their own mouths.

It's characteristic of Davis that along with Merian's beautiful drawings of plants and insects she wants readers to 'see' this. Merian doesn't reveal herself, though –

> Just as she did not arrest insects in their flight to depict their insides, so she did not stop to reveal her own. Describing God's creatures on the outside allowed them to keep living and changing.

Merian's fascination with the metamophoses of moths and butterflies makes her the book's mascot – for though Davis disclaims a 'favourite', it's clear she much relishes the *absence* of intimate material from Merian, who 'preferred the freedom of concealment and discretion'.

So perhaps I was wrong in saying at the outset that *Women on the Margins* avoids piety. It does have its own reverence for history as narrative. If the story is compelling enough – she exiles scholarly references to copious endnotes – then we will be able to glimpse something of the real nature of difference, of what pluralism might mean . . . There are several deities in this book, including the fashionable God or Goddess of dying Nature and the ecologists, and they are forced into improbable coexistence by Davis's patient and imaginative narrative. A marvellous book, then, with no end of other stories waiting in the wings – for example the one about Vladimir Nabokov, who came upon Merian's butterfly books in the attic as a small boy.

The Goddess of More: Parallels between ancient novels and the new womanism

The True Story of the Novel

MARGARET ANNE DOODY

THE NOVELS OF ANTIQUITY are famous for their excesses. Achilles Tatius from Alexandria made such a meal of the scene where Clitophon watches his sweetheart Leucippe being disembowelled by cannibal robbers who proceed to eat her liver for luck, that the Loeb Classics translator, Mr Gaselee, was moved to a footnote disclaiming responsibility: 'The appalling ill taste of this rhetorical apostrophe prevents the English translation of it from being anything but ludicrous,' he wrote. He was not shocked by the gory event in itself, which turns out, once we have enjoyed it to the full, to have been a theatrical stunt arranged by our hero's trusty servant Satyrus and a passing actor, who happens to have all the Homeric gear for sham murders in his luggage – 'You see the mechanism of this dagger; if it is pressed against a body, the blade retreats into the handle, as into a sheath', and so on. It is more Clitophon's instant and eager garnishing of the whole spectacle with well-chosen words that upsets him – particularly the bit about how additionally awful it is that he can't reassemble his virgin love's corpse in order to mourn her, because she's now buried in the thieves' stomachs ('Horrible and new-fangled banquet!'). Perhaps the date of Gaselee's edition – 1917 – has something to do with his squeamishness. But more likely it is a matter of offended classical taste.

These books must have been designed for readers addicted to the inward pleasure of the text. Tragic catharsis and the shapely containing of suffering (civic rituals, according to Aristotle) would be a lot less interesting to them than the pursuit of hybrid, tragicomic plenty. The next course always beckons. Gaselee knows this – 'Compare Chapter

V where the hero prays for burial, together with his beloved, in the belly of the same whale', his footnote continues; it is just that he despises this kind of writing for its lack of generic integrity. Petronius had been allowed to get away with it in the *Satyricon* because Trimalchio's feast is so self-consciously emetic (and anyway his text's integrity was mauled by *time*, not shapeless indulgence), but you cannot save the whole motley 'tradition' by assimilating it to satire, because too much of it is too wholeheartedly kitsch. Margaret Anne Doody loves it for just these reasons, however. For her, the antique novel, whether in Greek or Latin, is fascinating just because it's so unclassical, spiced with dark and doubtful hints (of which she makes fashionably much, in 'Black Athena' mode) of 'polyglot energies ... multiracial origins'. From Chariton's *Callirhoe* in the first century BC through to 'Algerian' Apuleius' *Golden Ass* in the second century AD, novels about 'erotic suffering' featuring star-crossed lovers and plots punctuated with shipwrecks, martyrdoms, resurrections and blissful unfulfilments of all kinds, chart the emergence of 'New Age' values that united decaying paganism and emergent Christianity – all about 'a desire to overcome the world, or at least in a kind of thought-experiment, to modify it'. This is Virtue as a kind of eating disorder, where you experiment with your own body's phobias and appetites – via, for example, 'a voluntary and extravagant chastity' – in order to assert control. The prospect of pain is, for these adepts, a key to their own special form of power. There is Leucippe herself, who has been sold into slavery this time, confronting a would-be seducer. Give her a taste of the lash, his servant has just said nastily, that'll tame her, little suspecting that on the contrary he's given her her cue:

> Set out your tortures, bring up the wheel ... Feast your eyes on a new sight; one woman contends against all manner of tortures, and overcomes all her trials ... I am defenceless, and alone, and a woman; but one shield I have, and that is my free soul ... That is a possession I shall never surrender ... !

Small wonder the villain feels so queasy that he has to rush out of the hut. Doody acknowledges, of course, that the posturing is in some ways 'comic'. 'To love oneself is, like loving God or one's neighbour, a religious activity – so the Novel says, in its prosy, comic and *un*priestly voice.' But if you thought that she was genuinely disposed to mock the narcissistic and masochistic mores her texts espouse, you would be very much mistaken. For her, these distant forerunners of Richardson's *Clarissa* and the Sadean woman are the very characters of psychic fulfilment. Her line is not that the books are more fun than they've been made out to be; she wants to make a much grander claim: that we have, in this unclassical writing, a special sort of 'wisdom literature' in which for the first time 'the human body could stand out as a clearly marked locus of free choice' and 'the sacredness of individuality' was messily and mysteriously affirmed.

There is a plot under the plots, Doody argues, and it has three main strands – a new emphasis on equality between (heterosexual) lovers, for 'the males . . . are as emotional as the females'; a new understanding of the meanings of freedom, based not on manly civic values of action and sovereignty, but female victim-values, which are very like slave virtues turned inside out; and third, underpinning these feminizing transformations, 'an alternative source of power . . . the priesthood of Artemis', the generative divinity who had survived official paganism and was about to take on a new lease of life in Christianity through her son's anti-patriarchal cult ('Eros is full of surprises'). These books, read her way, constitute 'claims to sacred self-disposal underwritten by the Goddess'. It is not at base a new argument at all, this one, indeed the antique fictions positively *lend* themselves to such free-floating suggestions, which were picked up by nineteenth-century mythographers, proto-Jungians, and such. The novelty of Doody's born-again version lies in the gusto and shameless bad faith with which she pursues her ends. For her, the novels are gnostic gospels – 'The essential story is the salvation of the soul through the experience of death and resurrection to new life.' The amorphousness and opportunism of the texts are for her not a problem but a promise. They allow and even invite a kind of careless appropriation that does indeed give the reader a heady sense of freedom.

So, though Doody retells their stories in loving, leisurely, digressive style, she still contrives to gloss over the possibility of alternative or competing interpretations. For instance, her claim that the meaning of slavery was only fully realized by women, because in the ancient world 'males are threatened with death on the battlefield, not enslavement in defeat' is unsupported by any direct historical evidence. The texts themselves, in fact, show heroes and heroines both routinely enslaved as part of the vicissitudes of the plot, but this is taken, perversely, as evidence for the new spiritual economy (these enslaved heroes are the new men of their day, sharing the burden of inward and spiritual freedom). Then again, the notion that the heterosexual heroes and heroines are equals in love is also open to objection: true, they are usually both young and both beautiful, but this mainly serves to make them objects of desire to other characters (and to the voyeuristic reader), who is thus offered two for the price of one, depending on his or her sexual orientation and appetite. And as for the Goddess, she is everywhere and nowhere, for the characters seem willing to believe in any divinity that provides a pretext for self-dramatization.

The rhetorical surface of the stories acts for Doody as such an irresistible seduction that occasionally she even gets the plot wrong in her anxiety to believe the characters. One example: Leucippe's foiled seducer, we are told, believes her to be dead, murdered by his jealous wife. In fact, this is a story he makes up in order to persuade her lover Clitophon to desert her. Not that one detail in an orgy of intrigue matters much, but getting it wrong is a small sign of Doody's eager credulity. In a sense, she is too good a reader of these books, she is too opportunist and gullible and a pushover for cultish rhetoric – 'The Goddess blesses the selving of the flesh' is one memorable line that she cannot quite find in the texts, so has to compose for herself. The search for origins turns out to be a rite of initiation into late twentieth-century New Age mysteries, after all. Gradually, as you're led by the hand back into the cave, into the cosy labyrinthine dark where anything goes, you realize that the purpose of your journey is not to find out what the ancient novels were really 'about', but to peer into their mirrors. They are prophetic dreams, or magic movies – 'Nothing is more cinematic than the novel from the beginning'; 'reading time' is 'mythical time . . . some form of deep time that is not really anybody's time'. And the conventions of criticism give way to a sort of crooning incantatory tone that means to re-create the delights of getting in touch with 'the earliest and latest levels of our consciousness':

> Suppose there were in these antique fictions and in other novels some other effects and meanings . . . ? running beneath and within these things. Suppose – to put it strangely – there were an undersong to these novels, which we could hear? . . . And if so, then whatever that other errand is may be the task also of the Novel of Now.

It's a small step from here to a revisionist 'history' devoted to liberating the Novel of Myth from the particular lower-case novels which mistook themselves for a literary genre (particularly in the eighteenth and nineteenth centuries) and got lost in a literal-minded deviation into realism. Part Two, 'The Influence of the Ancient Novels', explores their afterlife, adaptation, translation and dissemination. Earlier on, their actual presence in people's heads is sometimes a matter of conjecture, but that is grist to the mill: 'it is almost harder to believe that Boccaccio did not know Heliodorus (in some form) than that he did'. Later, in the High Renaissance and the seventeenth century, ancient fiction is securely circulating and widely loved and imitated. Until modernizing realism gets a grip, and hides from writers the dark origins of their art. *The True Story of the Novel* aims to put prose fiction back in touch with its deep structurelessness.

It is a game of mystification and hide-and-seek which involves quarantining the sacred Novel, and isolating it from the contagion of other kinds of literature: poetry and prose, she says darkly, 'serve different gods'. Novels (upper case) are guides to the voyage inwards, though this truth has been systematically and mischievously suppressed by Eurocentric authors and critics with their worldly, colonizing and materialist agendas. Ian Watt's *Rise of the Novel* is perhaps the clearest enemy text, though Doody would equally dislike Bakhtin's very different reading of the novel genre for its extrovert, dialogical, topical and satiric emphases. The critical thinker she is closest to, in an odd way, though she never (Eros forbid!) mentions him, is Harold Bloom. Her Novel of Now is almost exactly his rivalrous canon turned on its head – a sort of enormous and prolific matrix of 'tropes' (caves, labyrinths, food, rebirth), which equally seeks to efface the distinction between cultures and past and present experience.

The cumulative effect is vertiginous. While accusing realist novelists and worldly historians of literature of a great act of exclusion – 'one of the most striking aspects of the new domestic novel (of the eighteenth century) . . . is its ability to exclude' – Doody maintains that 'every novelist . . . repeats the tropes of the Novel itself'. In other words, there is endless difference, and no change at all: the realm of the Goddess, as she says, is bigger, not other. Novelists who were under the delusion that they were doing something quite different can be saved despite themselves, and so can readers – 'the novel's ritual acts can be efficaciously undergone in a state of unawareness'. With some mystic chivvying, a surprising number of books can be induced to deliver the rudiments of 'pilgrimage' – 'being cut, dirtied, muddied by some viscous mixture of wet and dry . . .'. Doody's Part Three looks at the recurring 'Tropes of the Novel', and yes, we have been here before. But the provenance of this particular mythic pattern doesn't have to be sought as far back as antiquity. Its affinities belong very much to history, and recent history at that; echoes that multiply in these caves come from a lot closer to home. We are back in the Women's Room, with Marilyn French, whose huge holier-than-thou classic of matriarchal masochism invoked just this mental landscape back in 1977. Take the trope of the seashore, for instance – 'My head is full of voices,' says French's narrator. 'They blend with the wind and the sea as I walk the beach as if they were disembodied forces of nature . . .' She too thinks of novel-writing as the genre of spiritual pilgrimage, the stuff of life itself:

> It has no shape, it hasn't the balances so important in art. You know, one line goes this way, another must go that way. All these lines are the same. These lives are the threads that get woven into a carpet and when it's done the weaver is surprised that the colours all blend: shades

of blood, shades of tears, smell of sweat. Even the lives that don't fit,
fit.

Though French is never mentioned, this memorable sermon is echoed
everywhere in Doody: 'A novelist's primary calling is to give a *representation of what it feels like to be alive*. This can be done in many ways. But
the sense of being alive, as an individual in time, is a mythic affair – no
matter what the religious belief or absence of belief of novelists or
readers.' All these lines are indeed the same – 'the same old salt tears
and sperm' (this is French), 'the same sweet blood and sweat she'd
wiped up for years'. Reading, says Doody, 'is an erotic activity that
mimics and reinforces the fundamental erotic desire of living itself'.
Or again, 'Our love of story . . . is related to our felt need to continue
living.' And French: 'Art is what nourishes, what feeds, art is food.' In
her mammoth moral history, *Beyond Power* (1986), French charted 'male'
civilization as a suicidal conspiracy, and concluded that 'the end of life
is the continuation of life'.

  Of course, there are differences. French's tone was anguished and
accusing, whereas Doody's is knowing and playful, since she has let
the Goddess out of the closet and exchanged the moral high ground
that used to be associated with documentary and consciousness-raising
for magic and myth – 'We wander through the labyrinth, we cross
water, we partake of holy food . . . The Goddess presides over and
sustains the body and soul in this life of being and becoming . . . She
may not seem "realistic" or "naturalistic" but the Goddess underlies
all realisms . . .'. For Doody, 'erotic suffering' is pleasure, and so is the
mystification of power as a quality of being and repetition. Perhaps
the most significant and striking thing she and French have in common
is the size of their books. As Doody says, 'The goddess is the assurance
that there is *more*.' The Goddess means – well – just about everything.
Except that she doesn't, she has rules of her own that – for instance –
deeply discourage scepticism, multiple meanings that threaten to engage
with each other, contradictions, alternative hypotheses, negotiable differences and true disagreements alike. The Goddess doesn't care what
you think you mean, she knows better. Doody seldom acknowledges

this aspect of her mythic mentor. However, some dissenters do bring her out in her true colours. Camille Paglia, for instance, provokes this admirer of Isis to a revealingly banal psychotherapist's snarl: 'Certainly, to see the Mother as God is hard on people who do not get along with their mothers . . .'. The Goddess is correctness itself, and to doubt her wisdom is to convict yourself of a whole series of sins, including very possibly 'Aryan' prejudice, as she weirdly and threateningly remarks at one point.

In the end, *The True Story of the Novel* is curiously claustrophobic for such a big book, its story is so very local, a story of the past twenty-five years, of nostalgic womanism and born-again correctness. Doody's way of reaching back through time to the ancient fictions of the age of credulity in which Christianity was born reveals a deep contempt for historical change. This is not a matter, as she would portray it, of religious sensibility in itself, but of the very particular style of beliefs she subscribes to. 'As a Christian, a participant in certain regular and mystical enactments and a hearer of stories regarded by the enlightened as myth, I see both mystery and myth as enabling conditions of insight and change,' she finally confesses on page 481, thus revealing that she has quite as little respect for the history of revealed religion as she does for the history of literature. What she is interested in is neither of these things, but the marshy, semi-fictional, semi-scholarly land that has been reclaimed for credulity by our habits of revisionism. She may be a very odd Christian, but she is an absolutely predictable *presentist*. 'It is almost impossible to resist the conclusion that we have here one of the late survivals of the cult of Cybele–Attis (alias Venus–Adonis, Isis–Osiris) associated with the blood of the bull . . .' Well, no, it's not, and the more you get of the Goddess of More, the more resistible she becomes. The road of excess leads to the palace of wisdom by more routes than one.

Learning new titles

Critical Condition: Feminism at the Turn of the Century

SUSAN GUBAR

R ECENT STATISTICS IN THE United States have apparently revealed that fewer women are being murdered by their husbands, not because there's less misogyny abroad but because there's less marriage. This is a good example of the way in which there have been enormous changes in the patterns of people's lives, which seem only loosely or mockingly related to what we projected. No wonder the postmodern picture of the individual as a passive construction of occult power at large seems plausible. Susan Gubar, looking at the relation between what 1970s feminist teachers and scholars wanted, and what has actually happened, is caught in a similar paradox; there are more women students, teachers, women's-studies programmes in universities, particularly in the Humanities, than anyone would have dreamed, but there is less and less common ground on what women mean.

Some of the reasons for this are obvious. Feminist academics first got jobs, and tenure, in significant numbers 'at exactly the moment when the profession itself came under intense pressure to downsize'. The result was that competition, the pressure to publish, and the need to distance yourself from your predecessors in the name of originality, were all savagely increased. Susan Gubar describes the situation – 'fissures ... between women of different ranks, between older and younger women, between women within traditional departments and those in multidisciplinary programmes ...', and so on – with exemplary restraint and even humour. She deliberately doesn't extend the grim picture, as she might well have, to point out that the very consciousness-raising that brought so many more women and previously excluded minorities into higher education itself led to the rationing. Women in women's-studies programmes came up against the limits of official inclusiveness with particular force. It is no accident that the kind of post-structuralist theory that Gubar feels most ill at ease with is very well equipped to explain how exclusion works and how divisions proliferate. Though a lot of it is notoriously obscurely expressed, its accounts of endlessly deferred meaning and compromised agency uncannily resemble the real world, or at least the real academic world, that oxymoron. Theory promises to give you symbolic capital, in other words, the only kind most of us are going to accumulate much of. Privilege your powerlessness is one of its messages.

If Gubar avoids this kind of careless fighting talk, it is because she is intellectually and temperamentally disposed, despite all, to read the situation constructively. The form of *Critical Condition* – a collection of essays – means she doesn't have to produce an authoritative overview of the whole story. You can piece it together, though: first, the phase (Kate Millett's *Sexual Politics*, 1969) of showing how women were characterized in male-dominated histories and stories; second, the building of female traditions (as in her own *The Madwoman in the Attic*, in 1979, written with Sandra M. Gilbert); third, African-American and lesbian identity politics (speaking 'as a . . .'); then with queer theory and post-colonial theory in the 1990s 'those very terms . . . themselves underwent a sort of spectacular unravelling'. And here we are, back to square one, with the best work in the field addressing itself to 'the perplexity of women's fractured, divided, multiplied and contradictory modes of identification'.

So where next? Some have given up on the whole game of identifying. Elaine Showalter is quoted as saying 'I don't care what the latest development is in feminist theory or gender theory. It's completely irrelevant to me.' Gubar, though, reads this as an understandable reaction to the kind of raw hostility that has become a feature of relations among feminist critics. She herself has, as she tells us, fought to resist cynicism, and the pieces that manage to digress from the question of 'What Ails Feminist Criticism' show that she has struggled to good effect. The essay on the reflections on race and colour in the work of visual artists like Faith Ringgold is subtle, funny and heartfelt; and the analysis of the work of Marilyn Hacker, Jeannette Winterson and Rebecca Brown, in which Gubar finds a 'metalesbian' message is very smart. Though there is something a bit odd about the implication that you need visionary sapphic abilities 'to leap over historical facticity'. Can't heterosexual writers do the daring illusions any longer? Perhaps Gubar is just being a good reader, showing she can learn new tricks herself. That is what she does in the book's potentially most interesting piece, 'Eating the Bread of Affliction', about teasing out the relations between her Jewishness and her feminism, when she reflects on the impact of African-American Studies:

> After black scholars convinced feminist thinkers about the importance
> of race, identity politics provided a vocabulary for Jewish women to
> take seriously their own hyphenated identities.

True to form, however, she wants to point to the Jew as one of modernism's most representative outsiders, whose fortunes she and Sandra Gilbert partly traced in their mammoth *No Man's Land*. There is some fascinating work to be done on American feminism's links with Jewish immigrant and diaspora culture, and un-American Activities, only hinted at here.

But at the same time, this gently personal piece marks a retreat. 'Has "What is to be done?" been replaced by "Who am I?"' she asks, and the answer must be partly yes. Not entirely, though, for the paradoxical reason that – judging from her tone – she is indeed a kind of Jewish Mom in the quarrelsome household of academe. She can't retire into herself, can't bring herself not to interfere. Her determination is her most powerful argument for continuing to search for common ground, or at least new ways of disagreeing, since fractures and faultlines are not going to go away. Any overview is a grand-scale act of will and ingenuity, but it is an act, something you do, not something you are.

Academic women edit texts, do archival research, write literary biographies, teach writing and review books, as well as engage in the 'mind-numbing battles' that Susan Gubar deplores. There is room to live intellectually, in other words, without having to compete over who's more marginal than whom. And there is even a book to be written on the perverse pleasures of claustrophobia for academic anchoresses that she is altogether too caring to contemplate.

Mother's back

What Is a Woman? and Other Essays

TORIL MOI

FEMINISM IS FIFTYSOMETHING IF you start counting from *The Second Sex*, and, like Toril Moi, a lot of academic women are taking stock. The good news is that wherever positive discrimination in favour of men has been suspended, there are many more women in universities than there used to be, as students, teachers and even tenured professors. What's been lost is the sense of connection with utopian politics. Part of the fiftyish feeling is to do with having to recognise that the future – *that* future, the classless, melting-pot, unisex, embarrassing one – is now in the past. Or, more painfully, that it has been hijacked by obscurantism and academic careerism, which often amount to the same thing.

What Is a Woman? and Other Essays deplores this development. Moi is in a tricky position, however, for she herself is widely seen as one of the villains of the piece: the woman who trashed sisterhood in her 1985 book *Sexual/Textual Politics* by preaching post-structuralist demolition of the whole person, and dismissing American feminists as naive empiricists. 'With friends like these, does feminism need enemies?' Susan Gubar asks with uncharacteristic bitterness in her new stock-taking book *Critical Condition*. Clearly Moi is unforgiven, even though she has partly recanted. For instance: she used to argue that 'all efforts towards a definition of woman are destined to be essentialist'. Now she thinks definition is a red herring, and wields the very word 'woman' like a weapon. This will not endear her to the women whose work she so influentially pigeonholed. Nor will her insistence that her former savagery was fuelled by a euphoric sense that conflict was exciting and feminist writing should be rash, hand to mouth and excessive. This was intellectual *life* after all, and *vive la différence*. No harm was done, we were all playing the same game, weren't we? The moment fed, she says now, a recurring 'fantasy of being able to speak in a way that would genuinely be all-inclusive ... The fantasy is one of merger, in which one would not have the problem of separating one's voice from that of others, so that, ultimately, it would not matter who was speaking.'

Well, it has turned out to matter. The essays that make up this new book examine the question of how to speak for yourself, and not in quotation-marks as though you were the mouthpiece of an unstoppable dialectical process. Moi still recognises the author of *Sexual/Textual Politics*, but no longer accepts the way she operated, quoting with some incredulity herself quoting Luce Irigaray and Hélène Cixous. She/they were doing away with the old humanist self as 'constructed', in one of the book's most-quoted passages, 'on the model of the self-contained powerful phallus'. Now, she says: 'I don't think I can have believed this when I wrote it. I don't understand why every integral whole must be phallic ... It doesn't help that I say I have it from Irigaray and Cixous. This in fact makes it worse.' This new use of 'I' liberates her from having to pay lip-service to post-structuralist orthodoxy. She hasn't changed, she was just carried away, she implies, and there's no reason not to believe her. With hindsight, the first book's odd disapproving allusions to Cixous's personal style – 'ermine as emancipation' – take on more weight. There spoke the literal, serious and class-conscious Moi of the turn of the century, exasperated with the decadence and snobbishness of deconstruction – 'obscure, theoreticist, plagued by internal contradictions, mired in unnecessary philosophical and theoretical elaborations.'

The long title essay undertakes a patient, sometimes dogged diagnosis of how this impasse came about. Feminist theory took a wrong turn almost at the moment of its rebirth in the 1960s. Moi traces the problem to the enshrining of the sex/gender distinction, which was so useful as a bulwark against biological determinism, but developed a life of its own and spawned metaphysical pseudo-problems around the concrete historical body. Perhaps the most interesting encounter here is with the work of Judith Butler. Butler, too, finds the distinction between biological sex and gender specious, but she resolves it by arguing that sex is just as constructed as gender, thus (for Moi) compounding the damage. Butler's concept of 'performativity' – the daily script that ends up being written on the body and makes a woman seem solidly a woman – brilliantly obscures the matter of self-making, of 'a "doer behind the deed", an agent who actually makes choices': 'In Butler's picture . . . sex becomes the inaccessible ground of gender, gender becomes completely disembodied, and the body itself is divorced from all meaning.' There is nothing material in such arguments except language itself, Moi argues, and language works to cloud the issue: 'Butler thinks of a woman as the ongoing production of a congealed ideological construct.' What we need is a way out of these labyrinthine post-structuralist debates in which matter is an effect of power and 'power becomes a principle that works in mysterious ways behind the veil of appearances'.

So how do we extricate ourselves? Moi argues that we need to go back to the future – back, in particular, to Simone de Beauvoir, whose phenomenological understanding of lived experience will provide a way out. Her 1994 book on Beauvoir, *The Making of an Intellectual Woman*, paid implicit tribute to the continuing relevance of Beauvoir's ideas, but now she applies them directly as a kind of alternative therapy for feminism's sick and fissile state. Beauvoir writes and thinks with awareness of 'the concrete, historical body that loves, suffers and dies'. 'Woman', in the words of *The Second Sex*, 'is not a fixed reality, but rather a becoming . . . the body is not a thing, it is a *situation*, it is our grasp on the world and a sketch of our projects.' Moi concentrates on Beauvoir's language in order to rediscover her originality, and she often has cause to rewrite H. M. Parshley's English translation, as she does here, where he had the body as 'a limiting factor' rather than a 'sketch', thereby importing (she argues) a traditional idea of consciousness as merely inhabiting the body. Beauvoir's woman is realistically ambiguous, a sex-gender amphibian, subject both to natural laws and to the human production of meaning, 'a synthesis of facticity and freedom': 'The fact that Beauvoir refuses to hand the concept of "woman" over to the opposition is what makes *The Second Sex* such a liberating read.' Beauvoir's woman – resembling her author – invents herself. Not freely, or fantastically, in a void, but in a style of resistance and scepticism. This is what Moi is after: a theoretical position that gives us back the notion of agency. She returns again and again to the same point: 'Each woman will make something out of what the world makes out of her' is a sentence that recurs with minor variations at least half a dozen times.

Moi in fact has come to resemble Beauvoir in her distaste for anything that might smack of self-pity or titivation: she would rather repeat herself than doll the idea up in different words. The second big essay in this book – '"I am a Woman": The Personal and the Philosophical' – comes at the argument about how to get the whole person on the page from a different angle. It looks at the fashion for saying 'I' in academe that started with Jane Tompkins's 1989 essay 'Me and My Shadow', in which Tompkins confesses to finding theoretical writing 'incredibly alienating': 'I love writers who write about their own experience. I feel I am being nourished by them.' Philosophy – i.e. theory of any kind – is male and arrogant, on this view; or to put it less personally, Post-Modern thinking pictures all knowledge as located: you have to say where you're coming from because (in Linda Alcoff's immortal words) 'a speaker's location is epistemologically salient.' Moi has a fairly easy time exposing the double-think involved here ('in order to indulge in the luxury of the personal one needs to have tenure') and showing how token or kitsch some of these supposedly vulnerable and personal excursions are. More seriously, you need to work hard to speak or write cogently in the first person, and to acknowledge that 'there is always someone who is not speaking'. Be your own woman. At the centre of the argument is a comparative analysis of the opening paragraphs of *The Second Sex* and Luce Irigaray's *Speculum of the Other Woman*, in which Moi is able to show convincingly that Irigaray's strategy of ventriloquism leaves very little space for readers to dissent, whereas Beauvoir's 'I' lets in the ordinary, partial perspective. For Irigaray, a woman under patriarchy is doomed to mimicry, locked up in a language not hers; for Moi, one of the major strategies of sexism is 'to imprison women in their subjectivity' in just this way.

This second long essay complements the first. Just because Moi has had enough of theoreticism, as she now scornfully calls it, doesn't mean that she is anti-theoretical in currently correct style either. Confessionalism, she concludes, has become an academic sub-genre like any other, which is unsurprising, since it is 'a theory-generated attempt to escape from the bad effects of theory'. The problem was the way we posed the problem. What she wants is a radical spring-clean of feminist thinking. Let's go back and start again, we have nothing to lose but our mind-forged manacles. Beauvoir was a freelance, an independent, and Moi is too, in spirit – not a deconstructionist, more of a righteous wrecker. Beauvoir told her eager biographer Deirdre Bair (who came to resent her superior glumness, if you read between the lines) that when she wrote *The Second Sex* she was 'the messenger who brings the bad news'. Moi has assumed her mantle. So although she laments the reluctance of feminist theoreticians to listen to arguments that don't speak the right language (use the right quotation-marks), she can hardly be surprised. Beauvoir's own reception by later feminists was spectacularly mixed; among the most prestigious, like Cixous and Irigaray, it was violently hostile. Moi notes here the 'snub' Cixous delivered by simply never mentioning Beauvoir in her contribution to the special issue of the magazine *l'Arc* dedicated to Beauvoir in 1975. Beauvoir was already dead and buried, for Cixous. 'Beauvoir is not an enemy . . . she is no one, nothing.' Antoinette Fouque in a 1986 obituary article in *Libération* accused Beauvoir of 'intolerant, assimilating, sterilising universalism, full of hatred and reductive of otherness'. There are others, Moi doesn't quote as many as she could. Annie Leclerc, for instance, who has described her 1974 book *Parole de femme* as 'an anti-*Second Sex*', sets her own version of textual bliss against Beauvoir's bleak view of the hard labour of reproduction: 'To be this vagina, an open eye in life's nocturnal fermentation, an ear alive to the pulse, the vibration of the originating magma'. This is enough to send one back with relief to Beauvoir's trenchant description of the colossal bad faith of women who choose charm and bad writing.

These days, Anglo-American feminists, too, would mostly agree that Beauvoir has nothing to say to them. She didn't know she was 'different' is the line. Moi thinks that quite a lot of this stems from generational rage, rubbing out mother. Indeed, she thinks it's all a feature of all intellectual life, and that you can see it in relations between male thinkers – for example, in the relations of Bourdieu and Derrida to Sartre, and of René Girard to Freud. So perhaps there's nothing specifically female or feminist about the bind that theory has got itself into. Battling her way out of the forest of quotation-marks, Moi turns to Freud himself and one of his most quoted phrases, 'Anatomy is destiny', which is a travestied version of what Napoleon said to Goethe: 'What does one want destiny for now . . . Politics is destiny.' In other words, Freud is inviting us to think about what destiny means in the modern world: he probably didn't intend to say that anatomy overrides human agency, though it may well ironise it. Moi's argument is characteristically detailed and lucid, and arrives at a reading of the Freud texts (he misquoted Napoleon twice, first apropos of all human beings, later just women) that avoids bringing in timeless and ineluctable fate by the skin of its teeth. History and contingency count, she wants to say: indeed, Freud was a man of his time in his 'tendency to think of male sexuality as fairly easy to investigate, and to cast female sexual difference as an unsolvable mystery'. By this stage in the argument – and in the book, which only has three short literary essays on courtly love and (again) Beauvoir's brief novel, *The Woman Destroyed*, to go – we're out of the wood, and the moral is clear. Don't settle for getting used to the dark, don't write yourself further into the undergrowth, perversely addictive though it is. Hack your way through the thickets of theory.

What Is a Woman? is a kind of *Pilgrim's Progress*: most of the other critics and theorists you meet on the way represent obstacles or sophistical tempters – or as in Freud's case have to be lent on to yield a usable meaning. One of the exceptions is the social theorist Pierre Bourdieu, whose remark 'One cannot liberate the victims of symbolic violence by decree' Moi takes very seriously. What it means is that you have to spell out the arguments step by step, and that even then the class-system in the intellectual world, which rations attention, and ensures that those who already have symbolic capital tend to accrue more, makes it hard for dissent to get a hearing. Another friendly presence is Wittgenstein: 'A picture held us captive. And we could not get outside it, for it lay in our language and language seemed to repeat it to us inexorably.' And another phrase of his – 'language on holiday': that is, language that's not doing an honest day's work – serves to describe what she so distrusts in deconstruction's style: if people have *fun* rattling their intellectual shackles, that's even worse. Like Beauvoir, Moi is the messenger who brings the bad news. 'No, we have not won the game.' Put these words of Beauvoir's into her mouth, and they come out sounding right. *What Is a Woman?* is written out of a prim passion for freedom. For a book that argues for the resurrection of Woman, it is shamelessly individualist. No wonder Toril Moi is regarded by some feminist scholars as the new enemy, the enemy within. But her energy is positive and provocative, and in the best sense old-fashioned – modern, utopian, enlightened, or at least of a kind to let in the grey day.

IV

Classics

Daringly distasteful

Keats and Embarrassment

CHRISTOPHER RICKS

KEATS AND EMBARRASSMENT IS about the continuous, prickling warmth generated in human interchange, and it hands over its sensations without apology to the reader. Christopher Ricks is adept in stirring up the small, satisfactory, argumentative relations that make critical dialogue look alive. He draws Keats into a sticky web of responses and insights culled from all over the place, not just glossing the poems (though he does that), but setting poems, case-histories, criticism, novels, into abrasive and productive contact. His own style of analysis is sharp, appreciative and irreverent, like William Empson's, and he is immensely good at turning respectable critical positions inside out. For example, he quotes Lionel Trilling's elegant description of Keats's 'dialectic of pleasure' – 'Keats . . . may be thought of as the poet who made the boldest affirmation of the principle of pleasure and also as the poet who brought the principle of pleasure into the greatest and *sincerest* doubt' – and goes on to argue, mischievously and entirely seriously, that 'the challenge is not a challenge *to*, but the challenge *of* pleasure'. The manoeuvre is characteristic (this is the way most points in the book get made), and enlightening: Professor Ricks's main target, so far as criticism goes, is the high-minded, queasy aversion to poetry that is simple, sensuous and passionate. (Though 'simple' for him means undifferentiated, whole and full, not unintelligent or unanalysable.)

More exactly, it is Keats's restive, redeeming greed that the book focuses on: his capacity to take his own pleasures (as a person, as a poet) and other people's too. This means that he is always uneasily, voyeuristically, infringing the careful codes that divide the private from the public, always insinuating his imagination, his words, into the moist, wordless intimacies of sensation. 'So said, his erewhile timid lips grew bold. And poesied with hers in dewy rhyme.' This insinuation, Professor Ricks suggests, requires a different sort of courage from objectifying or ironizing – it means daring to be distasteful, managing to register that grimacing withdrawal, and yet enclose it in a larger, more generous appreciation of the inevitable awkwardness of the machineries of joy. Keats is especially a challenge, moreover, because the textures and secretions he immersed his imagination in were not decently, saltily, abruptly organic. He 'breeds' on his own. His eroticism is a sort of generalized pang; it doesn't issue in action but in looking and dreaming and writing, and that makes it most difficult to take, allied as it is with an incipiently Victorian predilection for dawning blushes and milky kisses and gentle squeezes ... In short, Professor Ricks readily persuades one that this particular warm, damp corner of sensibility is embarrassing. But is that embarrassment, as he would claim, vital to our cultural tradition, and our present capacities for imaginative experience?

This is where the argument of *Keats and Embarrassment*, so admirably forthright on slippery details, becomes oblique and evasive. The agile use of quotation smuggles in some large unquestioned assumptions. For instance, the most substantial creative presences from this century are Aldous Huxley and Samuel Beckett, each celebrating in his own way the grotesque implausibility of human intercourse. You gather that 'we' need Keats's warm wetness because we, collectively, are arid, middle-aged and dried up. Only by braving the prickly heat of embarrassment can we recapture each other's pleasure and our own; or, to put it another way, can we stop being alienated voyeurs and become participatory ones. Voyeurs we must be, the book assumes, so best learn the art from Keats. Which seems, to say the least, a peculiarly donnish predicament.

Or again, instead of analysing the more metaphysical implications of stickiness (as a way of thinking about one's mortal relations with the world – and about the relations between thinking itself and perception), Professor Ricks quotes at length from Sartre on *slime*: 'Slime is the revenge of the In-itself. A sickly-sweet feminine revenge . . . That sucking of the slimy substance which I feel on my hands outlines a kind of continuity of the slimy substance in myself.' The quotation is tremendous, and obscure, and there is an awkward gap between the abstract issues its attenuated metaphor raises, and the concrete, localized vision of Professor Ricks's own analysis. One suspects that Keats's flutter and ooze of sensation is a refuge from the barren waste of literary metaphysics, too. The trouble is that quotation is not a way of ceasing to be dogmatic or abstract. It simply gives the generalities a more numinous, elusive status. Professor Ricks's interest in embarrassment seems much narrower, more professorial, more personal, than the book tries to suggest.

Thus the most striking claim – 'the case for some of Keats's most impassioned poetry is essentially the case for a purified and liberated scopophilia [voyeurism]' – turns out to be a lot less radical and adventurous than it sounds. Professor Ricks is not really in the Alex Comfort (*Gourmet's Guide to Love-making*) territory, or at least, his is a gourmet's guide for puritans. 'Purified and liberated' mean that Keats's voyeurism does not translate into crude, literal-minded doing, but generates a complex regression, a wilderness of mirrors – Keats talking about Porphyro watching Madeline undress, and us writing and talking about Keats's writing. What is the relation between this 'liberation' and, say – it's not an irrelevant or frivolous question – a shabby experience currently advertised on Great Windmill Street: 'Your Own Studios. Take Your Own Glamour Photos of our Beautiful Girls. First Floor. Camera Supplied'? Only in an enclosed, even cloistered context (which the book does not admit to) does it make sense to say that embarrassment is the source of our poverty, and the key to imaginative freedom. As though the problem were to cope with and control our attitudes to pleasure, rather than exploring the nature of the pleasures we propose to ourselves.

And so, for all the freshness and liveliness of its beginning, *Keats and Embarrassment* ends by invoking a familiar claustrophobia:

> Keats sets such store by the attempt to imagine a writer or a reader because doing so will release reading and writing from the inevitable

anxieties of solitude – narcissism, solipsism, lonely indulgent fantasizing. It is for such reasons that many of us set such store by the public discussion of literature. To write about literature, argue about it, teach it: these, though they bring other anxieties, are valued because they can help to restore a vital balance of private and public in our relation with literature.

Keats's acrobatics on the dangerous edge of mawkishness, his deliberate immaturity, are the specific for our dry, nervous culture, just as once irony and maturity were the correctives for left-over Georgianism. The difference is that Professor Ricks's seminar sounds more like group therapy than an investigation that hopes to get somewhere. I. A. Richards and Professor Empson expect literature to tell them which are the best experiences – 'Words', Richards said grandly, 'are not a medium in which to copy life. Their true work is to restore life itself to order.' The difference is important, and can be exemplified in the case of Byron, whose savage comments on Keats Professor Ricks quotes: '. . . such writing is sort of mental masturbation – he is always f—gg—g his imagination . . .' His way of dealing with this is the therapist's way: that is, he says to Byron, 'How interesting that this poetry should make you so angry. Let's consider what (in you) makes you so disturbed.' But may not Byron be *right*? To turn all judgments back on their speakers is surely to assume that 'lonely, indulgent fantasizing' is all anyone is capable of and to degrade critical dialogue to a species of timid exhibitionism.

Gay old times in Greece

Greek Homosexuality

K. J. DOVER

As Sir Kenneth Dover says in his preface, it has been difficult
to find out much about Greek homosexuality from classical
scholars, for the obvious reason that they had been inhibited either by
covert commitment or distaste. Either way, the end product has been
a depressing mystification of the whole topic.

Practical pederasty, it's implied, was a sordid minority vice, and
regarded as such; at the same time and on the other hand, it was
somehow – you hear this a lot from commentators on Plato – essential
physical fuel for metaphysics, given the secluded lumpish condition of
all respectable women. And anyway, weren't there always courtesans
at the symposium, to preserve a decent illusion of naturalness?

Dover's approach is tactless, literal-minded (even clinical) and – so far
as one who isn't a classicist can judge – genuinely and rudely exploratory.
Having confessed himself almost alarmingly free from ethical hobbles
and erotic prejudices ('I am fortunate in not experiencing moral shock or
disgust at any genital act whatsoever, provided that it is welcome and
agreeable to all the participants') he sets about describing what people
did, and how society treated them. Since he concentrates on vase paintings, graffiti and lawsuits as much as on literature and philosophy, the
picture that emerges is untidy and unideal. Greek sexual mores were
eclectic, inventive and exuberant, and different city-states developed
extraordinarily diverse habits. None the less a distinct type of the
sex-object and a pattern of homosexual courtship do emerge.

The desirable youth or boy (he was supposed to be at years of some
discretion but perhaps no one worried too much in a culture where

girls were marriageable at 12) was thoroughly redolent of the gymnasium, with huge thighs, tiny genitals and flat but highly developed pectoral muscles. Down to the mid-5th century BC he is such a powerful presence that he assimilates even female pin-ups to himself, so that they too develop sprinter's muscles. Girls, though (except at Sparta), didn't run: they were slaves, *hetairai* or wives.

If a Greek 'was to enjoy the triumph of leisurely seduction (rather than the flawed satisfaction of purchase) he must seduce a boy,' Dover points out; and he did it through persuasion, blandishments, presents, caresses and personal prestige. At the same time he was almost certainly married and probably made free with his female slaves. There was no word for 'a homosexual' in the sense of someone permanently orientated that way and the boyfriend too was expected to grow up into a similar versatility.

Not that it always worked. Agathon and Pausanias seem to have been notorious for sticking together (Agathon shaving his beard down to emulate boyish fuzz). And there was (at least) one glaring psychological-cum-legal problem: in a society so geared to the ideal of the male warrior-citizen (women were disenfranchised, along with slaves and foreigners) anyone who plays a passive sexual role 'detaches himself from the ranks of male citizenry'. Male homosexual desire is 'natural' only for the active party.

Dover explores this through a tortuous legal case in which Aiskhines discredited Timarkhos by claiming that he had been a boy prostitute: Aiskhines draws a fine distinction between 'legitimate' Eros and the other kind – a distinction which rests, amazingly, on the assumption that 'good' boys don't enjoy sex. According to Xenophon, 'the boy does not share in the man's pleasure in intercourse, as a woman does' – and so does not share, either, in female civil disabilities. Whether Timarkhos enjoyed sex, or did it so often for the money, he has forfeited his right to speak in the Assembly.

Suddenly, in the midst of so much seeming evidence for Greek adventurousness, you arrive at a spookily Victorian vision of a blushing, reluctant boy semi-raped by a triumphant lover. There was even an approved 'missionary' ('intercrural') position which looks very uncomfortable but preserves the manhood of both participants by avoiding anal penetration. Add to this the notion that the 'good' lover was the boy's teacher (whether in the Socratic sense, or simply an adult mentor – as Dover says in a footnote, 'in the Greek world those who could not only did but also taught') and you have a situation as tense, potentially wretched and rule-bound as a nineteenth-century long engagement.

Greek Homosexuality is a fascinating book, with much more detail than I've been able to indicate, not to mention a stimulating attack on Plato and pages of 'explicit' illustrations. If in the first flush of excitement at being able to demystify his theme Sir Kenneth Dover sometimes praises the Greeks for playboyish callousness ('enjoyment of *both* females *and* males affords a richer and happier life'), he does in fact show that they created their own nasty tangles of sexual politics, even after shelving the woman question.

Victorian fun and games

No Name

WILKIE COLLINS

WILKIE COLLINS'S SPLENDID CRIME mysteries – *The Moonstone, The Woman in White* – have kept his reputation alive over the years. The lush, paranoid plots and counterplots and feats of detection he pioneered (with a little help from Poe) are models of how to pull off a major success in a minor genre.

His powers in this direction, though, may have distracted us from his larger, untidier and more interesting ambitions. For Collins clearly meant to take on the major Victorian themes (money, marriage, crises of personal identity), and in his raffish underhand way he does some disturbing things with them.

No Name (first published in 1862) is the most ranging and penetrating of his 'Victorian' novels, and the funniest. The title (a knowing nudge about identity problems) is a joke along the same lines as Dickens's *Our Mutual Friend* three years later, and indeed Collins is openly influenced by Dickens and (on the documentary side) Mayhew: like them, he's getting very interested in the fictional roles people play in life, their lies and self-images (Mayhew's beggar impersonating a shipwrecked sailor, standing freezing in his artistically arranged rags until he catches cold out of professional dedication; or Dickens's dockland scavenger who, when asked what he 'does', replies 'waterside character'). The exotic, hybrid distortions of 'character' bred out of free enterprise, hypocrisy and repression provide Collins with mysteries just as titillating as the crime plots (whoisit instead of whodunnit) and revelations even more perverse.

Not that you'd think so in the opening chapter of *No Name*: the

Vanstone family are handsome, prosperous and solid, complete with (ungrammatical) servants, (faded) governess, and all the other appropriate properties. Collins describes them with bland benevolence, as they get up (late) and breakfast (in leisurely fashion), and then, slowly at first, he starts to strip away your comfy certainties. Mrs Vanstone, ideally middle-aged and elegantly frail, discovers she's pregnant – again; daughter Magdalen reveals a sinister talent for private theatricals, where she brings the house down by impersonating her quiet, pleasant older sister Norah (who wilts into repressed misery as a result) and falls for a silly fellow-actor.

Jovial Mr Vanstone, undismayed, sets out to fix up Magdalen's dowry, only to be killed in a train crash (Collins is warming to his task now, everything speeds up) whereupon Mrs Vanstone dies in childbirth, and the family lawyer arrives to reveal to an (understandably) distraught governess that the Vanstones weren't married until a few weeks ago (a small matter of another wife), so that Magdalen and Norah will be cast out into the world with no family, no money and, of course, no name.

This is where the novel proper starts, with the frantic struggle to acquire an identity (having 600 pages to play with, Collins can afford such tricks). Norah does the dull, decent thing and becomes a governess herself; Magdalen the improper thing, and becomes an actress. It's her career that Collins follows, since what fascinates him is the element of grotesque theatricality you begin to discover in 'real' life once you're outside the solid minority. You get the impression, suddenly, of a cast of thousands.

It's not just that Magdalen's personality fragments and dissolves as she starts to 'act' off-stage, in her scheme to marry the spindly neurasthenic, miserly cousin who's inherited 'her' money: but she finds herself conspiring and competing with characters who themselves are virtuoso performers – most notably Captain Wragge, a brilliant comic invention, a professional con-man with a whole wardrobe of what he calls 'Skins To Jump Into,' who rapidly establishes himself as Magdalen's 'manager' and threatens to take over the novel.

Collins doesn't quite let him, but is obviously tempted, because

Wragge affronts both bourgeois and novelistic decencies so satisfyingly: he can appropriate any role, *be* (almost) anything, since he's nobody, an outsider, a collection of contradictory attributes. He has one green eye, one brown one, from the back he looks 35, from the front 50; and while he (like Satan) is legion, he has a wife who hasn't quite managed to acquire even one self, a six foot three ex-waitress whose mind has been finally blown by trying to remember too many orders at once. (Mrs Wragge deserves a monograph all her own – she's one of the most frightening and hilarious versions of female mindlessness in nine-teenth-century fiction.) Anyway, to stop Wragge having it all his own way, Collins invents foul, ingenious, witch-like Mrs Lecount. She's the widow of a Swiss naturalist, and still keeps his toad to aid and abet the neurasthenic cousin in fending off Magdalen's advances.

She succeeds, more or less. That is, Magdalen marries the cousin and kills him (simply by marrying him, apparently) but still (for complicated reasons) doesn't get the cash; instead her dowdy, nice sister wins the love of yet another cousin and (repression pays) gets it all.

Collins is, of course, too mischievous to let it go at that; his plot somersaults through many more twists and turns (including a special prize for undeserving Magdalen) before the end. What he's after, both in narrative and in characterisation, is a series of contradictions so hectic and vividly felt that they will upturn all the reader's certainties about money or society or sex. His limitation, I suppose, is that he's really *unable* to believe in people, so seeing through them threatens to become too easy.

No Name, though, keeps just ahead of its creator's manic scepticism, and so achieves a dizzy balance between invention and destruction. Marvellous that it's back in print – it should provide a compulsive New Year's read, as well as freshening up a lot of tired courses on the Victorian novel.

Villette

CHARLOTTE BRONTË

*V*ILLETTE INTERESTS ME MORE and more, partly because it's such a *miserable* book. If *Jane Eyre* claimed the right to happiness and fulfilment, *Villette* claims the (equally important) right to be lonely, unfulfilled and crochety. Not a nice novel at all, indeed a bitterly, sardonically old-maidish one, but the braver and more brilliant for that.

It was published in 1853, and was Charlotte Brontë's last novel. It harked back, though, to her first strange and messy effort *The Professor* seven years before, and dealt with the same very difficult material – her time as a 26-year-old schoolgirl/teacher in Brussels, and her disturbing attachment to Monsieur Héger, who taught her there, and whose formidable wife owned the school.

It was this experience she first turned to when she attempted a publishable novel, and still, in 1852, despite the Reverend Arthur Nicholls poised matrimonially in the wings, this experience (the discovery that she must work and suffer alone, the conviction that she was an old maid) was at the centre of her consciousness.

She was of course alone in a quite other sense too: Branwell, Emily and Anne were dead, and she was writing in a new kind of void – '... there was no one to whom to read a line, or of whom to ask a counsel. *Jane Eyre* was not written under such circumstances, nor were two-thirds of *Shirley*.' This, I think, must have a lot to do with the special power and edge of *Villette*. She'd been forced into self-containment and self-definition. She had also, as a result of the fame of *Jane Eyre*, seen something of the world:

> On Thursday, the Marquis of Westminster asked me to a great party
> . . . but this I resolutely declined. On Friday I . . . met . . . Mr Monckton
> Milnes. On Saturday I went to see and hear Rachel . . . She is not a
> woman; she is a snake; she is the—. On Sunday I went to the Spanish
> Ambassador's Chapel, where Cardinal Wiseman, in his archiepiscopal
> robes and mitre, held a confirmation. The whole scene was impiously
> theatrical . . .

The consequence of these bouts of wide-eyed, sceptical socialising
seems to have been, hardly surprisingly, that she was confirmed in her
sense of being an anomaly. She became at once more introverted, and
more sharply, maliciously aware of the otherness of others, the social
'theatre'. And she invented Lucy Snowe, one of the most interesting
narrator-heroines of the century.

Lucy is mean, humorous and miserable. 'Quiet Lucy Snowe', people
think, 'a being inoffensive as a shadow', and she takes a perverse delight
in allowing them to think so. She's like an 'unobtrusive article of
furniture', people notice her no more than 'carpets of no striking
pattern'. In the social/sexual theatre she gets at best the supporting
roles ('I am a rising character: once an old lady's companion, then a
nursery governess, now a school-teacher'), and if she's sometimes asked
to play the man – as in the school play, opposite one of her pretty
overripe pupils – she sees *that*, quite accurately, as less a compliment
to her self-reliance than a comment on her sexual nullity, her failure
to be a womanly woman. The yawning gap between her sense of herself
and others' (non) sense of her generates some very bleak, modern-
sounding observations: 'He wanted always to give me a role not mine',
for instance.

She's a Protestant in Catholic Brussels, and a determined heretic
in the religion of love that keeps Mme Beck's school going: 'All the
teachers had dreams of some lover; one (but she was naturally of a
credulous turn) believed in a future husband.' She herself sternly
represses and internalises her dreams. Twice she breaks down – once
she goes to confession, and once she allows herself to love Monsieur
Paul. The love-plot, indeed, is a measure of how far Charlotte Brontë
has moved on since *Jane Eyre*. Dr John corresponds roughly to austere

St John Rivers, except that he's a great deal nicer and there's not the slightest chance of having him, and so: 'Goodnight, Dr John. You are good, you are beautiful, but you are not mine.' Irascible Monsieur Paul is the Rochester figure, but Lucy won't allow herself him either: at the end, merging finally into Charlotte Brontë, she disposes of him in a storm at sea, and mocks readers who want happy endings – 'leave sunny imaginations hope ... Let them picture union and a happy succeeding life'. She will not.

Lucy is, in the best sense, a grotesque, full of contradictions, covered in awkward angles, only prepared to reveal herself ironically, by indirections ('I, Lucy Snowe, plead guiltless of that curse, an overheated and discursive imagination ... of an artistic temperament I deny that I am'). One of the most extraordinary things about the book is the way that Charlotte Brontë's sense of the relation between her prickly self and the world has invaded Lucy's style at every point: she exists within the bounds people set for her, but makes her own idiosyncratic, introverted sense of them, savours her drabness, and aches on purpose.

After getting the first instalment of *Villette*, the publishers suggested that Lucy might seem 'morbid and weak'. Charlotte Bronte agreed: 'Her character sets up no pretensions to unmixed strength and anybody living her life would necessarily become morbid.' In other words, there's a good deal to be said for bitterness and neurosis, and she's determined to say it: 'I never meant to appoint her lines in pleasant places.' One of the things to be said for an old maid's eye-view is that she has a unique vantage point on the socially and sexually powerful.

Perhaps the most impressive portrait is that of Paulina, the Victorian child-woman stereotype. We see her at 7 and at 17 – and the similarities are more striking than the differences. She's fragile, almost weightless (she wrestles with sugar-tongs, sews invisible cambric) and she's greedily, obsessively, irretrievably dependent, first on her father, then on her lover: 'The child had no mind or life of her own, but must necessarily live, move and have her being in another.' She's clearly a monster, a 'fairy' perhaps (as she's often described), but still a revelation of how *weird* such an ideal is.

People have become stranger to Charlotte Brontë – more vivid, more dreadfully distinct. Paulina's opposite, the incubus/witch, is played by Mme Walravens:

> three feet high, but she had no shape; her skinny hands rested upon each other, and pressed the gold knob of a wand-like ivory staff. Her face was large, set, not upon her shoulders, but before her breast; she seemed to have no neck; I should have said there were a hundred years in her features . . .

Mme Walravens is repressive, social/religious power, I suppose. Charlotte Bronte is getting her own back on the world – but without in the least suggesting that she herself has not been distorted by her own exclusion and repression.

Thackeray, whom she much admired (she dedicated the second edition of *Jane Eyre* to him, unaware he had a mad wife, and caused an interesting scandal) made a cruel diagnosis of *Villette*:

> rather than have fame, rather than any other earthly good or mayhap heavenly one she wants some Tomkins or another to love . . . But you see she is a little bit of a creature without a penny worth of good looks, thirty years old I should think . . . a genius . . . longing to mate itself and destined to wither away into old maidenhood . . .

But *Villette* can take this sort of comment. It faces the ironies and absurdities of aloneness with ingenuity and thoroughly individual intelligence. Critics have talked of 'acceptance', an automatic pious hope for a great writer's last novel. Charlotte Bronte didn't know it was her last. Her marriage, pregnancy and death (1855) followed very fast, but she and the world had unfinished business.

When two melt into one

Sexuality and Feminism in Shelley

NATHANIEL BROWN

THE 'FAIRY SLUG' VERSION of Shelley is one we are all familiar with, if only because his critics feel bound time and again to refute it. A fairy slug is at once unmanly, irrational and grossly slimy: or, in short, a bit of a woman. Nathaniel Brown, feeling the 'slow turning of the zeitgeist' at his back, has decided boldly to agree. The time has come for the rehabilitation of the male feminist and the feminine man.

Sexuality and Feminism in Shelley is involved in roughly the same sort of manoeuvre as Christopher Ricks's *Keats and Embarrassment*: taking some of the most conventionally discordant and traditionally shameful aspects of the poet and showing them to be virtues. But even the titles suggest how differently they proceed. Professor Ricks, via Sartre on slime, suggests you into admiring Keats's appetite for 'slippery blisses' without in the least implying that you can become liberated from your shudders: you learn instead to enjoy them ('liberated voyeurism'). Professor Brown, who takes the zeitgeist seriously, means to establish fairly straightforward links between Shelley, present feminist arguments, and a possible androgynous future when there will be sexuality without repulsion.

For some readers, this will make him sound crazy (probably a bit of a fairy slug himself) so I'd better say now that this is a sane and scholarly study, written in a style of slightly pained neutrality, not a millennial romp. If it is true that there is a feminist bandwagon, it is also true that feminism is revising parts of literary history, and making us read many writers differently and often better, and so on. Shelley is a promising candidate for re-reading through 1960s and 1970s spectacles for several reasons (I remember with affection a critical study that admitted despairingly, as though all were lost, that Shelley was *the sort of man who would distribute pamphlets on street corners*); his possible lack of a 'fixed or exclusive gender identity' especially is no longer likely to seem so nastily eccentric, and his theoretical speculations on the matter become interesting by virtue of the very range and literalness that made them embarrassing.

Like most people interested in the third sex (or is it the fourth? the fifth?) Shelley started his researches with Plato's *Symposium*. He translated it in 1818, and wrote an introductory essay on *The Manners of the Ancient Greeks Relative to the Subject of Love* which was uncharacteristically cautious, but still sluggish enough not to be published in full until 1931. He was particularly fascinated (again, like most people) with Aristophanes' fable about originally spherical humans – three sexes, male, female and hermaphrodite – split down the middle by the gods for cartwheeling too blissfully and generally getting above themselves, and so now each a mere splinter doomed to seek its essential other half.

This is why, says Aristophanes, when lovers meet they clasp each other so desperately: each wants (in Shelley's translation) 'intimately to mix and melt and to be melted together with his beloved, so that one should be made out of two'. It is, of course, as Shelley recognized, a description of homosexual ecstasy (hermaphrodites are jokers), and this – since both his reading of Plato and his delight in androgynous late Greek sculpture had convinced him that the Greeks knew what romantic love was – set him two main problems. First, why was this archetypal need not focused on women? And second, what did the men *do*?

His answer to the first of these questions is an aggressively feminist one: women in Greek society were the victims of such thorough-going patriarchal repression that they were not only spiritually unbeautiful (in some sense unrecognizable), but actually physically dull. (Professor Brown has some interesting detail here on Shelley's reading of eye-contact: he claimed to be able to tell from statues that Greek women, like modern French and Italian women reared in convents, had a blank,

shallow gaze.) On the second question, which has seldom been properly answered, he is more surprising: despite Eton, he finds buggery
unthinkable (because it degrades the lover) and supposes that, given
the intensity of the need, and the dream-pressure behind it, Greek
lovers arrived at spontaneous orgasm. This is the sort of thing that
makes critics cringe, and mutter 'Adolescent!' However, Shelley's
hypothesis is at least more generous than the most recent version, an
entirely plausible one, from Sir Kenneth Dover: that the boy was indeed
not supposed to enjoy it, and was thought of as something of a whore
if he did.

Though Shelley seems never to have contemplated waking wet
dreams as a model for present sexual relations, he does, as Professor
Brown points out, take 'ordinary' wet dreams (for example in *Alastor*)
as evidence that one's like, other half, soul-mate, is generated out of
inner loneliness. In other words, he takes the Aristophanic myth seriously, applied now to women, and as a result takes women seriously.
Only if they are free to achieve intellectual beauty (he may have
borrowed the famous phrase from Mary Wollstonecraft) can one find
one's second self. His willingness to think of himself as partly feminine
obviously makes this more plausible. There's another ingredient here,
though, that the book might have mentioned: the long-naturalized
tradition in English poetry (deriving from Plato, again, but with the
added persuasiveness of 'domesticity') that achieving this wholeness is
a means to poetic creation. The poet's very poetry may depend on his
marriage. Shelley would have found Aristophanes' rather forlorn third
sex apotheosized in Spenser:

> Lightly he clipt her twixt his armes twaine,
> And streightly did embrace her body bright,
> Her body, late the prison of sad paine,
> Now the sweet lodge of love and deare delight:
> But she faire Lady overcommen quight
> Of huge affection, did in pleasure melt,
> And in sweete ravishment pourd out her spright:
> No word they spake, nor earthly thing they felt,
> But like two senceles stocks in long embracement dwelt.

Had ye them seene, ye would have surely thought,
That they had beene that faire *Hermaphrodite*
Which that rich *Romane* of white marble wrought,
And in his costly Bath caused to bee site:
So seemd those two, as growne together quite . . .

The erotic sublime here bears clear and moving traces of its translation
from an alien context, and reveals very honestly how curious it is to
think of heterosexuality this way. Spenser cancelled these lines, originally the climax of Book Three of *The Faerie Queene*, when he published
the poem's continuation, but not because the hermaphrodite worried
him: in later books Venus herself, and Nature, become bi-sexual, and
of course Mrs Spenser puts in her famous appearance.

   Shelley's first 'marriage' (I use quotation marks to suggest the special
meaning it had for him) had turned the nation of two into one to cruel
travesty. Shelley first galvanized Harriet into a dazzle with idealistic
electricity, and then accused her of having been a corpse: 'a dead
and living body had been linked together in loathsome and horrible
communion'; he felt himself diminished by contagion, 'sunk into a
premature old age of exhaustion, which renders me dead to everything'.
He is echoing the Milton of the divorce tracts, another vengeful victim
of the search for the antitype, though in Shelley's case disenchantment
followed from meeting another woman (Mary Wollstonecraft Godwin)
who revealed Harriet for the loving sham she was – mirroring back
his opinions so obligingly as to return him to his loneliness.

   In Mary he found himself convincingly redoubled ('in our family',
her sister Claire Clairmont said, 'if you cannot write an epic poem or
novel that by its originality knocks all other novels on the head, you
are a despicable creature, not worth acknowledging'). He had not
invented her, but nor was she too entirely other, which was very
important. For one of the odder side-effects of Shelley's acknowledgment
of his own 'female' nature was an equivocal and potentially mean
attitude to the masculine woman. His passionate friendship with Elizabeth Hitchener had been the test case here. Hogg described her as 'tall
and thin, bony and masculine . . . and the symbol of male wisdom, a
beard, was not entirely wanting. She was neither young nor old; not

handsome, not absolutely ill-looking'. And Shelley, after trying for a while to take her as all mind, rejected her as (alas) an 'ugly, hermaphroditical beast of a woman'. (It took Wilkie Collins, in *The Woman in White*, to fall convincingly for a heroine with a moustache.) 'To mix and melt and to be melted together': creative love is recognition, like to like. According to Hume, says Professor Brown, our closest sympathies will always be for those most like ourselves. Mary Shelley's inspired comment on this was *Frankenstein*. She must, of course, as the poet's other half, write ('He was forever inciting me to obtain literary reputation'), but what she produced was a fantasy of otherness and rejection. 'My hideous progeny', as she called it with maternal pride, depicts not only the injustice by which a creator corrupts his creature, but also (picking up the inevitable metaphor) a man who feels himself tied to a walking corpse, which happens – as critics have often pointed out – to be more human, more rational and more imaginatively versatile than himself.

Shelley's closeness to women, as friend, lover, husband, mentor, brother, did involve a breaking-down of gender boundaries. It also, however, involved a distaste for whatever *was* bounded – the aggressive, alienated, privatised 'male' ego. It's a kind of dissolution he's after (in this like Lawrence): he imagines intellectually and practically heroic women, but their true value (anyone's true value) lies in the oceanic connection. His passages of cosmic sex are extraordinary and (if you can stand it) marvellous:

> The snow upon my lifeless mountains
> Is loosened into living fountains,
> My solid oceans flow, and sing, and shine . . .
>
> It interpenetrates my granite mass,
> Through tangled leaves and trodden clay doth pass
> Into the utmost leaves and delicatest flowers . . .

In this love-duet between the (female) moon and the (male) earth from *Prometheus Unbound* it would be difficult – amid the general melting – to distribute the genders at all confidently. Professor Brown quotes Margaret Fuller, the American feminist, writing in 1845. Shelley's life, she said, '. . . was one of the first pulse beats in the present reform-growth'; his imagery promotes 'a plant-like gentleness in the development of energy'.

This vegetable love is undoubtedly one of the more tenacious feminist growths, but it is at odds, as Professor Brown's chapter on Mary Wollstonecraft admits, with the rationalistic and individualistic arguments for women's economic and civil rights. He suggests that both Wollstonecraft and Shelley tended, despite a conscious commitment to enlightenment values, towards just this 'feminist transvaluation', which would set the female sensibility up as a model for the male. He doesn't convince me on Wollstonecraft, who may have been passionate and impressionistic but was also – and simultanously – thoroughly reasonable, and as a result often writes like a misogynist. On Shelley, however, he's much more persuasive: women's autonomy could never have struck Shelley as a desirable thing, separateness for him was the primal curse.

The book's final chapter spells out the connections of all this with current feminism. There are two main directions in which the sympathetic love tradition points: towards (feminist) androgyny, and – unsurprisingly, given its background – homosexuality. The latter is 'perhaps a more logical resolution', writes Professor Brown, since the whole thing is based on 'same sex identification', but that way lies disaster and violence (SCUM raising its ugly head): only convergence holds out hope. There is here, as there was in Shelley (even more in Mary) an underlying despair. Relationship means incest or identification, or cannot exist. But in actuality, surely, the breakdown of gender boundaries (such as it is) spawns much more variegated monsters than this, people not only divided from each other, but psychologically motley in themselves. If you abandon the zeitgeist, and organicist metaphors about growth (and feminists have little reason to trust them) then Shelley becomes a particularly fascinating piece in a puzzle whose 'solution' isn't yet in sight. Professor Brown would doubtless accuse me of nostalgia for the sex war. Certainly his careful, rather solemn exposition of Shelley does seem to invite a perverse bout of misogyny.

A Scribbler comes of age

Lord Byron: The Complete Poetical Works, Volume 1

EDITED BY JEROME J. McGANN

THIS FIRST VOLUME OF the new Oxford English Texts *Complete Poetical Works* of Byron raises an old question: just how did the fat boy from Harrow turn himself into a poet? The flab is, of course, even more in evidence this time round with thirty-five previously uncollected bits and pieces helping to swell the volume; and the daunting scale of the textual apparatus (the last 'thorough scholarly edition', was done almost eighty years ago, as Jerome J. McGann points out) makes Byron's dreadful juvenilia look all the more dim. To begin at the beginning is to wonder at its being a beginning at all:

> Thro' thy battlements, Newstead, the hollow winds whistle;
> Thou, the hall of my fathers, art gone to decay;
> In thy once smiling garden, the hemlock and thistle
> Have choak'd up the rose, which late bloom'd in the way.

'On Leaving Newstead Abbey', the poem that opened his first publicly printed volume *Hours of Idleness* (1807), was proudly dated by Byron '1803' (when he was fifteen). He obviously felt this should impress readers the right way at the outset, but the silly jauntiness and the arrogant parade of 'ancestors' (including at least a couple of whom, as the commentary notes, 'there is no record') have quite a contrary effect – even if you don't know that Newstead was rented at the time to Lord Grey de Ruthin (who seems to have made a humiliating pass at him), and that he was painfully at odds with his fat, passionate and vulgar mother (who, he suspected, fancied Lord Grey), and awfully conscious of the shakiness of his station.

The second poem, on leaving Harrow (1806), took the same unpromising line:

> Ye scenes of my childhood, whose lov'd recollection,
>   Embitters the present compar'd with the past;
> Where science first dawn'd on the powers of reflection,
>   And friendships were form'd, too romantic to last.

His title and his youth (*Hours of Idleness* described the author as 'George Gordon, Lord Byron, a Minor') moved him to an ecstasy of self-caressing sadness and self-admiration. He saw himself as brilliantly boyish and said as much in his Preface: 'the poems are the fruits of the lighter hours of a young man, who has lately completed his nineteenth year'; he will, he says, content himself 'with the not very magnificent prospect of ranking "amongst" the mob of gentlemen who write, my reader must determine, whether I dare say "with ease" . . .' His snobbish squirming and his wincing tenderness for his work elicited a corresponding sycophancy from the first reviewers: ('ample evidence', said the *Critical Review*, 'of a correct taste, a warm imagination, and a feeling heart'). However, the *Edinburgh* reviewer (Brougham) did a splendid if slightly belated job on the whole production especially on the subtext of the Preface:

> He possibly means to say, 'See how a minor can write. This poem was actually composed by a young man of eighteen and this by one of only sixteen!' . . . So far from hearing, with any degree of surprise, that very poor verses were written by a youth from his leaving school to his leaving college . . . we really believe this to be the most common of occurrences; that it happens in the life of nine men in ten who are educated in England; and that the tenth man writes better verse than Lord Byron.

Brougham possibly fixed on the word 'common' with a particular relish. He was out to undo Byron's sense of his own specialness, and to suggest how very vulgar 'the noble minor' was in his insistence on it.

He was absolutely right at the time (though *English Bards and Scotch Reviewers* in 1809, also in this volume, was to prove him wrong): the main interest of Byron's earliest writings is winkling out, with hindsight, any sign of something that was not 'common'. Brougham, of course, had not seen the even earlier, privately printed things – the libertine poem that set his mother's circle in a flutter ('Now, by my soul, 'tis most delight/To view each other panting, dying./In love's *extatic posture* lying . . .'); or the 'tender' lyrics to his boy loves. But they would hardly have changed his mind. 'To E —' (an all-purpose love poem according to Professor McGann, who coolly consigns it to both an anonymous tenant's son of 1802 and to Edleston, Byron's Cambridge choirboy of 1805) sets the tone.

> And though unequal is thy fate
> > Since title deck't my higher birth;
> Yet envy not this gaudy state.
> > *Thine* is the pride of modest worth.

'Fugitive' early Byron is perhaps even more smug than dilettante Byron. Edleston moved him to lines that should at least be camp, but aren't ('he who seeks the flowers of truth/Must quit the garden for the field'), and his gallant 'gather ye rosebuds' verses to girls betray him into farcical revelations:

> 'Tis this, my beloved, which spreads gloom o'er my many features,
> Tho' I ne'er shall presume to arraign the decree,
> Which God has proclaim'd, as the fate of his creatures,
> In the death which one day will deprive you of me.

You of *me*? By some dreadful vengeance (the god of rhyme perhaps) his poetical machine seems for once to have said what he really meant. The poem 'To My Son' (not printed until after his death, addressed according to Professor McGann to an otherwise unrecorded bastard of 1807) suggests even more unsavoury possibilities:

> Oh, 'twill be sweet in thee to trace,
> Ere age has wrinkled o'er my face,
> Ere half my glass of life is run,
> At once a brother and a son . . .

This sounds to me like Humbert Humbert dreaming of engendering a line of Lolitas, though it may be what Wilson Knight meant when talking of Byron and Christian virtue – kindness to children and pets.

Things were going on that didn't get into his poems. He was filled
with revulsion – against his impoverished inheritance, and against
himself. In April 1807 he wrote to his lawyer John Hanson from his
mother's rented home:

> You speak of the *Charms* of Southwell, the place I *abhor*, the Fact is I
> remain here because I can appear no where else, being *completely done
> up, Wine & Women* have *dished your humble Servant, not a Sou to be had
> all over*, condemned to exist (I cannot say live) at this *Crater* of Dullness,
> till my *Lease of Infancy* expires . . . you will be surprised to hear I am
> grown very thin, however it is the Fact . . . I have lost 18lb in my
> weight . . .

Though Brougham's review came as a shock he had in a sense prepared
for it. He was plotting his escape from minority (despite the Wine and
Women boast) and from England; and, coincidentally, getting into
shape for Grub Street. He began 'The British Bards' in October, feeling
pleased with himself, and completed 'English Bards and Scotch
Reviewers' almost a year later in September 1808, smarting furiously
(Brougham had intervened) but, poetically speaking, a new man:

> I, too, can scrawl, and once upon a time
> I poured along the town a flood of rhyme . . .

His slimming methods were drastic ('I wear seven Waistcoats & a Great
Coat, run & play at Cricket') and so were his operations on his style:
he turned meanly on the writers he had lovingly pastiched; on Scott's
'half-strung harps', Moore's 'melodious . . . lust', Bowles as 'the oracle
of tender souls'. You can almost see the lard melting away.

He was pared down to genuine nausea and self-contradiction. 'English Bards' is, textually, the most complicated case in the volume, in
part because of Byron's chronic indecision about who and what to
abuse and how much. He maintained the aristocratic stance over the
matter of accepting cash for your work – 'No! When the sons of song
descend to trade/Their bays are sear, their former laurels fade' – but
otherwise he acknowledged that he was in the business. And given
that, universal spleen followed almost automatically:

I printed – older children do the same.
'Tis pleasant, sure, to see one's name in print;
A Book's a Book, although there's nothing in't.
Not that a title's sounding charm can save
Or scrawl or scribbler from an equal grave:
This LAMB must own, since his Patrician name
Failed to preserve the spurious Farce from shame.
No matter GEORGE continues to write,
Tho now the name is veiled from public sight,
Moved by the great example, I pursue
The self-same road, but make my own review
Nor seek great JEFFREY'S yet like him will be
Self-constituted Judge of Poetry.

Byron thought Jeffrey was responsible for the Edinburgh piece; but really Byron, in attacking others, was attacking himself. His malice against noble authors and Scottish taste in this passage for instance must have been considerably sharpened by the memory of writing – only a few short months before – lines like these:

I would I were a careless child,
Still dwelling in my Highland cave,
Or roaming through the dusky wild,
Or bounding o'er the dark blue wave ...
Fortune! take back these cultur'd lands,
Take back this name of splendid sound ...

There was also his Ossianic effort. *English Bards* puts Byron on the spot, though he only occasionally pauses to notice it ('Every Brother Rake will smile to see/That miracle, a Moralist in me!'), and hides behind Gifford (editor of the Quarterly, 'some Bard in virtue strong') when this position becomes unbearably embarrassing. His own private notes from 1816 – 'Unjust', 'Misquoted', 'Too ferocious – this is mere insanity', '*Fool* enough, certainly then and no wiser since' (on himself) – reflect wryly on his hit and run tactics. The only passage that wins his mature approval ('Good') is the one (lines 632–7) ticking off the Society for the Suppression of Vice.

Professor McGann in an uncharacteristically opinioned 'note' of his own, suggests that Byron 'really had no intense satiric quarrel with his age', which seems right when you consider how many of his objects of attack were later woven into his life. Monk Lewis, for example, who gets some memorable lines:

> All hail, M.P. I from whose infernal brain
> Thin sheeted phantoms glide, a grisly train . . .
> Even Satan's self with thee might dread to dwell,
> And in thy skull discern a deeper hell.

Perhaps this was always included as something of a compliment; certainly Lewis later became a friend and so of course did 'Immoral' Moore. Lamb ('Damned like the Devil') was the husband of Byron's noisiest mistress, and the son of his confidante, Lady Melbourne. Lord Holland, here the arch-patron of hacks ('HOLLAND's banquets shall each toil repay;/'While grateful Britain yields the praise she owes/To HOLLAND'S hirelings and to Learning's foes') became enough of an ally by 1812 for Byron to supress the eighth edition of *English Bards* altogether. Joseph Blackett the hapless and briefly fashionable cobbler poet, ('How ladies read and Literati laud!'), might have seemed a safely distant target, but he had as it turned out been patronized by the clever and rich Miss Millbanke.

For the moment however, Byron felt justifiably exhilarated at coming of age and getting out of England. His parting doggerel on the Lisbon packet is splendidly euphoric – for once he isn't the one who is sick:

> Hobhouse muttering fearful curses:
>   As the hatchway down he rolls,
> Now his breakfast, now his verses
>   Vomits forth and damns our souls.
>   Here's a stanza
>   On Braganza;
>   Help! – a couplet – no a cup
>   Of warm water –
>   What's the matter?
> Zounds! My liver's coming up.

Even his Greek fever in 1810 found him congratulating himself. – 'Poor B-r-n sweats – alas! how changed from him/So plump in feature, and so round in limb,/ Grinning and gay in Newstead's monkish fane . . .';

by the time of *Hints from Horace* (1811) he can openly jeer at the 'mob of gentlemen'.

> Shall I, thus qualified to sit
> For rotten boroughs, never show my wit?
> Shall I, whose fathers with the quorum sate,
> And lived in freedom on a fair estate,
> Who left me heir, with stables, kennels, packs,
> To *all their income*, and to – *twice* its *tax*!
> Whose form and pedigree have scarce a fault –
> Shall I, I say, suppress my Attic salt?

This splendid piece of parodic bluster, he must have felt, freed him from Brougham's accusations, made him a professional. The same year, on his return, he is quite clear (in a letter to Augusta) what his role is to be.

> Nothing so fretful, so despicable as a Scribbler; see what I am & what a parcel of Scoundrels I have brought about my ears; & what language I have been obliged to treat them with to deal with them in their own way: – all this comes of Authorship but now I am in for it; & shall be at war with Grubstreet till I find some better amusement.'

It would be convenient if the story, even of Volume One, stopped here, with Byron a convinced and useful (and slender) 'Scribbler' who had put Harrow and Cambridge behind him. In Greece, pickled in real 'Attic salt', he had been sure of it – 'all my old school companions are gone forth into the world and walk about in monstrous disguises in the garb of Guardsmen, lawyers, parsons, fine gentlemen, and such other masquerade dresses' – but England proved a different matter. And of course the emotional dandy had not withered away, he was rehearsing for *Childe Harold*, in poems on the death of Edleston, and a poisonous 'epistle' about Mary Chaworth, whom he loved at fifteen:–

> I've seen my bride another's bride,
> Have seen her seated by his side.
> Have kiss'd, as if without design,
> The babe which ought to have been mine. . . .
> But let this pass – I'll whine no more,
> Nor seek again an eastern shore;

> The world befits a busy brain,
> I'll hie me to its haunts again.
> But if, in some succeeding year
> When Britain's 'May is in the sere',
> Thou hear'st of one, whose deepening crimes
> Suit with the sablest of the times. . . .
> One rank'd in some recording page
> With the worst anarchs of the Age. . . .

And at about the same time Byron writes to an old Harrow chum, regretting 'the state of Society, in the World everyone is to steer for himself . . . but I do not think we are born of this disposition, for you find friendship as a schoolboy, & Love enough before twenty'. Though he had changed himself radically, the plump and mawkish minor was still inside trying to get out, and succeeding – using bitter 'experience' indeed as a cover, writing *good* bad poetry. That, though, is Volume Two. With a full chronological text to set alongside the *Letters and Journals* Byron's awesome, perhaps awful capacity to experiment with the contradictory ingredients of his personality is going to become more difficult to cope with, and more fascinating, tome by tome.

This volume ends with a Latin lament for Edleston ('What remains for me now? only groans, or a brother's vague dreams . . .') uncollected before, and only once published, in the Catalogue of the 1974 V & A exhibition, as if to stress the importance of establishing a new text of the complete poems. And obviously it is important . . . though the price (£35 for Volume One) relegates it to libraries – which, though one has become used to it, is an absurdity. There may be other lurking absurdities too: it seems that the standards of accuracy and the elaborate textual apparatus which 'justify' the price may now be becoming beyond the reach even of Professor McGann and the Clarendon Press. Certainly the lists of the contents of each of Byron's first four books of poetry ('for those who wish to reconstruct the complete sequential texts') which appear on page 363 are complete nonsense: each of these collections started, we are told, with poem number thirty; but look up poem number thirty and you will find that it is one of Professor McGann's

special prizes – a piece *unpublished before*, a nicely scurrilous 'portrait'
of a hated lady, which comes from a 'draft MS at Texas'.

> Doats yet the hag that from her form so vile
> A race shall quicken to enrich our isle,
> Her poisonous blood thro' other channels roll
> And spread pollution in each new born soul?
> Forbid it Heaven – but yet a thought, more wild
> Ne'er fixed the fancy of the veriest child. . . .
> See her each old one fold in close embrace,
> And flattering hopes from drivelling tales inhale,
> Tales that Dependents barter by wholesale;
> Each herb, each philtre idling art employ
> How to produce a much longed lovely boy.
> Her phantom form now doubly rendered spare
> With drugs on drugs – she almost lives on air.
> Now costly viands, cordials lend their aid,
> Now Matron throes weigh down the teeming maid,
> Now sickenings, languors, faintings, longings press
> But still instead of quickening she grows less. . . .

The scholarly industry that reclaimed this emetic fragment is impressive.
All the more irritating then to discover the trivial blunder over number-
ing. It is not hard to work out what went wrong: earlier lists which
did not include ladies from Texas have crept unnoticed into the final
text. Easily done – except that it really should not, and *must not* be, if
scholarly projects on this scale are to remain credible or feasible. I have
not spotted any other mistakes of the same kind, but to suspect they
are there is enough. The least the Clarendon Press can do is issue a
pleasantly Byronic sheet of 'errata' with the next volume. While they
are at it, I offer a couple of innocent literals: a misplaced line on p. 371,
in the notes to lines 57 and 64 of *Thoughts Suggested by a College
Examination*, and a spoiled joke – 'poor as *Irus* or – an[d] Irish mine!'
on p. 308.

Weaving, deceiving and indecision

Heroines and Hysterics

MARY R. LEFKOWITZ

CLASSICAL STUDIES ONCE SEEMED to imply a vaguely androgynous aspiration but over the last ten years or so they have become a focus for much more radical speculations about sexual roles and sexual difference – neatly reflecting (as they always did, perhaps precisely because they were supposed not to) current preoccupations. Semonides of Amorgos, poet-philosopher of the seventh century BC, for instance, can seldom have been so oft quoted:

> From the beginning the god made the mind of woman
> A thing apart. One he made from the long-haired sow;
> While she wallows in the mud and rolls about on the ground,
> Everything at home lies in a mess.
> Another doesn't take baths but sits about
> In the shit in dirty clothes and gets fatter and fatter.
> The god made another one from the evil fox. . . .

Semonides was a prize example in Sarah Pomeroy's 1975 *Goddesses, Whores, and Slaves*, a bitterly enthusiastic exercise in literary archaeology, laying bare the foundations of misogyny. The maddest myths about the creation of women acquire a new piquancy these days:–

> Of the men who came into the world, those who were cowards or led unrighteous lives may with reason be supposed to have changed into the nature of women in the second generation. And this was the reason why at that time the gods created in us the desire of sexual intercourse . . .

Well, *obviously*. This is Plato's *Timaeus*, and one can see why scholars interested in women's 'nature' have found it in a way heartening, partly because it so clearly suggests, as Noel Coward used to put it, that things might have been organized better. The rest of the passage is just as interesting. The penis is like a troublesome animal, a domestic parasite:

> and the same is the case with the so-called womb or matrix of women; the animal within them is desirous of procreating children, and when remaining fruitful long beyond its proper time, gets discontented and angry, and wandering in every direction through the body, closes up the passages of the breath, and . . . drives them to extremity. . . .

Eventually, their parasitic animals bring man and woman together. Perhaps. The bringing together involves a disputed reading, a textual crux, as well it might.

As this kind of material undergoes a new 'translation', the extraordinary difficulty of finding out what Greek women were, or felt themselves to be, becomes increasingly pressing. The wandering womb is the subject of one of the most interesting pieces in Mary Lefkowitz's *Heroines and Hysterics* and, as she shows, the doctors were no more troubled by actual anatomy than Plato. Women, in more senses than one, were a vagrant, suffering *space* in the culture, only safe or 'well' when child-bearing: 'Treatment of the disorder involves giving the womb what it wants, to receive seed and to produce offspring.' Doctors behaved, Ms Lefkowitz suggests, more like priests than anything else, explaining 'the nature of the powerful forces beyond man's control', and certainly beyond woman's. Woman's biology, like so much else about her, is obscure and fugitive – a matter of absences and uncertainties. The wandering womb, in short, is a fitting emblem for classical women's most unclassical status, and *Heroines and Hysterics* mirrors its subject matter by stressing the (probably permanent) fragmentation and indirection of our knowledge about them.

In this, it's very different from Sarah Pomeroy's aggressive analysis of misogyny, and also from Sir Kenneth Dover's book, *Greek Homosexuality*, of four years ago. Dover was able to be robustly demystificatory: homosexuality was elaborately tied in with all aspects of cultural life, and had complex rules and mores (for example, that 'nice' boys didn't enjoy it – in many ways he produced an almost Victorian picture), and our ignorance was a matter of our own repressions, Even he, however, was defeated when it came to women – 'That female homosexuality and the attitude of women to male homosexuality can both be discussed within one part of one chapter reflects the paucity of women writers and artists in the Greek world and the virtual silence of male writers and artists on these topics.' The more we investigate, the less, it almost seems, there is to look at.

Ms Lefkowitz would not put it quite so strongly. Not all her heroines are hysterics. None the less she insists, with her own brand of stoicism, that the visible women are experts in passive suffering:

> the *Iliad* ends not with a description of debate or of battle, but with funeral lamentations of Hector's kinswomen. His wife Andromache . . . talks of the life she will lead as a slave, and suggests that her son will also be enslaved or even killed by the Acheans; his mother, Hecabe, speaks of Achilles' brutality, and of the other sons that he killed; Helen tells of his kindness, when all others reproached her. So the epic ends with reflection on the fate of the victims, not of the victors of the famous war . . . the women who cannot take action for themselves . . . have the last words.

These women on the sidelines stand somewhere between audience and actors, and – perhaps – between actors and the 'forces beyond man's control' that the epics and the tragedies seek to encounter: precisely because they 'endure the consequences of the action in the arena', they 'are best able to interpret its meaning, and, as survivors, to demonstrate its consequences'. A woman's view of the action is essentially choric. For Ms Lefkowitz, the tragic heroines who break the rules, like Antigone ('I am not a man', says Creon, 'she is a man if she can have this power without suffering'), actually prove the rule. The moments from tragedy that she peculiarly savours are those when women demonstrate their exclusion from the action, as in Euripides' *Andromache*:

> She has taken refuge at Thetis' shrine, along with her son by Neoptolemus. Neoptolemus' wife Hermione . . . wants to murder her. But because both she and Andromache are women, they must wait for their male relatives to arrive on the scene before anything can happen.

Women encounter the impossible (or the inevitable) at almost every stop and so, in a sense, arrive by a nasty short cut at the end of wisdom, without the heroic delusions of the real actors. Euripides seems so convinced of 'traditional dangers' that in his work women's passive heroism sometimes becomes the model for men.

It will be seen that this is a double-edged argument. Ms Lefkowitz admires Penelope's virtues ('weaving, deceiving, indecision') and finds even in Sappho a predilection for 'the special weapons of the oppressed, miracles and patience'; and her own strategies are similarly underhand. Active heroism (when was it anything else from the point of view of the chorus?) is dangerous, crassly public behaviour. On the sidelines, we at least know we live marginally, precariously, provisionally:

> If ancient women had written as much as men, our impression of what mattered in the world would be greatly altered: conversation might count more than physical appearance, punishment be more often internalized, and greater stress be placed on the effect of one's actions on others.

The separation of male and female cultures in the ancient world, on this view, starts to look less a matter of misogyny and exclusion than of a (still) unsolved mystery. The hysteria question, the wandering womb, for instance, takes Ms Lefkowitz, via some tactful 'weaving', into the consideration of arguments about women's education towards the end of the last century. Intensive courses of study, it was feared, indeed shown by 'research', would lead to menstrual disorders, an atrophy of the womb even; certainly an intense fear of childbearing. Greek, Hebrew and higher mathematics were especially suspect, and so were single-sex colleges, as having a more or less direct effect on women's pelvic economy. The learned doctors were anxious, like their ancient predecessors, to ensure that women wouldn't somehow lose touch with their dubious biology, their obscure link with the human race. Ms Lefkowitz, if I read her indirections right, wants to suggest that in a way they were right to be anxious, and that bringing men and women together is proving almost as tricky as Plato imagined.

*

She has, here, a special advantage, since she was herself educated and now teaches at Wellesley, one of the New England women's colleges established in the face of womb-envy, and one that was conservative enough to stay a women's college during the 1960s and early 1970s. Her piece on 'Education for Women in a Man's World' meditates on the contrasts between this 'strange Utopia' and the effect of a semester spent teaching at the University of California at Berkeley, where 'you can be whoever you want to be . . . as if in an intellectual communal bath'. Perhaps the quotation says almost enough: Berkeley drives women *as* women underground; 'they keep hearing this message that says their biological make-up is at odds with their intellectual or professional role . . .' The great majority of their teachers are male ('since the 1930s the proportion of PhD's earned by women has decreased'), and academic mores, however unheroic, make assumptions about women's roles that sound remarkably Greek:

> In classics . . . married men write significantly more books and articles than unmarried men, or unmarried women, and married women, with a few exceptions, write the fewest of all.

The wry conclusion being that higher education has merely postponed marriage and children, for women; and that acquiring wives, or at least the support of communities of women, starts to look like the only (provisional) answer.

This is a thought which has increasingly occurred to feminists over the last decade. The notion of separate spheres, once a betrayal into marginality, has taken on a new, and newly embittered, relevance. Ms Lefkowitz doesn't sound particularly bitter, it's true, but her continued insistence on the shadowy otherness of women's lives and meanings places her firmly in the tough-minded camp as well as on an all-female campus. The book's two final essays – 'On Becoming a Cow', 'On Becoming a Tree' – set out the ground rules as it were. They are both about translation, and translation seen most radically as metamorphosis – a traumatic, infinitely problematic change of state. The 'cow' is Io in Aeschylus' *Promethus Unbound*, horribly deformed into a fly-bitten heifer by her union with Zeus: 'Her deformity is the result of the war that cannot be fought' – a literally *intestine* battle: she is indeed hysterical, schizophrenic. Translators, Ms Lefkowitz argues, have nearly always diminished her paradox by turning the chorus's description of her sexual terror into a familiar idiom – 'What will become of me?' Whereas it should read 'What should I become?', or even, 'Who should I become?' Only Gilbert Murray (perhaps, she suggests, because he was writing 'during the years when women in England achieved . . . political equality') did Io's tragedy some justice with the words, 'I know not how I should be changed'. For the most part, our translations have decently veiled Io's translation into a female animal: 'Union with Zeus has dire consequences . . . Marriage even to a mortal, with its usual consequence of pregnancy, inevitably involves physical transformation.'

'On Becoming a Tree' looks, with a certain wryness, at the alternative scenario, in the form of the Tree Day ceremony at Wellesley, a bridal procession without a groom, at which students plant a tree to commemorate their life together, before graduating. (Again, like the college itself, this custom has survived long enough to acquire what one might call a post-feminist force.) The ceremonial songs culled from the college archives have a sadly *fin de siècle* tone about them – love-lyrics to *Alma Mater*:

> The message . . . is at best discouraging: that one must love one's beloved, but must leave her, even though the relationship is aesthetically satisfying, offers sustenance, and engenders respect. Everything after is more sinister,
> . . . other years may bring us tears
> Other days be full of fears.
> But the songs offer no suggestions of how to deal with these inevitable difficulties to come.

Which is rather Ms Lefkowitz's position, too. She wishes her readers, I think, to see in these pastel rhymes a distant echo of the female chorus in Greek tragedy, and to draw what strength they can from, as it were, facing the worst: 'As Persephone discovered when Hades carried her off to the Underworld, *marriage is death*'.

Links in a mystic chain

Lull and Bruno

FRANCES YATES

THIS FIRST VOLUME OF her *Collected Essays* was already under way when Dame Frances Yates died last autumn at the age of 81. Its posthumous appearance points up, by sad coincidence, how very long she always had to wait for her work to receive its due.

The earliest essays now handsomely reprinted in *Lull and Bruno* date from the late 1930s and their freshness reveals, a touch ironically, her special distinction as a scholar – her sympathetic penetration into ideas out of step with the orthodoxies of their own age and hers.

You can trace, here, something of the painstaking process by which she disinterred the occult philosophies (Platonist-Hermetic-Cabalist) and reinstated them in the history of Renaissance thought. Her studies of Bruno in particular – which were issued in her book *Giordano Bruno and the Hermetic Traditions* in 1964 – were all along accumulating the evidence that was to turn the martyr in the cause of modern science (he was burnt by the Inquisition in 1600) back into a Magus and heresiarch. Bruno in her version indeed espouses Copernican theories about the material universe – but because they confirm the magical sun-centred world picture he derives from ancient 'Egyptian' sources.

A 1938 essay here on a typical conflict that arose during his whirl-wind mission to England from 1583–85, as self-appointed ambassador on behalf of the magical universe, rehearsed the whole scenario in miniature. Bruno attacked the Oxford natural philosophers for their shallow enlightenment (all Ciceronian rhetoric and – this time – *Prot-estant* hatred of 'superstition'), and teased them with numinous hints about 'barbarous' pre-classical wisdom being actually, secretly, radically modern – not to say ecumenical.

Bruno became one of Dame Frances's favourite figures precisely because of his gift for systematically levitating across the frontiers erected by the intellectual establishment. His self-description, in his account of the row with Oxford, obviously delights her: carelessly dressed, with the odd button maybe missing, he confronts the gowned dons in their gold chains, who look, if you adjust to his focus, rather like the absurd dignitaries who visited Thomas More's Utopia – dripping with finery, they are blissfully unaware that in that land of the mind gold was a substance specially reserved for the manufacture of chamber pots.

She has changed our picture of Renaissance thinking, more or less literally. It's impossible now to imagine the mental life of the period without recalling the labyrinthine diagrams and maps of mystical memory theatres which always illustrate her books and which she explicates with daunting and paradoxical clarity. Bruno talks of 'making everything out of everything' ('since all is in all, as the profound Anaxagoras says'), which sounds like a recipe for terminal intellectual chaos – certainly a nightmare for any interpreter not equipped with inexhaustible patience and (there seems no other word for it) faith.

This point is also made even more forcibly in the essays on Ramon Lull, the thirteenth-century Catalan philosopher-mystic whose metaphysical algebra, set out in a forest of bizarre tree-diagrams, preoccupied Dame Frances over the past 20-odd years. Lull was a missing link in the chain that led back from the (occult) Renaissance to (occult) antiquity. He was also – and this explains something of Dame Frances's 'faith' – a thinker who brought together Jewish, Muslim and Christian traditions, in the hope (like Bruno later) of synthesising an ancient, perennial and universal rite.

From this angle Dame Frances's scholarship, which can seem so determinedly esoteric, confesses itself a response to the history of her times and ours: a search for the forgotten formulae of toleration, occult indeed.

Ravishment related

The Rapes of Lucretia

IAN DONALDSON

THE FIRST THING YOU notice – as you are meant to – in the plates that illustrate *The Rapes of Lucretia*, is that Lucretia is lavishly naked, her ravisher Tarquin elaborately clothed. Thomas Rowlandson's untraditionally undressed Tarquin looks, as Ian Donaldson writes, 'curiously, indeed almost risibly, vulnerable and lacking in menace'. The myth requires a rapist whose body is concealed, a creature of the shadows (as in Titian's painting), clothed in plush and brocade, his (possibly risible) sex displaced on to the knife with which he threatens the naked innocence of his victim.

It is of course, a famously voyeuristic effect (Tarquin has his clothes on *like us*) and one that flatters the male viewer ('had Narcissus seen her', thinks Shakespeare's Tarquin, 'Self-love had never drown'd him in the flood'). The slave who obligingly holds the bed-curtain back in several paintings (including Titian's) adds to the salacious implications. Even more so, if you remember that in the story Tarquin threatens Lucretia, if she resists, with not only death but dishonour: he'll kill the slave too, and swear he found them *in flagrante*, so that she'll lose her good name for eternity. Which in turn (by making it useless for her to court instant death) gives her the chance to rewrite the plot by publicly killing herself and loosing revenge on Tarquin. This, though, is to anticipate Donaldson's account of the narrative's verbal metamorphoses. What the paintings of the rape-scene reveal is that it's a myth about hiddenness – hidden lusts, hidden motives. Again, Shakespeare's poem (itself so interested in painting) spells it out: women, for men, are the exposed, the readable –

> Their smoothness, like a goodly champaign plain
> Lays open all the little worms that creep:
> In men, as in a rough-grown grove, remain
> Cave-keeping evils . . .

The human topography of the paintings works like this, with rich expanses of lighted flesh overhung by a violent figure in shadowed and concealing clothes.

Tarquin, though, isn't the only 'hidden' man in the story. The transformations Professor Donaldson is tracking through history spring from a myth that in its earliest versions (dating from the first century AD, five hundred years after the supposed event) already enshrined a certain duplicity. Lucretia's tragedy is also the triumph of Lucius Junius Brutus (her husband's friend, and like him related to the Tarquins) who, on witnessing her suicide, swears to drive the princely rapist's father, and the whole race of kings, from Rome. Brutus is a dark horse in several ways: he has (in a folklore motif) feigned idiocy until this moment to avoid political dangers; and he goes on, as Consul, to preside over the execution of his own sons for plotting Royalist treason. Thus Lucrece's story has a further end. Brutus turns her rape into a symbolic outrage against Roman civil rights, and founds the Republic. In Botticelli's 'The Tragedy of Lucretia' her body, decently shrouded now, is on display in the forum, under a statue of David with the head of Goliath, surrounded by a thorny forest of raised, naked, revolutionary swords. On this view, as Simone de Beauvoir said, Lucretia joins other heroines of history who have been 'pretexts rather than agents'; her suicide 'has had value only as a symbol'. And much of the book's interest lies in uncovering such changes in focus, with Lucretia conquering her rapist, only to be edged from centre-stage by her avenger.

Donaldson postpones this outcome, however, and concentrates first on treatments of the rape and suicide which focus on the heroic woman, and the paradox of strength-in-weakness: 'Despite her apparent passivity, subservience, and self-destruction, Lucretia is the ultimate victor.' In companion panels by Cranach, a Lucretia holds the knife to her breast and a Judith daintily dandles the severed head of Holofernes; a Raimondi engraving makes her lone suiciding figure into a type of

Christ, arms spread wide; a splendid Tiepolo rape scene contrives to confuse Tarquin's threatening gesture with Lucretia's later suicide, by intertwining their figures to make it appear that she's already holding the dagger. She becomes a triumphant martyr, achieving her destiny. Donaldson points out that even one of the very few women painters to treat the theme, Artemesia Gentileschi (who had herself, as it happens, been raped by her art teacher), goes along with the conventions. Though if he had juxtaposed Gentileschi's saintly and sexy Lucretia with her Judith, recently on show at the Royal Academy, he might have detected signs of scepticism. In this painting, all the conventionally gratifying ploys are reversed: Judith's maid holds Holofernes down, while her mistress saws at his neck, in a strange, spreadeagled perspective that forces you to wonder, sickeningly, how far off his head is. For Gentileschi, possibly, activity and passivity meant rather different things.

Usually, though, when the paradox of heroic passivity is questioned, it's from quite different angles. Augustine argues that if Lucretia's will did not consent she was guiltless until she became guilty of self-murder. Shakespeare's 'Rape of Lucrece' arrives at an inspired stalemate by deploying tensions between Christian and pagan attitudes: 'immaculate and spotless is my mind' says his Lucrece, but only once she's made up her mind to kill herself. Richardson 'solves' the suicide problem – Clarissa, clearly triumphant in her moral victory over her rapist, dies of natural causes. We don't, however, know what they are, and in side-stepping one problem, he's exposed another. Rape is apparently, despite Christianity, still 'a lethal act', as Donaldson succinctly puts it. But why? In ancient Rome, he suggests, intercourse with any man other than her husband magically polluted a woman (and indeed her husband and any subsequent children) whether it was voluntary or not. However, from his own account, something like this 'magical' theory survives into the eighteenth century and beyond, more than he is prepared to admit.

He stresses 'will', though it seems precisely the point of rape that women raped are revealed to be not what they will, but what happens to them: 'For men have marble, women waxen minds.' When Shakespeare's Lucrece stabs herself the blood flows into two puddles, one red and clear, the other black, and polluted by Tarquin. She's on the way to becoming flesh of his flesh, as though his sperm had permeated her. Donaldson talks of pregnancy fears, but it's more than that: the woman herself seems in some sense 'fathered' by her men – stamped with her husband's (and now Tarquin's) mark as surely as by her father's blood. It's this feeling that makes sense of the silly squabble – 'She's mine', 'O, mine she is' – between Lucrece's father and husband after her death in Shakespeare's poem. It's a real question whether these most soulful women, from Lucretia to Clarissa, *have* souls to call their own. They, apparently, suspect not: their 'souls' of 'minds' are not free agents inhabiting their bodies, like men's minds, but much more intimately and passively intertwined with their flesh, only to be liberated in death.

In this context the 'soulless' jokers and sceptics, whom Donaldson rather looks down on, aren't so much of an anti-tradition after all. Their line tends to be that Lucretia obviously enjoyed it, which is why she killed herself (if she did). Machiavelli, naturally, is prominent here, and so are Restoration libertines. As the epilogue to Southerne's *The Fatal Marriage* (1694) has it – 'all must own, 'tis most egregious non-sense/To dye for being pleas'd, with a safe Conscience . . . .'. Aphra Behn is also sceptical:

> Who applauded the Chastity of *Lucretia* (whom all the world now cele-
> brates for a Vertuous Woman) till they made it a subject of private
> Revenge, and the occasion of the Liberty of *Rome*?

Aphra, though, not only casts doubt on Lucretia's chastity, but questions the motive for having her in the story at all, and so returns us to the second man 'hidden' in her destiny, Brutus. Lucretia is not only a victim of Tarquin's tyranny, but also, in a sense, of Brutus's revolutionary plot. Machiavelli (who takes this seriously) says the king was driven out, not because his son had raped Lucretia, but because 'he had violated the laws of the kingdom, and ruled tyrannically'. The change in perspective, as Donaldson points out, can be seen 'in a quite literal sense, in many drawings and paintings'.

And so we move openly from 'the world of women to the world

of men'. Brutus, paralleled with his later namesake (who was thought to be killing his father in killing Caesar) takes over centre stage, as the executioner of his own sons in the name of the Fatherland. It's a myth that is much more useful in France than in England (where every treatment is accompanied by anxious noises off about constitutional monarchy) and its central moral event – the stoical sacrifice of mere physical paternity by a *Pater Patriae* – distances Brutus's story from Lucretia's in a nicely symmetrical way. Again, however, shades of the other story (the women's story this time) creep in. Not everyone could quite take Madeleine de Scudéry's vision in *Clélie* (1654–60), in which Lucretia and Brutus had been (just) chastely in love, and 'he minded not the liberty of *Rome*, but in order to avenge the death of the innocent *Lucretia*'; but in many other versions his feelings are displaced on to a wife and daughters. Jacques-Louis David's painting 'Lictors Returning to Brutus the Bodies of his Sons' (1787–9) is finely described:

> At the left the lictors, representatives of the state, move past carrying the bodies of Brutus' sons, as though along a public thoroughfare. Under the ominously darkened figure of Rome Brutus sits tensely and in shadow ... On the right of the painting, bathed in quite another light and behaving in quite another manner, are the women of the household: Brutus' wife and daughters ... within a single composition David is depicting the tragic separation of two worlds: the private and public worlds, the worlds of men and of women, of duty and of love, of calculation and spontaneity. The worlds are divided as though by an invisible wall. The women's gestures can touch nothing, alter nothing, that the men have already decreed and done. Yet to express a grief that Brutus also shares, ... the women seem to authenticate in a sense Brutus' humanity ...

This change in perspective, though, is fittingly itself 'placed' by a final chapter on the cognate story of Cato (a suicide like Lucrece, and a stoic like Brutus). Cato was not celebrated for domestic sensibility, as Byron's pleasant couplet reminds us – 'Heroic, stoic Cato, the sententious / Who lent his lady to his friend Hortensius'.

Byron reminds us too of the basic rules of the game which *The Rapes of Lucretia* so learnedly and fascinatingly documents. Donaldson brings out a vivid life in the mutations of his stories and images, in their alternations of light and darkness, their hidden and overt messages. He has time too for incidental delights, like the cat ('emblem of liberty') who keeps the suiciding Lucretia company in the 'Storia di Lucrezia' in the Ca' d'Oro in Venice; or Quarles's version of Tarquin's fate (sung to death by nightingales, who then pick out his eyes). The only possible quarrel one can have with the book is that, in covering so much ground, in looking for changes, he understates and under investigates what doesn't seem to have changed, at least within his enormous time-scale up to the eighteenth century. In short, it would have been interesting to have more speculation on the role of Father almighty. The narrative tapestry of tales and pictures hides, as well as reveals. But why not, after all? Since (as I'm sure Professor Donaldson would remind me) the story of this story isn't finished.

From our spot of time

The Unremarkable Wordsworth

GEOFFREY H. HARTMAN

Wordsworth's Revisionary Aesthetics

THERESA M. KELLEY

Dorothy Wordsworth and Romanticism

SUSAN M. LEVIN

Wordsworth's Historical Imagination: The poetry of displacement

DAVID SIMPSON

WORDSWORTH'S 'PROSPECTUS' TO *THE EXCURSION*, promising to show 'How exquisitely the individual mind ... to the external world / Is fitted', seemed to Blake so wrong-headed that according to a fascinated Crabb Robinson, it gave him a bowel complaint that 'nearly killed him'. Geoffrey Hartman, responding more circumspectly, but in similarly apocalyptic vein, famously picked the Wordsworthian mind out of the mud in *Wordsworth's Poetry* in 1964. He set Romantic imagination at odds with the order of nature by demonstrating 'the continuous purging of fixities' that went on in the real poetry. That book, as Donald G. Marshall points out in his foreword to the Hartman essays collected in *The Unremarkable Wordsworth*, was part of the 'ivory palace revolution' that led to the present dominance of 'literary theory'.

Marshall himself puts quotation-marks round theory to indicate a revolution that went wrong. The 'continuous purging of fixities' has indeed proved continuous, and now it's 'the disseminated play of signifiers' that gives Hartman's kind of thinker a pain. It's as though

Hartman's revolution, which aimed to make the relations between critic and poet more intimate, fraternal and democratic, had let in the Robespierres and Napoleons. Marshall says nothing so crude, but Hartman's own introduction sounds the note of betrayal:

> It says something about our moment in criticism that we prefer the preacherly and excited writing of French culture-critics to the sober lights of Wordsworth and Ashbery or even to Thoreau's *Walden* and passages in Emerson. How seriously are we taking our own traditions . . . ?

The thought is not new, of course (that is not its point), but it acquires a particular resonance in the context of these essays on Wordsworth, written over twenty-five years, and testifying to Hartman's fixation on the poet he unfixed; and his desire (Marshall again) 'not to decide on all those separations – spoken / written; inside / outside; metaphorical/ literal . . . – which must be asserted to give deconstructive analysis its purchase'. By returning again and again to those Wordsworthian 'spots of time' which 'describe a trauma, a lesion in the fabric of time' Hartman has turned what was once apocalyptic into a figure for stability.

Thus, the 1985 essay on 'The Unremarkable Poet' which gives the book its title revisits the sonnet 'Composed Upon Westminster Bridge, Sept 3, 1802' in order to explore Wordsworth's challenge to the culture of 'marks' or signs:

> the inscription of time and place is not innocent: the tradition invokes or re-animates a buried consciousness; it puts the genius of the writer into relation with genius or spirit of place . . .

Which is another way of saying that 'A reading which recovers the strange interplay of cultic feeling and modern self-consciousness will also recover the precarious subjectivity of the poet' – as he did in his piece on Riffaterre and 'The Use and Abuse of Structural Analysis' (1975) also reprinted here. The poet's subjectivity, his 'voice' ('a peculiarly Wordsworthian tone', in this instance, 'hovering between pompous cliché and sublime simplicity') turns out to be what holds the line against mere textuality. Unsurprisingly, perhaps – though the analyses that make the point, particularly in 'Words, Wish, Worth', an essay that addresses itself to post-structuralist assumptions, are elaborately hedged about with reservations: 'The life of Wordsworth's lines is often uneasy and as if somewhere else.'

One might apply the same description to Hartman's own writing in some of these pieces. His position, his habits of reading, haven't changed, but he's looking over his shoulder, conscious that the readings in themselves will no longer persuade unless they're 'pointed' in a theoretical direction. And since to abstract in this way is a kind of betrayal (of Wordsworth, of the reciprocity between thinking and imagining), the results are indeed 'uneasy'. Two essays not printed before, on Hegel and Heidegger in relation to Wordsworth, speak of 'the alliance philosophy can make with art', 'one that delays or multiplies endings and creates limits that prove liminal'. But the omens point another way:

> We too are faced with the 'undisciplined revelry' or 'stupor of conscious-ness and wild stammering utterance' which constitute the pseudo-infinity . . . Hegel tried to put behind him.

'Limits that prove liminal' and 'pseudo-infinity' may sound like much the same sort of thing. However, the second is for Hartman empty, lost to the subject. When he talked of 'continuous purging' it was, it turns out, in the faith that 'There is always a remainder that cannot be purged, whatever violence of intellect we employ'.

Theresa M. Kelley, untroubled by the complicity with the decon-structors that marks Hartman's generation, puts sublime violence in its place almost briskly:

> In Wordsworth's later poetry the dizzying, emptying detours and countersigns which are the errant sign language of the sublime yield to the beautiful, which sanctions and extends the task of gathering infer-ences and echoes from several frames of meaning.

Wordsworth's Revisionary Aesthetics argues that France and the revolu-tionary sublime of the Terror and the wars discredited in retrospect the vertiginous and apocalypic experiences on which Wordsworth was weaned; and that, in any case, one can detect from the beginning these two rival aesthetic models – the sublime and the beautiful – at work in his thinking and writing. Her terms are not as Burkean as they sound (they're filtered through Wordsworth's *Guide* to the Lake District, and the fragmentary manuscript on aesthetics that has acquired the title 'The Sublime and the Beautiful'). None the less her own revisionist aim (to put the imagination back into its time) is undisguised:

> Post-structuralist critics who have used the Kantian model to define Wordsworthian and Romantic sublimes have in effect tried to legitimise an absorption in and by the sublime, which Wordsworth and other Romantic writers could not afford.

The reason they couldn't afford it is 'the pressure of history on the sublime', despite its claim to exist outside time and society.

The argument centres on Wordsworth's mapping strategies, and in particular the figurative topography that re-inscribes and recuperates apocalyptic energies. Kelley too is interested in 'spots of time', but for what they reveal of 'how the mind defends itself against the sublime'. As she announces succinctly apropos of Wordsworth's restless reclassification of the *Poems* of 1815, 'what interests me is the strategy of limitation'. In a sense, she's reading Wordsworth back into himself in order to focus on the frames that were always there, even though they were broken. Reading this way, you spot the 'signs that stabilize families of meaning' and restore the writing to decipherability and a kind of referentiality. In Kelley's terms, you arrive at the 'code of beauty, sociability and representability', rather as, in the sonnet 'To the Torrent at Devil's Bridge', the initially singular and nameless 'force' is domesticated and named as one of 'a family of floods'.

One obvious problem is that in rescuing Wordsworth from singularity and all that is *unheimlich* (or, in showing how he rescued himself) she may merely be discovering something duller. It's not an issue the book addresses directly, though the tone does register that when 'the code of representability' really takes over, as in *The Excursion*, the results are dire – 'a sublime vision well *supervised* by the beautiful', 'the speakers . . . are very nearly unrelenting in their *management* of sublime figures and values' (my italics: this is what gave Blake's bowels such a turn). Kelley, however, would want to defend her visions of *The Prelude* or the Tintern Abbey poem on the grounds that 'a larger temporal and social arena submits sublime images to scale, making them serve a widened perspective and reality'. She'd argue, against Hartman (in many ways her mentor), that one's not condemned to 'liminality': 'fallen beings – including those fallen from sublime visions into discourse about the sublime – can and do develop new, more insistently human vocabularies . . .'

This is a reading that has stepped (back) across the threshold, in every sense a *domesticating* argument. Kelley quotes De Quincey's description of Dorothy – 'she it was that first *couched* his eye to the sense of beauty, humanised him by the gentler charities' – and though she does not pursue it, the possibility that 'the beautiful' is aligned with feminine values is allowed to hover gracefully in the background. Susan M. Levin's *Dorothy Wordsworth and Romanticism* tackles this question head on, with more conviction than subtlety. She looks again at Dorothy's writing life, stressing the travel writing and the poetry rather than the more familiar journals, and prints in appendices all the known poems, plus the tale of 'Mary Jones and her Pet Lamb', in order to argue for a distinctively 'feminine romanticism'.

The poems produce some creepy transformations of William's lines. The baby-sitting poem *The Mother's Return*, for instance, invokes Lucy and death, as well as the 'five years' of Tintern Abbey:

> Five minutes passed – and Oh the change!
> Asleep upon their beds they lie,
> Their busy limbs in perfect rest,
> And closed the sparkling eye.

It is often hard to be sure of Dorothy's tone. Some lines ('I *reverenced* the Poet's skill, / And *might have* missed a mounting Will') sound very knowing, particularly when you picture the old woman who copied them out and recited them obsessively, a Dorothy 'filthy, fat, selfish, and crazed' who (according to Mary Wordsworth) lost all interest in family life: 'She says she is too busy with her own feelings'. Levin wants to argue both that Dorothy's madness is an expression of suppressed ambitions, and that the suppression itself produced a feminine idiom shared with other women of the period 'characterized by refusal: refusal to generalise, refusal to move out of a limited range of vision . . .' Paraphrasing Hélène Cixous, she hails it as a process 'of representing the external objective world in a non-dominating nurturing way'. This is, of course, itself a sub-Romantic and essentialist position (men and women are 'equal but opposing forces'). It's also – as you realize when she describes Mary Shelley's *Frankenstein* as 'a horrible warning against the power of creative genius' – a thoroughly sentimental simplification. Celebrating limits ought to be much harder work, particularly for a feminist.

David Simpson certainly labours hard at it – as befits a good materialist – in *Wordsworth's Historical Imagination*, where he deploys a much-modified Marxist perspective to accommodate Wordsworth's alienation. He writes with considerable verve and ingenuity, and an attention to detail that's resolutely designed to localize the issues. Wordsworth's poetry

> continually falls short of what it aspires to be, but reveals in that falling short its greatest intelligence and most coherent messages.

This view of how the writing functions – 'intersubjectively', as a specialized set of ripples in the 'language pool' – means that, for example, you could substitute 'incoherent' without worrying Simpson very much. His Wordsworth is an exemplary disaster area, a version of 'the creative mind as the site of errors, conflicts and uncertainties'.

There's a good deal of exhilaration to be got out of his analyses – particularly when he is closest to writing about what's *not* there, as in the opening reading of *Gipsies*, a fairly shocking 1807 poem in which Wordsworth, who is out for a stroll, berates the travellers for idleness. Simpson's reading, tracking down vagrant echoes (especially Miltonic-Satanic ones) and using compromising snippets of biography (who was paying Wordsworth's bills?), produces a guilty and richly confused tangle of feelings associated with the *topoi* of toil, liberty and the rejection of revolutionary innocence. He is convincing, more or less. What is disturbing here and elsewhere is not the vision of Wordsworth in the Laocoon grip of the 'historical unconscious', but the unmistakable implication that where all this leads is to a revaluation of the later Wordsworth, where of course the suppressions are yet more massive and (in a sense) satisfactory. In short, back to *The Excursion*: 'We have yet to rediscover', Simpson concludes ominously, 'the energies behind that light fallen, or falling'. Here he's close to Hartman, and indeed to Kelley – and this slightly improbable consensus gives one pause. What is it about our own 'spot of time' that makes failure so attractive? Or that makes the later Wordsworth's bad faith into a kind of shelter for the critical mind? The answer seems to be our own 'French Revolution'. Wordsworth's very untranslatability, his stubborn Englishness (or rather, 'Englishness' – he's become very nearly American), his way of withdrawing from the visionary brink, may well be timely for an academic world that wants the purges to stop.

Peace with a vengeance

Witness Against the Beast:
William Blake and the Moral Law

E. P. THOMPSON

THIS POSTHUMOUS BOOK ON William Blake is a fitting post-
script to E. P. Thompson's sweet-tempered and argumentative
career. 'I shall not cease from mental strife/Nor shall my sword sleep
in my hand . . .' Thompson, like Blake, was for peace with a vengeance;
his commitment to the peace movement was one side of a coin whose
other side was a robust appetite for controversy, paradox and contradiction.

'Robust' is a word he likes, in fact, and *Witness Against the Beast* is
a book about Blake as a substantial, endlessly energetic man, a literal-
minded visionary who throve on complexity but hated Mystery. So not
the Neo-Platonist Blake, nor the Gnostic Blake, but the historical man
who inhabited late eighteenth-century London of tiny religious sects
and Universal Churches with a score of members. This Blake was
opposed not only to the organic Toryism of Burke, but also to the
Enlightenment rationalism of Tom Paine and of Mary Wollstonecraft.
His mum was possibly a Muggletonian.

Part of Blake's fascination for Thompson is that he represents the
survival and even re-birth of a tradition of antinomian radicalism that
was outside 'polite' discourse, not the property of intellectuals, but of
tradesman, artisans and petit-bourgeois, independent fixers. These
people handed down ideas from the seventeenth-century's Ranters and
Levellers – via caches of manuscripts and printed sermons and polemics.

Often notions ran in families, it was that local: you can nearly name
the members of some churches, they run at most into hundreds, and
the relevant ones are, like Blake, mostly London-based. These people

bandied about symbols, 'which appear to be grand or profound when presented as part of hermetic and Neo-Platonist thought', but are actually common property on the radical fringes of Dissent. The antinomian idea that God actually became Christ (i.e., ceased to exist as the Father at the coming of the Son), and that this Christ vindicates the Divinity of Man – William Empson in *Milton's God* suggested that this was a heresy cherished by Milton – helped give such humbler believers confidence in their visions, and sustained their imaginative independence.

Thompson is not given to picturesque anecdotes, but he clearly cannot resist some, like the story of seventeenth-century Thomas Tany: 'A goldsmith in the Strand, he read some of Boehme's work, and, in 1650, announced that it had been revealed to him that he was "a Jew of the tribe of Reuben" . . . As a necessary preparation, he circumcised himself . . . He claimed first the throne of England and then the throne of France, had an armed affray at the houses of parliament, and finally seems to have disappeared, perhaps in 1655, or later, in a home-made boat in the Channel, crying "Ho, for the Holy Wars".'

The adjustment of focus it takes to make such individuals historically visible is obviously congenial to the author of *The Making of the English Working Class* (30 years old this year). 'I like these Muggletonians,' he says, for instance, 'but it is clear that they were not among history's winners.' Which is very much his line – only a rather wimpish historian, you're meant to feel, would always go in for the winners.

On the other hand, Thompson is very clear that a century and a half in the wilderness had done little good for the antinomian tradition – 'Where seventeenth-century antinomians, Familists or Seekers had laboured with sweat on their spiritual brows through forests of vivid imagery . . . most eighteenth-century mystics and antinomians relaxed into anti-rational postures and gave up the struggle . . .', Blake magnificently excepted. The high point of Thompson's reading of the poems is a look at 'London', where he persuades you to share Blake's densely symbolic vision of the streets and wharves. In 'Near where the chartered Thames does flow', 'chartered', which in earlier drafts was 'dirty' or 'cheating', takes on the aspect of something leased-out, a product (Blake

would have said) of the kind of pseudo-freedom Britons associate with
Magna Carta.

And then there are the '*Marks* of weakness', which are the marks
of the Beast, and in particular of commercialism, the sale not of goods
but of people, which leads to the child-harlot's giving birth to plague-
striken babies in the last terrible verse. Impossible to summarise the
full argument, but its originality lies in enabling you to imagine what
Docklands looked like to a visionary who took it for granted that
London streets were inhabited by signs of our psycho-history, the
wandering monsters of our creation.

Or to put it another way, you could say that Blake was engaged on
the 'symbolic analysis of market relations'. Thompson prefers for the
most part to stick closer to Blake's own language, however, since Blake's
value is precisely that he acts as a reminder that the 'formal, intellectual
culture' doesn't always have the last word. As Thompson points out,
the 'Left' establishment of Blake's generation were largely disillusioned
by the turn of the century, whereas Blake – buoyed by his strenuous
efforts to invent his own system – kept the faith. You don't need to
be a Neo-Platonist to spot the allegorical application of this particular
observation to our own *fin de siècle*.

V

Critical Tradition

The gay protagonist

The Homosexual as Hero in Contemporary Fiction

STEPHEN ADAMS

AFTER A LONG HISTORY closeted in code, Mr Adams argues, the homosexual in contemporary fiction can surely at last stop playing heroines and villains, and play the hero. 'Sheer ordinariness' lurks under the exotic disguises of the past: 'healthy eclecticism' is gradually eroding the heterosexual dictatorship.

It's a familiar liberal, liberationist argument, applied with considerable care and intelligence to a series of post-war novels. What lends it unexpected tension is that it turns out, apparently, not to be true. The more diligently and honestly Mr Adams searches for his commonplace homosexual hero, the more elusive he becomes. The contrast between the reasonableness of his own tone and the violence, mockery and *mauvaise foi* of his authors, is striking. They refuse to be translated into neutrality, or at least accepted with bad grace. Take, for example, this description of a famously frolicsome writer:

> He views homosexuality not as a cause meriting special pleading but quite simply as a normal, healthy, human response that has been distorted by society's prescription of the *right* sexual equation.

Who would recognise Gore Vidal? It's not that Mr Adams doesn't understand camp: in a sense he understands it all too well –

> the affectation of a camp style can be a way of mocking oppressive masculine stereotypes and of converting a despised effeminacy into a subtle form of attack.

This, though, is to 'see through' the surface of a style that exists in and for artifice, to imply that somewhere on the other side of Myra Breckinridge there's nature and simplicity, a quiet, solid individual no longer playing a part. And no longer writing fiction – not *this* kind, at least.

With James Baldwin, or with Forster's posthumous fiction, the approach works rather better, perhaps because they are themselves optimistic and didactic. Burroughs and Rechy again, though, expose a yawning gap between Mr Adams's enlightenment about 'stereotypes' and their own determined darkness: 'Most writers who portray male homosexuals sympathetically value tenderness and emotional sensitivity in preference to aggression, yet some ... have cast the homosexual male in the role of new frontiersman.'

And Genet, even semi-exiled in a final chapter, stubbornly advertises both his own importance to the tradition, and his fascination with the cruel old patterns. His vision, Mr Adams admits, 'may seem offensive to those who wish to assert the sheer ordinariness of homosexuality.'

Offensive too – and this is surely relevant – to anyone who wanted to assert the *ordinariness* of heterosexuality. The example of Genet, actually, suggests that there might be a rather different way of understanding homosexual 'melodrama'; not as a sideshow somehow deprived of authenticity by the existence of a 'straight' world where people are tautologically people, and don't play roles, but – possibly – as an act among acts.

Mr Adams wants, I know, simply to put his writers, and homosexual themes in general, on a level with everyone else, and it's perhaps mean to stress his difficulties when the detail of his readings is often persuasive. But why does he assume that the rest of us are on such solid ground? A heterosexual hero – or heroine – has to be pretty well acquainted with unreality, has to learn to swap masks to get by these days. 'Camp' and 'Gothic' are hardly terms of the ghetto; the sideshow, if you think of contemporary fiction at large, often looks to *be* the show.

Or perhaps I'm substituting an illiberal pessimism about role-playing for Mr Adams's liberal optimism. There is, however, a real problem for someone who takes on this sort of critical position: that in the search for a 'hero,' for a model of 'how the individual homosexual might achieve a satisfactory life-style', one's liable to turn the actual (fictional) achievements based on radical dissatisfaction into forms of merely transitional therapy. Are they really practising to be ordinary?

Seminal semantics

Dissemination

JACQUES DERRIDA

TRANSLATED BY BARBARA JOHNSON

STRUCTURALIST LANGUAGE IS STILL an alien dialect in Anglo-Saxon criticism – sometimes doubtless for good native, pragmatic, sceptical, etcetera reasons, but sometimes for less elevated ones. We've an uneasy sense that our French accents aren't quite in order, that we don't properly belong to the intellectual common market. We still analyse our texts rather than deconstruct them, and when we graft on the tell-tale hyphenations – 'in-scribe,' 're-mark,' 'de-compose,' what someone called the 'poststructuralist chant,' the refrain of the new(ish) theoretical doubts about meaning – we move to do it with a certain stiffness and reluctance, victims of slow culture-shock.

Jacques Derrida, *philosophe* of l'Ecole Normale Supérieure and coiner of the terms 'deconstruction' and '*différance*' (with an 'a' not an 'e'), is perhaps – outside the *avant-garde* in fiction, though the distinction has long been lapsing – the most disturbing of the avatars of fracture, now that Roland Barthes is dead. Barthes, one realises, was a mainly benevolent presence, for though he inhabited the hall of mirrors of infinite regress, texts that rewrite themselves and other texts and so on, he salvaged out of it a kind of creativity, an endless (fore)play of signs, the pleasure of the text. The gloomy prospect of the lack of 'final' or 'whole' meaning got iced over (the mirror turned into a skating rink, on which the charismatic critic does his figures). Barthes made a virtue of frustration. Whereas one's tempted to say that Derrida, so much more laboured and rigorous in hunting down our atavistic yearnings for meaning and truth, has made frustration a virtue.

Certainly, since in this company a critic's own text must enact the language games it talks about, Derrida binds himself to be (sometimes horribly) difficult. His particular preoccupation has always been with the divorce of written language from speech, from life and breath, from the particular speaker or author: 'a structure cut off from any absolute responsibility, or from consciousness as ultimate authority, orphaned and separated at birth from the support of the father . . .' However, as the father/son metaphor implies, there is indeed a drama going on here: Derrida, like Barthes, is skating on thin post-Freudian ice.

'Deconstruction' – a practice of reading that 'must always aim at a certain relationship, unperceived by the author, between what he commands and does not command of the patterns of language he uses' – also opens up ego, authority, 'natural' hierarchies. Writing and reading impose order, wholeness and simultaneity of meaning, but they will also turn, given a chance, into vagrant, wasteful, 'unnatural' practices. Patricide, for example, and masturbation.

Which is where *Dissemination* comes in. The title deploys one of the abortive puns (spilt seed/the proliferation and scatter of written language/signs that never get to signify, just to play with themselves) that Derrida uses to think with, and that must have given his lucid and unwearying translator no little trouble (*La Dissemination* came out in 1972). This pun's seminal force is best illustrated in the book's major piece on Plato, the 'father' of truth-addiction in Western philosophy, whose books are anti-books (in praise of the spoken word, dialogue, and good – i.e., 'truthful'—writing) but who in Derrida's re-reading reveals himself as also the guilty 'son' (writer, pederast) whose books subliminally 'rehearse' the role of the outlaw and patricide even while in the act of 'mastering' it.

It's a dizzying analytic performance, taking in Plato's use of the Egyptian myth of Thoth (patron of writing, drugs, funeral arrangements and cosmetics) and Athens's use of Socrates, its doctor and scapegoat, swallowing his hemlock to be locked in written words. Plato writes obsessively about writing: he also has another hidden metaphor, the one that for Derrida blows everything: the text, he discovers, 'is all about fathers and sons, about bastards unaided by any public assistance, about glorious, legitimate sons, about inheritance, sperm, sterility . . .'

The traditions Plato 'fathered' through his spilled seed/written word have, like Father, covered up this messy primal scene, denied their origins in duplicity, and sternly given priority to 'nature' and 'being' . . .

This is exhilarating stuff, to which I'm hardly doing justice and from which there are obviously lots of ways to go. One way that has already been taken by French feminists is an analysis of the official languages of Western culture as 'logo-centric' and 'phallocentric' modes of 'intercourse' exclusively between men, which must be radically recomposed to end Father's rule. Derrida himself in 'Dissemination' goes on to analyse, in Mallarmé and Philippe Sollers, male texts that practise absence, disjunction, self-dissection. Such texts, says Derrida, are 'rich with a kind of poverty': they cheat the critic of his interpreter's role, allowing him no final meaning to (even) chase.

One final quotation, to illustrate Derrida's special, and specially dubious, glamour. Plato, the old quack, contemplating the alchemical birth of 'Platonism':

> Plato mutters . . . The walled-in voice strikes against the rafters, the words come apart, bits and pieces of sentences are separated, disarticulated parts begin to circulate through the corridors . . . translate each other, become rejoined, bounce off each other, contradict each other, make trouble, tell on each other, come back like answers, organise their exchanges, protect each other, institute an internal commerce, take themselves for a dialogue. Full of meaning. A whole story. An entire history. All of philosophy . . .

Derrida is supposed to be the de-mystifier of all this, but actually, one suspects, it's precisely like this that we see him – the Magus of post-structuralism, a source of strange spells and stranger spelling. To date, we de-compose, most of us, in rather bad faith.

Men against women

The Rape of Clarissa

TERRY EAGLETON

R ICHARDSON'S *CLARISSA* (1747–48) created the first great suffering virgin. This is how Terry Eagleton summarises its action:

> . . . a young woman of outstanding intelligence is made to suffer under a violently oppressive family, is tricked away from home by a notorious sexual predator, deceived, imprisoned, persecuted, drugged and raped, and finally impelled to her death.

What, he asks, have the critics made of this? In his view, they've ritually re-enacted it: 'Cavaliers, deconstructionists and debunking liberals' (shorthand for old-fashioned Tory scholars, new-fangled theoreticians and, well, liberals) alike have systematically collaborated with the rapist Lovelace to read their hostile meanings into the text. Rape squared.

It turns out, though, that the critical record has not been quite so criminal. A good deal of what Eagleton has to say in his brief polemic is familiar from the work of (for instance) Ian Watt, Christopher Hill or John Preston: that *Clarissa* is not merely obsessive, or morbid, or one-sided, but 'dramatises the contradictions of ruling-class patriarchy'. Her rape by an aristocratic libertine makes her a martyr for the emergent ideals of the middle class; and her martyrdom in turn exposes bourgeois values ('the commitment to individual freedom') as viciously incoherent, particularly in the case of women, who are at once sensitive souls and squalid commodities. As Eagleton says, 'the pedestal is never far from the pit.' Richardson's distinctive medium – letters – reveals written language itself, however 'private,' as the site of continuous power struggles, and of Clarissa's inevitable alienation (an alienation so total that she spends almost a quarter of the book dying and writing her will).

But what makes Terry Eagleton identify with Clarissa (for he does)? His approach, he says, combines three methods of reading: post-structuralist, feminist and Marxist. However, they can't be said to cohere very convincingly. To take one particular strand of argument – Clarissa in her role as representative of the emergent class shares Richardson's puritan and transparent view of language ('I always speak and write the sincerest dictates of my heart'); her claim to integrity is fetishised, by Lovelace (who is all scepticism, seductive invention and onanistic language games) so that she becomes for him 'the "phallic" woman' whom he must reveal (by rape when seduction fails) as 'castrated'. Lovelace is thus 'a hopeless prisoner of patriarchal false consciousness' and is roundly abused by Eagleton: 'Thoroughly narcissistic and regressive, Lovelace's "rakishness", for all its virile panache, is nothing less than a crippling incapacity for adult sexual relationship.'

It's not just the echo of Leavis that gives one pause here. Surely Clarissa herself in Eagleton's account is also 'a hopeless prisoner of patriarchal false consciousness', father's dutiful daughter? Surely her self-regarding masochism is as grotesque in its way as Lovelace's Don Juanism? Such 'goodness' (witness Sade's *Justine*, a loving tribute to Richardson) looks like a particularly nasty myth for women. Any feminist reading must, one would think, explore its negative tendencies.

However, Eagleton makes remarkably little of it. This is partly, perhaps, to do with his (Marxist) temptation to identify with the rising class regardless (at least they're on the side of history), plus a touch of temperamental puritanism. Thus, while he opens by declaring much of Richardson's ideology 'repellent and irredeemable', a few pages later 'Richardson seems to me pious and high-minded and nothing more'. But there's something odder going on as well: like Clarissa, Eagleton the critic is anxious to keep himself pure from the deconstructive tendencies Lovelace represents – from critical fantasy, from promiscuous and exotic speculation, in short, from fashionable ways of talking about writing as self-pleasuring play, 'virile panache'. Like Clarissa, he's playing the very dangerous game of corresponding with the enemy, speaking his language, while at the same time trying to retain his Marxist virtue.

And so Clarissa for him becomes a go-between 'Writing, like women, marks a frontier between public and private, at once agonised out-pouring and prudent stratagem; or again, women, like letters, are 'that circulating property which cements the system of male dominance'. Eagleton is here describing the currency of eighteenth-century patri-archy, but his own strategies seem embarrassingly similar. I want to feel sisterly solidarity when he says, of Clarissa's dying out of her world, 'In this society death is indeed the only place of inviolable security', or quoting Raymond Williams, 'There was not, as yet, any available or adequate social response' to the woman question. But somehow I can't.

When Clarissa dies to (in this reading) symbolise the future, I find myself full of nasty suspicions: for example, that feminism is here standing in for working-class radicalism, and that that is a sign of a complicated crisis in academic Marxism, which is less about accommod-ating the woman issue than about the stubborn unreachableness of the working class.

To put it crudely, English departments are very short on working-class students, but full of middle-class women in danger of being seduced by Lovelacian theoreticians. *Clarissa*, argues Eagleton, reveals the importance of the old historical imperatives; it is 'a warning that the trading of such imperatives for the short change of eroticism and *écriture* delivers you to the political enemy'. Female virtue, after all, is about self-sacrifice.

Cavalier and roundhead

Essays on Shakespeare

WILLIAM EMPSON

Valuation in Criticism and Other Essays

F. R. LEAVIS

William Empson had nearly finished assembling and revising his uncollected Shakespeare essays when he died two years ago. That he left it so late in the day is doubtless an indication of his reluctance (likeable, but inconvenient) to turn himself into a critical institution.

Also, he had other things to do: there's a new, long essay here, hugely elaborate and entertaining, on the Globe Theatre, down to the last nut, bolt and trapdoor; and there is, according to editor David Pirie, another (not in publishable state) on *A Midsummer Night's Dream*, about the aerodynamic capabilities of fairies, and Shakespeare's heretical thoughts on 'global powers' in general.

A pity, because the anti-Christian argument (as in *Milton's God*) brought out some of his most moving and ingenious criticism. Still, his turn for irreverence is much on display, starting with Shakespeare's narrative poems (the Bard, he argues, is 'deliberately holding back the power to be funny') and going on to celebrate Falstaff. He is an apt tutor for this Prince (Machiavelli would have approved) because obviously Henry V 'had learned to be a good king by his experience of low life'. The famous Falstaffian charm ('presenting himself as a deliciously lovable old bag of guts') shouldn't be sentimentalised, and needn't be: one can begin to explain his popularity by recognising him as 'the scandalous upper class man whose behaviour embarrasses his class and pleases the lower class in his audience'.

Concern for what groundlings might think is an Empson hallmark. The *Hamlet* piece is about making the play's depth plausible in terms of Shakespeare's stage, and the self-conscious 'theatricality' involved in rehashing earlier Revenge plays. Empson is not a debunker, despite his tone (which the blurb understates as 'almost racy'); his favourite targets are scholarly simplifiers and academic disintegrators – 'I suspect the Wimsatt Law, which says a reader must never understand the intention of an author, has been at its fell work . . . a strange collapse of the sense of reality, another failure of nerve has been going on.'

This is à propos of conjectures about the Globe, but it puts a name to another Empson quality – 'nerve'. He has the nerve to pursue meanings to their most sublime and humble extremes at once and still expect them to hang together. Here he is, arguing about the height of the 'upper' stage, using the scene where Cleopatra and her servants pull dying Antony up to her tower:

> They can reach down to a point where the soldiers can reach up; the height is plainly about eight feet . . . the whole point of the scene is that they still behave nobly when reduced to the help of only a few faithful servants. Surely, unless [Cleopatra] . . . were pulling hard, it would be unbearable for her to say 'here's sport indeed'. Either eight feet or very bad taste.

He also has the nerve to make cruel fun of critical puritans. To ex-Scrutineer D. A. Traversi (who describes Perdita in *A Winter's Tale* as 'unprepared to come to terms with certain necessary aspects of mature experience') he retorts: 'The idea that young people can't have stresses and egotisms like middle-aged people is surely too absurd to discuss.' And Harold Brooks's use of the 'weasel-word "romance"' to describe what Bottom misses in Titania is mercilessly diagnosed: 'The real feeling of Brooks, I submit, is: Thank God we don't have to watch a lady actually giving herself to a stinking hairy worker.'

Empson is always surprisingly *practical* – probably the only truly 'Practical Critic' in the motley school that went under that name. He was a Utilitarian – a Benthamite, F. R. Leavis would have said. *Valuation in Criticism*, the new collection of Leavisiana, can't be fairly compared with the Empson volume, since a considerable amount of posthumous Leavis has already come out, and the bottom of the barrel is in sight.

Not that this is entirely a disadvantage. Though essays like the 1963 retrospect on *Scrutiny* assert the familiar heroism of principle, the earliest and latest pieces reveal an altogether less rebarbative Leavis. There's even a 1931 review of Empson ('alive . . . to the exciting strangeness of the present phase of human history') penned before Leavis had discovered that most of that 'exciting strangeness' was alien to him. Though it's perhaps significant that he coyly refused to quote ('I prefer to take no risks') Empson's comparison of analytic critics to two kinds of dog – 'those who merely relieve themselves against the flower of beauty, and those, less continent, who afterwards scratch it up.'

But then, Leavis was set to turn into a third kind – the Big Bow-wow, the Carlylean prophet who denounced 'aestheticisms and Flaubertianism and esotericisms', and demanded that we choose between 'life and electricity', Eliot and Auden, Lawrence and Joyce – and of course Leavis and Empson. You can trace the process: the withdrawal from Eliot's critical influence; the late inclusion of some – not much – of Yeats; the unending endeavour to cleanse the canon.

Perhaps the most engaging and interesting piece is the script of what editor G. Singh calls a 'partly extempore performance' from 1972 – 'Reading out poetry' – where the magisterial style breaks into appealing (in both senses) asides: 'there's no such thing as just "mind," you know'. As he introduces his readings from the poems that most move him, apologising for 'stumbling', you can glimpse what he was after, the speaking voice hidden under the black marks on the page, 'deeply, shyly, even obstinately tacit'. The author for him *breathes* authority. Which is one key to the difference between himself and Empson.

Harold Bloom:
Poetics of Influence

EDITED BY JOHN HOLLANDER

*P*OETICS OF INFLUENCE IS a Harold Bloom compendium, a fat cento of essays and excerpts from the books which charts his revisionary progress over approximately thirty years (a true Gnostic, he erases the dates) from Shelley to the Hebrew Bible, and from battles with the New Criticism to Armageddon ('it is very late in the West') and deconstruction. Bloom, as John Hollander points out in a long and tetchy introduction, is and has ever been an 'antithetical critic', at odds with prevailing orthodoxies, but in the name of an orthodoxy of his own. He describes himself as 'a sect or party of one', and though you're meant, I suppose, to focus on the lonely heroism of 'one', in fact the word 'sect' is here the most telling. Bloom believes in disbelief, and this is what has made him such a distinctive critical presence.

His long line of analytical love-affairs with those writers he likes to call, sword-and-sorcery style, 'the masters of misprision' all turn on the ultimate sectarian paradox: that heresy is a usurpation of authority as well as a defiance of it (which of course in turn generates further paradoxes – for example, that the 'alternative' tradition had better not become orthodoxy, since its very existence is sustained in struggle). *The Anxiety of Influence* was his most effective and eloquent book precisely because he there located a model which celebrated simultaneously impotence and authority – internecine strife within the Milton–Blake–Yeats tradition. The anxiety of influence guarantees originality by making its achievement nearly impossible. Similarly, the Neoplatonic notion that all poets are working on the same great poem attracts him because he can choose to read it as implying that they are all jostling for the same space. Modern poetry only exists because of 'a history of caricature, of distortion, of perverse, wilful revisionism' which supplants the Nobodaddies who got there first: 'What is the Primal scene, for the poet qua poet? It is his Poetic Father's coitus with the Muse. There he was begotten? No – there they failed to beget him. He must be self-begotten . . .' This highly characteristic Bloomian catechism reveals that for him each 'strong' poet or myth-maker also belongs to a sect of one.

Such a writer's position is legitimized not by his provenance (Father, whom he usurps) but by his own literary power, which imposes itself on readers and would-be rewriters. So 'we have become Freud's texts', for example. Though saying 'we' is always, for Bloom, a bit uncomfortable. 'Teachers? Students? Writers Readers? I do not believe that these are separate categories nor do I believe that sex, race, social class can narrow this "we" down . . .' It's easy enough to spot the problems here: I am a 'sect', you belong to a 'coven', they constitute the 'rabblement'. These are, however, problems endemic to his discourse, since by his own logic only the rhetoric of power (and the power of rhetoric) matter. The weak are therefore a much more real enemy than the formidable Originals, because they dilute and sidetrack the great questions of succession and renewal when they promote 'different' histories. So, for example, the following piece of apocalyptic sarcasm is in a sense seriously meant:

> I prophesy . . . that the first true break with literary continuity will be brought about in generations to come, if the burgeoning religion of Liberated Woman spreads from its clusters of enthusiasts to dominate the West. Homer will cease to be the inevitable precursor . . .

Bloom in this mode has proved God's gift to feminists like Sandra Gilbert and Susan Gubar, who are looking for evidence to prove that literary tradition has been exclusively phallocentric, and that undoing it will produce real change. He of course sees his 'strong' poets as the only defence against the disintegration of cultural identity in a welter of unconscious pastiche; a kind of return to nature, where nature equals 'an exhausted phantasmagoria'.

Bloom really comes into his own, though, when he is engaged in more intimate conflict with critical positions closer to home. When one surveys accumulated Bloom, it is striking how very timely the advent of deconstruction was for him. He was provided with precisely the right brand of opposition, a rival doctrine of discontinuity that commanded widespread fear and obedience, and yet denied its own will to power. So he was able to argue, in considerable style, that deconstruction's 'post'-ness ('belatedness' in his vocabulary) was itself part of the influence syndrome, the latest move in the revisionist game; not radically discontinuous at all. And the ground he shared with Derrida's disciples (basically, the notion that writing has been tradition-ally referred back to a God-like author, whose presence ratifies its authority as speech) enabled him to chart his own difference with renewed gusto:

> For the deconstructive critic, a trope is a figure of knowing and not a figure of willing . . . But what can a cognitive or epistemological moment in a poem be? Where the will predominates, even in its own despite, how much is there left to know? how can we speak of degrees of knowing in the blind world of the wish, where the truth is always elsewhere . . . ?

In short, poems lie. Their authors are avatars not of God, but of some Satanic demiurge, who from the beginning gets it wrong on purpose, in order to claim he's self-begotten. And the claim works, if it does, through the reader's own will: 'We believe the lies we want to believe because they help us survive . . . Strong poems strengthen us by teaching us *how to talk to ourselves*, rather than how to talk to others.'

Talking to yourself means cultivating a critical language so hybrid, strange and personalized that it resists assimilation to other people's discourse even when there are grounds for agreement. One of the incidental amusements of this book is the contrast between the early Bloom who jeers at the school of Yeatsian occult enthusiasts, who ask us to believe in a 'neo-platonised and cabbalized Yeats, whom to understand we must first master an august company that ranges from Cornelius Agrippa to Madame Blavatsky', and the later Bloom who derives his terminology from Orphic cults, St Paul, Empedocles, Greek fortune-tellers and Lucretius, not to mention Neo-Platonism and Kab-bala (now dignified with initial caps). At moments one is reminded of the dreamy, interminable battles of science fantasy: 'Poets – strong ones – are truly demonic, and frighten Sphinxes. The Covering Cherub is a demon of continuity; his baleful charm imprisons the present in the past'; 'The clinamen or swerve . . . is the Urizenic equivalent of the errors of recreation made by the Platonic demiurge . . .' Bloom did, of course, write a novel, *The Flight to Lucifer* ('A Gnostic Fantasy'), a few years back, and it is a pity that this compendium doesn't include the odd extract, since that narrative reveals more clearly perhaps than any of the pieces here his contempt for the reality principle. 'Except when he killed,' we are told of the quester Perscors, 'he seemed to be living in a vivid phantasmagoria.' Something similar, at a metaphorical remove of course, is true of Bloom's violence of vocabulary – words constitute a trap woven of other people's meanings, a mere 'facticity'.

The most damning thing he can say about our current demystifiers is that 'Negation also has become a facticity', its figurations fading – or should it be glowing? – into literalness. His dread (the word is melodramatic, but no other seems to fit) of the texts, or events, that 'read us' is profound. Here, you can trace it back to his early insistence that Romantic poetry is 'antinature' poetry, his distaste for 'the cyclic rhythms of a running-down natural world', and his paraphrase of Freud on natural love as 'a picaresque chronicle in which the ever-vulnerable ego stumbles from delusion to frustration, to expire at last (if lucky) in the compromising arms of the ugliest of Muses, the reality-principle'. (You can see from this the attraction of Gnosticism, which holds that the Creation was the Fall since it hid from us our divinity.) Later Bloom switches his attention from nature to culture, so that the contexts of tradition are seen as smothering us with 'brute facticity', 'brute fact', 'brute contingency', but his founding heresy hasn't really changed, only the claustrophobia gets more intense. Perhaps I have over-emphasized the eccentric mythology. There are pieces here on Stevens (the masterly misprision of *Domination of Black*), on Pope, Emerson, Whitman, which are less in-turned. However, the overwhelming impression created by cumulative Bloom is of someone writing himself into a corner where fear (there is a splendid essay full of fellow-feeling on Collins's 'Ode to Fear') generates energy and sets the adrenalin flowing. The antithetical critic needs to write in a context that leaves almost no room for manoeuvre; and he must, ironically enough, invoke it and elaborate its inescapability in order to set up his rhetorical levitation. The most disturbing feature of his arguments is the implication that freedom, the 'strong' individual voice, is a) nearly extinct and b) always saying the same thing. Possibly, if he is right, the second of these 'developments' may be the explanation of the first. But then what is right? Bloom has no answer except – the power to convince. This is what makes him exasperating, his perverse consistency in denying any appeal to consensus or (God forbid) an agreement to differ. But when you think about it, it is also what has made him despite himself a representative figure: our revisionist readings have tended (as Foucault suspected back in the 1960s they might) to remystify authority by exposing its arbitrariness. You couldn't wish for a better incarnation of this dilemma than Harold Bloom.

Oops, a lexical leak

In the Reading Gaol: Postmodernity, Texts and History

VALENTINE CUNNINGHAM

Once upon a time, back in the dawn of deconstruction, before it was called that at all, Roland Barthes attacked the traditional novel, Balzac's baby. Realism was all wrong, and so (he suddenly said, in a moment of euphoric iconoclasm) was our whole way of representing the world and parcelling it up in art-works. 'This operation occurs constantly in the whole of Western art', from the Greeks on, and it's got to stop.

You can derive from this gesture the grand rejection of the co-existence of realism and invention, story and history. From now on, increasingly, 'fiction' for the theorists leaks out of novels and dramas and poems into all forms of text; and texts in turn become reflexive, self-referring, echoes bounced off the walls of the prison-house of language.

It's this prison Valentine Cunningham has in mind in *In the Reading Gaol*, his spirited, funny and heartfelt response to academic criticism's loss of history, 'the world and things and people'. So prestigious and prevalent has become Barthes's kind of grand iconoclastic erasure that only gaps, voids, doubtful mysteries are proper objects of attention for literary intellectuals.

Only those texts that denounce the authority of the writer (via doctrines about the death of the author, etc.) have authority; only self-undermining meanings mean. Cunningham analyses with learning and awesome energy and persistence many of the great deconstructive truisms, and their authors (one of his neater ripostes to Derrida, 'the great guru of the lexical leak', is to turn him into nearly a character), in order to show, first, that traditional stories (Dickens, Hardy, Brontë, Eliot) were always a lot more self-aware and mysterious than critics claim; and second, that modern fiction and criticism have a lot more to do with messy world-stuff than they like to admit.

He does it by a process of reading and argument that's acrobatic, allusive, anecdotal, rigorous and playful by turns – a virtuoso perform-ance of the role of the reader, in fact, which goes a very long way to establish the very freedom theory likes to claim for readers, but (he would say) actually denies them by telling them what they'll find (a fashionable emptiness) in advance.

Punning is one of his favourite games, and in a sense he's saying that the relation between words and the world is just such a kind of coincidence. Things get into texts in unexpected ways for instance (this is a picturesque Cunningham obsession) the Huntley and Palmers bis-cuit factory in Reading (opposite the gaol) and the biscuits made there, and the tins they came in, get into all sorts of places, including Joyce's *Finnegans Wake* (Huntler and Pumar's) and Conrad's *Heart of Darkness*.

I despair of making this sound as convincing as it is: the point is the density of the detail, and the tensile strength of the associations. His title alludes more sombrely to Wilde's discovery of what a mere letter could do 'Misplaced faith in the prison-house of language, the reading gaol, landed Wilde in the Reading Gaol', an early martyr to post-modernism. On Dickens's *Hard Times* he produces a splendid peroration about the factory 'hands' pointing out that Dickens has in mind the hands chopped off in industrial accidents ('potently polemi-cal'), and that the name of the evil Bitzer puns on 'bits o'' people. Can you, like Barthes, he asks, reduce the author to a mere writing hand when you think of this?

There's one major Pun that deserves a capital, as well that is, the cunning and occasionally show-off way in which Cunningham is mimicking the playful procedures of the very postmodernists whose anti-faith he deplores. One can forgive him the showing off, on the grounds that it's almost always amusing and (anyway) demonstrates that he's not merely deploring their difficult and demanding manoeuvres on grounds of lazy 'common sense' or blokish boredom.

However, there's yet more to it, I suspect: a last chapter which takes us back to the interpretation of the Bible implies that he does, after all, share with the authoritarian anti-authoritarians a sense that what's happened to Western culture is a metaphysical disaster except that it happened a lot longer ago. 'In the beginning was deconstruction', so we shouldn't delude ourselves that we live in some post-script world that cuts us off from the great traditions. For my money, the argument from Huntley and Palmer's is more convincing.

The First Bacchante

The Ground Beneath Her Feet

SALMAN RUSHDIE

THE PHILOSOPHER PLOTINUS WAS such a good Idealist that he refused to have a portrait done – why peddle an image of an image? – and argued that the true meaning of the myth of Narcissus was that the poor boy didn't love himself enough. If Narcissus had recognised whose the reflection in the water was, he'd have lived and grown and changed himself, instead of being the helpless subject of a pretty tale of metamorphosis. Salman Rushdie's new novel is full of such Neoplatonic jokes (though this isn't one of them). *The Ground Beneath Her Feet* is vertiginous, perilous, on the edge, because it's all about pushing beyond the author's Other-love, and the techniques he has so far perfected for dissolving 'I' into 'we'. Here he is embracing what his enemies have always called his arrogance. He is taking things further, to that excess whose road leads to the palace of wisdom.

It's a winding road, though, with lots of digressions on the way. This is a novel crammed to bursting with allusions to mythology, particularly the myth of Orpheus and Eurydice, she gone before into the underworld, he trying to win her back with music. They are the hero and heroine of a plot about the history of imaginative life:

> In the beginning was the tribe . . . then for a little while we broke away, we got names and individuality and privacy and big ideas, and that started a wider fracturing . . . and it looks like it's scared us so profoundly . . . that at top speed we're rushing back into our skins and war-paint, Post-Modern into pre-modern, back to the future.

Mythology is the idiom of the times, the language of pre and post-fracture. The novel's immortals, its Orpheus and Eurydice, are idols of the music business: Ormus Cama, whose Parsi father Sir Darius is obsessed by comparative mythology that draws together East and West, and Vina Aspara, half-Greek-American and half-Indian. They are both vessels for the spirit of our age because they are rendered rootless early on by childhood tragedy. That's why people loved Vina, we're told, 'for making herself the exaggerated avatar of their own jumbled selves . . . The girl can't help it, that's what her position came down to.' She's a chimerical mixture of Madonna and (in death) Princess Diana, with other bits added on (a sting in the tail from Germaine Greer); Ormus has a dead twin brother who sings Western hits into his ear long before they burst on the rest of the world – but Ormus can never quite make out the words. When he first hears 'Heartbreak Hotel', which he's been humming for more than two years, he's furious with the American 'thief' of his inspiration, and as time goes on his private music of the spheres (78 rpm) teases him more and more cruelly: 'The ganga, my friend, is growing in the tin' has been haunting him, and 'sure enough . . . one thousand and one nights later, "Blowin' in the Wind" hit the airwaves.'

Ormus and Vina live in a world that's part India, part America, where the processes of mythification are far enough advanced to canon-ise 'science fiction by Kilgore Trout . . . The poetry of John Shade . . . The one and only *Don Quixote* by the immortal Pierre Menard'. It's a bit reminiscent of the hybrid Russian-American world Nabokov invented for *Ada*. Here, John Kennedy wasn't shot in Dallas but years later, along with his President-brother Bobby, by a magically bouncing Palestinian bullet, and the British Labour Government sent troops to Vietnam (which is called Indochina). Gradually the game of getting it just wrong reveals itself as a way of satirising the contradiction and double-vision we (ordinarily) take for granted. When Ormus finally makes it to America (you're an American, says Vina, you always were), 'It is evident from the daily newspapers that the world beyond the frontiers of the United States (except for Indochina) has practically ceased to exist. The rest of the planet is perceived as essentially fictional.'

And for that matter, 'a kind of India happens everywhere, that's the truth too . . . There are beggars now on London streets.' Ormus and Vina's double act – a rock opera on stage, a soap opera off – suits this brave new world.

By comparison with the state of chronic, euphoric uncertainty ('The uncertainty of the modern. The ground shivers, and we shake') the India Ormus grew up in was marvellously real and solid. Bombay seemed the capital city of hybridity: 'Good communal relations and good solid ground we boasted. No fault lines under our town.' But that diversity, too, has proved an illusion, has been earthquaked and developed and divided. Rushdie's tone about all this is a strange mixture of regret and revelation. Can it be that one's very image of rootlessness was a secret refuge from change? An imaginary homeland? Apparently so. Having left Bombay behind, you have to leave the displaced person who measured himself against it too. Time to change. In earlier Rushdie novels Ormus would have been the book's 'medium', the very type of the writer: 'There are too many people inside Ormus, a whole band is gathered within his frontiers, playing different instruments, creating different music, and he hasn't yet discovered how to bring them under control.' But here Ormus, although certainly a genius, is at the same time doomed to mythic finality. We're moving on, taking leave of 'impure old Bombay' for the nth time, but in a new spirit: 'I am writing here about the end of something . . . I am trying to say goodbye, goodbye again.' And this 'I' doesn't belong to Ormus himself, but to the novel's narrator, who is a new kind of character for Rushdie, not the spokesperson for all the 'others', but a more ordinary – and thus, in this context, extraordinary – 'I'.

He is called Rai, and he's a photographer, the only child of loving, hopeful, sceptical, humorous parents whose break-up symbolises the failure of Bombay to resist the fissile pressures of the age. And he's the book's Narcissus, the one who discovers the uses of mirrors, and speaks in an aphoristic style that marks him out as the ironic survivor, who chronicles the others' more (or less) than human fates. 'As we retreat from religion . . . there are bound to be withdrawal symptoms,' he remarks early on. And he is sometimes given an elevated, archaic-

sounding poetry to speak, like this: 'Among the great struggles of man
. . . there is also this mighty conflict between the fantasy of Home and
the fantasy of Away, the dream of roots and the miracle of the journey.'
But he's also allowed some splendidly vituperative lines, as in his attack
on the misuses of the word 'culture' as a weapon. What is it but a
smear of bacilli on a slide? 'Like slaves voting for slavery or brains for
lobotomy, we kneel down before the god of all moronic micro-organisms
and pray to be homogenised or killed or engineered.' Rai is not 'objective', not above or outside the world of 'mythologisation, regurgitation,
falsification and denigration'. He is Ormus's adoring friend, and Vina's
besotted secret lover. And before he follows them to England and
America, he goes on an assignment in rural India that pays lavish
tribute to the dream of roots: 'The size of the countryside, its stark
unsentimental lines, its obduracy: these things did me good . . . Politics
painted on passing walls. Tea stalls, monkeys, camels, performing bears
on a leash. A man who pressed your trousers while you waited. Ochre
smoke from factory chimneys. Accidents. *Bed On Roof Rs 2/=*. Prostitutes. The omnipresence of gods.' Word-play and rhyme (walls and
stalls, ochre smoke) are everywhere. And the whole adventure is based
on a kind of pun: Rai is being sent to expose a monster fraud – the Great
Goat Scam – which turns to tragedy, a word based on the Greek for
'goat-song'. The country is part of the con-trick. The moral Rai draws
from his excursion is that far from being 'solid, immutable, tangible',
reality is ever-shifting: 'Where the plates of different realities met, there
were shudders and rifts. Chasms opened. A man could lose his life.'
This seismic imagery is his, and the book's, most important metaphor
for the universality of change, and one of the title's main meanings.
Both Ormus and Rai adore Vina, but the ground beneath her feet opens
up and swallows her. And then Ormus goes after her. They are eaten
up by the violent mythologies of the times, myths they themselves fed.

Rai lives to tell their tale, and to put the case for imagination as
opposed to vision. 'The god of the imagination,' he declares, 'is the
imagination. The law of the imagination is whatever works.' The novel
is, in the old sense, a Defence of Poetry – like Sir Philip Sidney's in
the Renaissance, and Shelley's in the early 19th century. And like theirs,

it is premised on fiction's paradoxical truth. In the first book he published after the fatwa, *Haroun and the Sea of Stories*, Rushdie echoed
Sidney's famous riposte to those who accused the poets of being liars.
Those who purport to tell the truth (historians, for instance) can hardly
avoid getting it wrong, Sidney said, whereas the poet 'nothing affirmeth
and therefore never lieth' – he barefacedly makes it up as he goes
along. Rushdie's version went like this: 'Nobody ever believed anything
a politician said, even though they pretended as hard as they could
that they were telling the truth ... But everyone had complete faith
in Rashid, because he always admitted that everything he told them
was completely untrue and made up out of his own head.' It's often
said (of both Sidney and Rushdie) that this means fiction is a form of
play, fabulation for its own sake. But when Sidney goes on to tell us
that one of his favourite 'poems' is More's *Utopia*, it's clear that for
him fictions have designs on us, and that their modesty in the matter
of literal truth is more than made up for by their speculative ambitions.
Shelley's *Defence* makes the same point when it ends grandly by calling
poets 'the unacknowledged legislators of the world'. Rai echoes these
unapologetic defenders of poetry when he says: 'in our hearts we believe –
we know – that our images are capable of being the equals of their
subject. Our creations can go the distance with Creation; more than
that, our imagining – our imagemaking – is an indispensable part of
the great work of *making real.*'

But unlike Rai, Orpheus–Ormus and Vina–Eurydice are mystics of a
last-days sort, they mistake the meaning of their own performance,
particularly Vina, 'who took books by Mary Daly and Enid Blyton with
her when she went on tour', who believes in pretty well anything that's
on offer, and who loves America because

> You get to be an American just by wanting ... However you get through
> your day in New York, then that's a New York kind of day, and if
> you're a Bombay singer singing the Bombay bop or a voodoo cab driver
> with zombies on the brain, or a bomber from Montana or an Islamist
> beardo from Queens, then whatever's going through your head, then
> that's a New York day.

Vina is portrayed as irresistible, absurd and ultimately dangerous. Forget Eurydice, Vina is 'the first bacchante', a New Age primitivist, she'll be the death of her husband Orpheus. Professor Vina, as Rai calls her, can improvise a monologue on almost any topic, and in the end her rhetoric leads to a return to tribal consciousness, 'the battle lines, the corrals, the stockades, the pales . . . the junk, the booze, the fifty-year-old ten-year-olds, the blood dimm'd tide, the slouching towards Bethlehem . . . the dead, the dead'. It's his word against hers, against theirs. He draws a difficult distinction between myths and fictions, rather as Frank Kermode did in *The Sense of an Ending*. A myth you act out, a fiction you believe in knowing it to be a fiction. Kermode liked to quote Wallace Stevens, the aphoristic Stevens of *Opus Posthumous*, and Rushdie's Rai sounds rather like Stevens too – 'our love of metaphor is pre-religious . . . Religion came and imprisoned the angels in aspic.' Or again: 'When we stop believing in the gods we can start believing in their stories . . . the willing, disbelieving belief of the reader in the well-told tale.'

It's clear – this is why *The Ground beneath Her Feet* is such a strange and disorienting book – that belief and unbelief are in our era twins, according to this narrator and his author. The writing confounds seduction and scepticism. 'In a time of constant transformation, beatitude is the joy that comes with belief, with certainty,' and it's hard to resist. 'These are not secular times.' Once a writer like Apuleius, in *The Golden Ass*, could make 'an easy separation between the realms of fancy and of fact', but a writer who wants to follow in his jokey, mock-magical footsteps now will have a harder time. Presumably this is why Rai loves Vina despite seeing through her, he can't quite bear to draw the line. And Ormus he lets go with huge reluctance: 'He was a musical sorcerer whose melodies could make the city streets begin to dance and high buildings sway to their rhythm, a golden troubadour the jouncy poetry of whose lyrics could unlock the very gates of Hell.' This Orphic power faces both ways, towards the illusionist magic of performance and the bad faith of faith. Early on in the novel, Rai quotes from the libretto for Gluck's *Orpheus*, which gives the story a happy ending – 'E quel sospetto/Che il cor tormenta/Al fin diventa/Felicità' and explains that 'the tormented heart doesn't just find happiness, okay: it *becomes happiness*.' But he's mistranslating, I think. It's the 'sospetto' that tortures the heart that turns to happiness. His version reveals his eagerness for a miracle. Still, it's a trick a lot of Orphic lyrics pull – like the one from the play of *Henry VIII* that used to be attributed to Shakespeare, where the first two lines make Orpheus into a god ('Orpheus with his lute made trees/And the mountain tops that freeze') and the third demotes him, by completing the grammar: 'Bow themselves when he did sing.' A little exercise in illusion – it doesn't take all the artist's powers away, just makes them more like conjuring tricks.

Before he turns into a mythic hero, Ormus thinks that 'the solutions to the problems of art are always technical. Meaning is technical. So is heart.' The novel bears out this conviction, not least in the way its structure defies the climactic-apocalyptic mode. It starts with an ending, its middle is made up of beginnings (some of them false) and the ending finds Rai in the middle of his life, with a ready-made family. The characterisation, too, with even the three main figures in unstable focus, sometimes hyper-real, sometimes near-transparent emblems and allegories, is designed for 'disbelieving belief'. The 'great work of *making real*' – ironically enough – eats away at realism. Some while back, the (real-life) Indian-American literary theorist Gayatri Spivak, writing on *The Satanic Verses*, pointed out how effectively Rushdie incarnated contemporary ideas of anti-authoritarian storytelling – 'the writer-as-performer'. Even so, she went on to say, 'fabricating decentred subjects as the sign of the times is not necessarily these times decentring the subject'. In *The Ground beneath Her Feet* he is saying: yes it is, or can be, you can be a fictionist and a deconstructionist at once, and make the novel an 'anatomy'. Having become himself a representative figure – the emblem of literature's freedoms – he is turning the role inside out, calling his own technique into question, finding a new style for uncertainty, saying goodbye again. The effect is exhilarating, hard-to-take, heterodox, critical-creative with the stress on the critical: a fable for now.

A Simpler, More Physical Kind of Empathy

South of the Border, West of the Sun

HARUKI MURAKAMI, TRANSLATED BY PHILIP GABRIEL

The Wind-Up Bird Chronicle

HARUKI MURAKAMI, TRANSLATED BY JAY RUBIN

TALKING TO JAY MCINERNEY in 1992, the year *South of the Border, West of the Sun* was published in Japanese, Haruki Murakami said that he wasn't so much an international writer, as a non-national writer: 'You might call it the Japanese nature that remains only after you have thrown out, one after another, all those parts that are altogether too "Japanese". That is what I really want to express.' His pleasure in jettisoning the picturesque and traditional signs of 'roots' is of a piece with the fact that he was a fan of the work of Raymond Carver, and became his Japanese translator. *South of the Border* is a minimalist's novel. A 1984 interview with Carver is commemorated in a Carver poem:

> We sipped tea, politely musing
> on possible reasons for the success
> of my books in your country. Slipped
> into talk of pain and humiliation
> you find occurring and reoccurring
> in my stories. And that element
> of sheer chance. How all this translates
> in terms of sales.

Murakami would have appreciated the last gesture that switches from chance as a fictional device to the cultural lottery of late capitalism – it's a connection his own authorial avatars often make. They are determinedly not traditionalists: on the other hand, they are witnesses to the defeat of the radical movements of the Sixties and Seventies, and live in the real world of paradoxically empty freedom, mobility and disaffection. 'It's the way of the world,' says the cool narrator of *Dance Dance Dance*, 'philosophy starting to look more and more like business administration . . . things were a lot simpler in 1969. All you had to do was throw rocks at the police. But with today's sophistication, who's in a position to throw rocks? . . . You throw a rock and it'll come right back at you.' Murakami said to McInerney that he was now 'after something Japanese':

> I would like to write about Japanese society from the outside. I think that is what will increasingly define my identity as writer. By the way, do you know there is no equivalent in Japanese for the word 'identity'. That's why when we want to talk about identity, we have to use the English word.

However, as the Carver poem suggests, pain and humiliation are eminently translatable into Japanese, and vice versa, and they occur and reoccur in Murakami's fiction, too.

Western readers wouldn't necessarily have known this until the last couple of years, however, because his own identity was a pretty slippery one, and the first of his novels to be translated were parodic and playful, and crammed with distracting trophies of his love-affair with American popular culture: *A Wild Sheep Chase* (1982, translated 1989), *Hardboiled Wonderland and the End of the World* (1985, translated 1991). These books, together with *Dance Dance Dance* (1988, translated 1994), formed a loose trilogy of mixed-genre, jokey metafictions, texts that read very much as he said he wrote them, making it all up as he went along, saluting American detective fiction, science fiction and demotic fantasy (Vonnegut, Brautigan), as well as pop music and jazz and movies, and using brand names and other cultural imports as 'props' (in the theatrical sense: he did his degree in drama). In between, in 1987, he'd published *Norwegian Wood*, which sold two million copies in Japan. These books were obviously fun, and eerily recognisable (someone wittily rechristened the first 'The Big Sheep'). For the young Murakami, who used to like to tell people that his vocation as a novelist came to him out of the blue while he was watching a baseball game, the United States had been what Roland Barthes called Japan, back in 1970, an 'empire of signs', a place where signifiers floated loose from their signifieds. He says that his America was a virtual reality, he pieced it together in his head in Kobe, where the second-hand bookshops were full of American fiction traded in by the US Navy. His parents were teachers of Japanese literature, and he was an only child, both things that inspired him to levitate in his head into this alternative, charmingly fairy-tale place.

By the time he was having his conversation with McInerney, however, he was living in the States. He left Japan in 1986, when he was 37, for almost ten years, living first in Greece and Italy, then in Princeton and Boston. In 1996 he dryly summed up the round trip: 'In Japan I wanted personal independence. I wanted to be free. In America, I felt free. But Americans take individual independence for granted.' He could not, and the novel of his imaginative return, *The Wind-Up Bird Chronicle* (1994–95, translated 1997), which he researched in the library at Princeton, puts Japanese history – the history of the Sino-Japanese war, and of the Manchurian front in World War Two – back into the picture in inset stories. Violence, he told the *New Yorker*, which printed some peculiarly nasty episodes from the book, is 'the key to Japan': 'The most important thing is to face our history.' So these last two translated books belong, the one in minimalist style, the other in the style of what Patricia Waugh calls 'historiographic metafiction' (an appropriately baggy label for a sprawling sub-genre), to the literature of 'pain and humiliation'.

The first-person narrator of *South of the Border, West of the Sun* is in the middle of a good life: a happy marriage, with two small daughters he loves, and lots of 'props'. 'And here I was . . . savouring Schubert's *Winterreise* as I lounged in my BMW, waiting for the lights to change at a crossroads in ritzy Aoyama. I was *living someone else's life, not my own*.' He's the typical Murakami protagonist, a man who's *too* typical, almost abnormally ordinary, with just the odd quirk in his fate (being an only child in a generation where that isn't yet usual) that helps tip his lack of conviction over into existential crisis. Hajime (his name means 'Beginning': he was born in the first week of the first month of the first year of the second half of the 20th century, 4 January 1951) manages a bar, as his author did between 1974 and 1982, before his first literary successes turned him into a full-time writer. But this is not – or not directly – a portrait of the artist. Hajime has invested his imagination and his leftover idealism in his personal life, and now his sense of creeping unreality focuses on loves he lost in childhood and adolescence, before he turned into this plausible adult. Watching his own children grow, he feels his apartness – the only child – turning into mere mulch in a family line, 'as if a tree were growing inside my body, laying down roots, spreading its branches, pushing down on my organs'. And it's at this moment of crisis that Shimamoto, his lost best friend from childhood, walks into his fashionable bar, and reawakens a passionate conviction of affinity he has never quite recaptured since, not even with Yukiko, the wife who rescued him from pointless drifting, and whom he loves.

Shimamoto, too, was an only child, and walked with a limp back when they were 12, a precocious but infinitely receptive companion who mirrored and shared his loneliness. 'She gazed at me gently as I talked ... It was as if ... she were gently peeling back, one after another, the layers that covered a person's heart, a very sensual feeling. Her lips moved ever so slightly with each change in her expression.' Murakami lends his character Hajime a hesitant, lyrical eloquence that translates emotions into body-language, and makes this exchange as erotic as the later description of the long-delayed consummation of their desire for each other. In a sense that's the point, that there was a completeness about this childhood intimacy which was better than anything that came after. But as a result Shimamoto is for him a fatal woman, a kind of Lamia even, when she reappears – an emissary from the land of unlived lives, paths not taken. For here there's no middle way, it's total possession or nothing, 'her eyes told me she was already given up to death'; re-meeting and re-losing her, Hajime painfully lays bare to himself his own heartless character.

It's a plot about spooky empathy *v.* human sympathy. And it's

Hajime's offence against the latter that Shimamoto in a sense avenges, though she knew nothing about it – his unfaithfulness to his second love, Izumi, his high-school girlfriend: 'Izumi could never understand my dream. She had her own dreams, a vision of a far different place, a world unlike my own.' He discovered himself as a person who could do evil in the damage he did to her in pursuit of his personal castle in the air, and is doing now to his wife. From one angle – the angle of 'one', in fact – the book is a tale of romantic agony; from another, it's about renouncing the charm of the eternal return, rediscovering the reality of the order that says there's a beginning, a middle and an end. 'No one will weave dreams for me – it is my turn to weave dreams for others . . . If my own life is to have any meaning at all, that is what I have to do.' And here there is a hint of aesthetic life-writing, an apologia for the artist. The parting image ('Rain softly falling on a vast sea, with no one there to see it') has more in common with Joyce's 'The Dead' than with Carver's deliberate, prosaic poverty of spirit, even though in theory it's exorcising the specialness of 'I', making our hero just another character.

In *The Wind-Up Bird Chronicle* a sinister, minor Mephistopheles with a walk-on part, a cabaret performer, wakes up his inattentive audience with a didactic set-piece on the paradoxes of empathy:

He set his guitar on the floor and, from the guitar case, took a single candle . . . 'As you are well aware,' the man continued, his voice soft but penetrating, 'in the course of life we experience many kinds of pain. Pains of the body and pains of the heart . . . People say that only they themselves can understand the pain they are feeling. But is this true? If, before our own eyes, we see someone who is truly suffering, we do sometimes feel his suffering as our own. This is the power of empathy . . . The reason people sing songs for other people is because they want to have the power to arouse empathy . . . tonight, as a kind of experiment I want you to experience a simpler, more physical kind of empathy . . .' He held his hand over the lighted candle . . . Someone in the audience made a sound like a sigh or a moan. You could see the tip of the flame burning the man's palm. You could almost hear the sizzle of the flesh . . . Everyone . . . watched in frozen horror.

And then he clasps his hands together, produces a thin red scarf from between them, and reveals the whole thing as an illusion. Rapturous applause, he's a marvellous conjuror, he ought to be on TV, they say, but while they're savouring their relief he has disappeared. The novel itself, all six hundred-odd pages of it, pulls this kind of trick again and again, in revisiting horrors and atrocities from the last war – most memorably and terribly in the inset stories told by Lieutenant Mamiya, who describes watching a Japanese agent being flayed alive on the orders of a Russian, and the experiences, told by his daughter, of a vet who saw zoo animals being shot to bits by Japanese soldiers, and recaptured Chinese prisoners being bayoneted, and brained with a baseball bat.

These narratives are juxtaposed with the present-day quest of Toru Okada, another 'ordinary' Murakami narrator with a mid-life crisis, for his wife Kumiko, who has been having an affair with another man, has now left him for what turn out to be much more mysterious and deep-rooted reasons. Okada, coming unstuck in his own life, at a loose end, becomes the audience for other people's stories. He can't do empathy, it turns out – but that's not necessarily a bad thing. Instead, he searches his own psyche, and his personal experience, for traces and echoes of the kind of violence that came out of the closet in the war. Talking to Ian Buruma in the *New Yorker*, Murakami said that when he was a boy he heard his father (whom he doesn't get on with) reveal something terrible about his experience as a soldier in China, but he couldn't remember later what it was: 'I don't want to know the facts. I'm only interested in the effect my blocked memory has on my imagination.' The novel shows what he seems to have meant: Okada does his researches by exploring the alley to nowhere at the back of his house, and climbing down into the implausibly deep dry well in the back garden of an empty house where a retired general who committed suicide once lived. Alongside the sensation of empathy suggested by realistic, illusionist writing, Murakami sets a kind of translation or internal re-creation of the violence and pain of the past. It must be 'there' somewhere in one's character, his character Toru Okada reasons, as he turns into a psychic warrior, and learns to walk through walls.

Vertigo and disorientation overtake him, 'a throbbing deep in my head ... a lump of string in the pit of my stomach', and intensify to the point where they start to resemble skinnings and stabbings of the self. Like Marguerite Duras in *La Douleur*, which she claimed was a wartime journal she found in a drawer, but had no memory of writing, Murakami lays claim to a share in others' crimes against humanity. His character Okada becomes a kind of clairvoyant conscript, not only suffering the shame of rejection and powerlessness, but wielding a fatal virtual baseball bat against his enemies.

Chief among these is his brother-in-law Noboru Wataya, a Post-Modern economics guru turned politician, who is described with real dislike – 'Consistency and an established worldview were excess baggage in the intellectual mobile warfare that flared up in the mass media's tiny time-segments.' The novel may be sceptical about the good faith of realist writing, but it's also nauseated by Wataya's kind, cultural vampires, the new undead. Maintaining this balancing act doesn't subdue its exuberance: it has the usual metafictional company – the truanting teenage sidekick, the prostitute of the mind, the sweating, chain-smoking gangster go-between, the missing cat, even the sheep. The teenager, May, provides a handy description of the formal rules of this writing: 'So then one disconnected thing led to another disconnected thing, and that's how all kinds of stuff happened.' There's even some nice 'hardboiled' pastiche for old time's sake: 'She dropped the cigarette on the ground as if testing gravity conditions for the day.'

So what does Murakami's return to a Japanese 'identity', and facing up to history amount to? It's edged around with irony, certainly, and scrupulously disconnected and rootless in its structure. At the same time, Okada is much closer to being a hero than earlier protagonists. May, whose disaffection and youth give her a special authority in this upside-down world, says to him: 'I can't help feeling that you are fighting for me ... that, in a way, you are probably fighting for a lot of other people at the same time you're fighting for Kumiko.' But it's perhaps too easy from the outside to seize on signs of representative Japaneseness, especially when they come in the form of 'reverse anthropology', returning from foreign parts to look at your own culture with an estranged eye, as so many Western writers have done since the war. How do Japanese readers react to his return home? Do they empathise, or do they see him as still the international writer? Is his history theirs? In *South of the Border, West of the Sun* Hajime wonders whether the real purpose of inventing alternative realities, fictions, castles in the air, afterlives in the underground (Murakami's own jazz bar was in a cellar), is to sustain by contrast the reality of here and now. The danger is, he muses, that then you need a third reality to serve as grounding, and so on and on. Nonetheless, it's only by maintaining that chain that we keep the uncertain world of memory and sensation in business. This has the air of an *apologia pro vita sua* as a Post-Modern success, but it saves the conjuring tricks, too. The story of Murakami's oeuvre is itself fascinating, a great contemporary triumph of translation, in more senses than one.

VI

Italy

Fighting Fascists in bed

ALITALIA AIR HOSTESSES RUN a feminist collective. So do 14-year-old girls in half the schools in Rome. Since 1970, Italian feminism has emerged from nowhere to become a seething, vociferous movement that puts down new local roots each week, and can muster mass rallies in the big cities at impressively short notice (10,000 in six hours last year in support of Claudia Caputi, who brought a charge of rape against a gang of youths, who raped her again for bringing the charge).

The first demonstration for free abortion on demand in 1971 involved ten rather jokily desperate people, six women and four men, picketing a hospital; by December 1975, 30,000 (women) were on the march. And last month parliament, anxious to avoid a traumatic referendum, passed an abortion law which, though it still requires 'reasons', is more liberal than the British one.

Abortion, of course, is the symbolic issue, the tip of a Titanic-sized iceberg of other demands, from wages for housework to free contraception, crèches to control of cottage industries. On the face of it, Italian women seem to have condensed the routine 150 years of slow struggle into seven.

The lack of a substantial history does have some advantages. 'Siamo realiste, vogliamo l'impossibile' ('We're realists, we want the impossible'), as one of the more philosophical graffiti puts it: there's no tradition of gradual amelioration to encourage compromise. The arguments for liberation arrived in a lump, ready-packaged, in the aftermath of the 'events' of 1968, and they seem to have taken root so effectively for two main reasons. First, because a lot of women were used to thinking politically (though not about themselves), and second, because of the archaic – almost operatic – nature of male and female roles in the home.

Most active feminists are naturally of the Left, and one of their earliest rallying points was the collective 'discovery' that their (Communist or Socialist) men might fight against the oppressor in public, but turned into bosses, managers, the leisured class, in private: 'Comrades in the piazza, Fascists in bed.'

A typical true life confession in the feminist broadsheets comes from the girl who finds she's pregnant, and tells her boyfriend: 'All his fine ideas about solidarity and social justice suddenly evaporated when I told him, because he left me straight away.' In this society, the sex struggle cuts across the class struggle with a particularly sharp and ragged edge, and while it's true that plentiful translations of *The Hite Report* or *Fear of Flying* in the bookshops don't necessarily signify much (the average Italian reads only half a book a year anyway), the number of small groups and collectives does. A lot of the ideas and slogans are imported wholesale, but the anger is native.

One immediately visible result is that old and new life-styles clash daily, in small matters as well as large. In a liberated household in Florence, for example, Joanna's boyfriend cooked the lunch (a bit self-consciously, but in a practised manner) while she and I talked; however, the first course he didn't cook – that was minestrone, lovingly brewed and sent over by his mother from across the road, because she was afraid that he didn't get enough to eat.

The power of the image of a white wedding, and the myth of the sanctity of motherhood (upheld, according to the women's estimates, by a million clandestine abortions a year) are notorious, but none the less real for all that. And as every female tourist knows, there's nowhere you can get sicker, faster, of being a sex-object. Once, Italian women used to offer sour advice on how not to get molested (wear a headscarf if you're blonde, carry a shopping bag, don't catch anyone's eye, scurry modestly from A to B without loitering); now, they're learning to be tourists, aliens, in their own country.

According to Joanna, young girls at last are starting to dress unself-consciously (messy hair, flat shoes, 'almost English or American') and to behave as though they were not 'on stage', part of the line-up auditioning for marriage or seduction. They still are, though: rape is on the increase, not just because it's reported more, but also because 'liberated' manners (i.e., what most women in Northern Europe would regard as normal behaviour) are taken as provocation.

You have to allow this fact of Italian life its full weight in order to understand why women's collectives and cooperatives have sprung up so seemingly magically. There's safety in numbers, and once Italian women do manage to transcend the mutual jealousy and suspicion which come of defining themselves exclusively in relation to men, the time-honoured separation of sex roles makes it much easier for them to think in sexist terms on their own account. 'Autogestione' (self-government) and 'autocoscienza' (consciousness-raising, or more accurately, consciousness of self) have flourished, both in theory and in practice, though you won't find them in the dictionaries.

Study groups extract the goodness from economics, psychoanalysis, anthropology and so on; neighbourhood centres form pressure groups to re-educate the local social services (maternity units, schools, police), and where – as with abortion – the services are an illegal racket, they've tried to fix up alternative facilities. They also provide an untidy but effective information network, through which the mass campaigns are orchestrated because there is no one national organisation.

The absence of centralised organisation is something women boast of as a sign of liberation from male habits of hierarchical, totalitarian thinking, and something they bemoan as an administrative weakness. It certainly produces a ferment of activities and aims that's nearly impossible to map; the abortion issue came so much to the fore because it answered the need for a common cause, as well as the need (which is deeply felt) for taking charge of one's own body. In order to by-pass the law, and keep each other informed, the movements developed considerable expertise and resources. Package abortion trips to London were worked out down to the last detail, with deliberate and reassuring neutrality – don't take a taxi from Gatwick, because it's too expensive;

if you want the coil fitted, that'll be a £2 surcharge; and so on. This advice appeared in *EFFE*, a monthly magazine written and (since '75) produced by women in Rome. I talked to one of the editorial cooperative, Daniela, and she acknowledged that now the abortion problem is partly solved, *EFFE* is trying rather hard to keep the momentum going by, for instance, anticipating the backlash from the Catholic 'Movement for Life', who are already collecting signatures for a referendum to repeal the new law. 'You know how they do it?' she said. 'My maid told me that the priest was watching as she came out of mass, to see if she signed. She's had three abortions, but of course she had to sign.' Like a lot of Catholic women, the maid obviously treats her sex life as none of the Church's business.

The Casa delle Donne is an enormous palace in Rome where any number of radical splinter groups squat, and where I thought I might encounter some militant scorn of my own lukewarmness. The women occupied it two years ago, and it once housed Beatrice Cenci. 'Forbidden to Men' is the legend on the door, and I found myself, much to my own surprise, inwardly cheering.

Perhaps that feeling conditioned my view of the people I'd come to see, a collective that had just brought out a new, exceedingly grass-roots and exceedingly ill-produced newspaper called 'Quotidiano Donna'. Anyway, they seemed both wise and likeable, though their views were frighteningly simple and rigidly held: that the 'historical feminists' of the 1968 generation were not feminists at all, but emancipated women who worked like men; that feminist women worked collectively, without competition or aggression; that the study-groups had produced a technical jargon that cut them off from ordinary women; that professionalism in general was suspect.

Their obvious pleasure in each others' company was the only thing that made any of this plausible – a pleasure, interestingly, that had none of the lesbian edge that would certainly have been there if they'd been English or American. For all their stress on separate development, they were all married, just about.

The particular 'generation' they belong to has nothing to do with age; it's measured from the time, two or three years ago, when feminism acquired mass support, and it includes middle-aged housewives and schoolgirls like Silvia, who simply wandered in. She was 16, she said, and had belonged to a group at school for two years; the older girls tried to influence them against feminism, but failed. She was slight and scruffy, and looked younger than she was, and she spoke in a husky Roman accent, at a pace that made everything she said sound like a lesson she'd learned by heart. Her mother's generation were convinced that nature made them for a traditional role, but they were conditioned to think so, because it was convenient for the men. At home she sometimes refused to do housework to force her brother, her father and her grandfather to pull their weight, but of course they didn't, so her mother ended up doing everything, which meant that she herself was exploiting her mother too.

She feared quarrels between the various strands of the feminist movement because disagreement would destroy all they believed in.

Silvia, with her militancy and her insecurity, represents a problem that the 'historical feminists' are all too aware of. They haven't succeeded in transmitting their stress on consciousness-raising to this new generation. Biancamaria Frabotta, a writer and academic, and Serena Rossetti, a journalist on *L'Espresso*, both told me that the present mass support was misleading, and that for all their stress on working as women, with women, the new generation lacked the necessary core of self-knowledge to keep male politics at bay, especially given the multiple crises of Italian economic and political life which would encourage them to make common cause with the men. They themselves are becoming more inward, less part of the public battles. Both in their different ways seemed to be shoring up personal defences against the day when the feminism they believed in would wither away as rapidly as it grew. Mass support, for them, has come too fast and at a bad time. They may be right, but for all their pessimism, a lot has been achieved.

Displaced persons

Flight from Torregreca: Strangers and Pilgrims

ANN CORNELISEN

Ann Cornelisen didn't invent 'Torregreca'. It exists (though that is not its name), a town in Lucania, the poorest and least picturesque region of southern Italy, parched in summer, sodden and freezing in winter; a foggy town like 'something out of a vicious fairy tale' as she says, that has taken possession of her imagination, and made of her its fascinated, saddened chronicler.

Such a town's life is secret, obscure, almost out of reach. Centuries of indifference on the outside, and of illiteracy and grinding poverty within, have given its people a settled habit of suspicion. When Ms Cornelisen first went there as a social worker for Save the Children just over 20 years ago, she thought she'd never gain enough of people's confidence to function at all. But she did, and as they talked to her about their lives, her social worker's mission became overlaid with another, more subtle task – to give these people so long inarticulate a voice, to describe their experience, and who they are.

Ironically it's an English voice, or rather an American one, but then Italian would hardly be more appropriate, since the Torresi speak an unwritten dialect of their own. What is special about her documentary style, indeed, is that she knows and acknowledges the distance she's trying to bridge, the sheer otherness of her characters, however intimate their revelations.

Torregreca (1969, now reissued) and *Women of the Shadows* four years ago portrayed a starved medieval culture where the only evidences of the twentieth century were a faltering electricity supply and a few treasured shards of formica, where black-shawled women old at 30 beat their washing on the stones. Now, in *Flight from Torregreca*, she describes the bizarre 1970s 'miracle' that has filled the town's streets with traffic jams and its bleak houses with furniture, without giving its people any access to the identity, the personal substance, they yearn for. Because Torregreca has become a ghost town for all but one month of the year: the Torresi have become migrants, 'guest-workers' on the building sites and in the factories and warehouses of northern Italy, Switzerland, West Germany. They are, if anything, more 'lost,' more invisible than ever. Official statistics minimise the migration (so that politicians can claim they still have a population to administer); for their 'hosts' they have almost no civil existence. While acquiring their 'consumer durables' they are actually becoming nomads – swapping one archaic style of life for another.

There is no concealing the sadness of it all, and Ann Cornelisen doesn't try: Gaetano, for instance, surrounded with 'things,' feeding beer to his ulcer, with two children born in Germany who refuse to speak Italian, or understand it, or him. She listens, dreading that 'this man, not yet 50, would tell me again what he saw as his only reward, his only reasonable hope – that he might "last" until he had his pension and could go home to Torregreca . . .' Or Lucetta and Paolo, living still in squalor, converting their hard-earned marks into lire that are 'quietly inflating, evaporating where the emigrants know they are safe – in Torregreca.'

The children struggle in German schools – some even *look* German (they seem to keep their baby blondness, she says, through some curious chemistry of 'climate, diet and unconscious imitation'), but they have little hope of integration. An Italian school supervisor tells a German headmaster, 'They were born in the mud of the *mezzogiorno*, let them die in the mud of Germany'.

And yet – and this is Ann Cornelisen's special gift – she portrays the Torresi as alive, surviving, despite all. She is alert to the stubborn, lying ways in which they preserve their hungers:

They have ignored much that would have been of value . . . bought, gorged on much that was useless. They lie to each other about what they are and what they have ... They want so desperately to live, and they *know* they have not; so far.

She sees signs of life in the strange new vernacular they speak – a mish-mash of southern dialects and building-site German, but none the less, for the first time, a language they can share with other Italians. She marvels at their ersatz splendours – an apartment without windows decked in lace curtains with concealed lighting, a kitchen of *antiqued* formica. Most importantly, she rescues them, by the quality of her attention, from the jargon and statistics surrounding 'social problems'. She is these days, one gathers, something of a displaced person herself, a long-term exile in Italy, and shares more and more her Torresi's sense of strangeness.

Our Lady of the Accident

SILVER HEARTS, DISCARDED LEG irons, crutches, dented helmets, exploded shotguns, bent steering wheels, shreds of shirt – the Madonna of Montenero specialises in accidents, and her sanctuary on the hill above Livorno is hung with the macabre but theoretically cheery debris of lives almost lost, dusty votive offerings that commemorate moments when the routine horrors of life were suspended by the grace of Our Lady. Inarticulate offerings, too – it seems impossible to imagine the donors. Or it would, except that at Montenero there developed a tradition of offering not just objects but paintings. They line the sanctuary's corridors, often six deep, and insist on the graphic reality of what happened, when, and exactly whom it happened to. They were done, almost all, by local craftsmen from 1800 on, and they provide an extraordinary sub-history (life-through-accidents) of Livorno and environs, a bit of Tuscany pictured without glamour for once, miles mentally, if not physically, off the tourist track.

It all started with a painting of a rather different kind. On 15 May, 1345 – when Livorno was a wretched village surrounded by malarial fen – the altar painting of the Madonna from the island of Eubea appeared miraculously at a cross-roads at the foot of Montenero. It was found by a shepherd who, prompted by inspiration, carried it up the hill, until it suddenly became too heavy for him. There, under the brow, on the spot she had chosen for herself, a shrine was set up to the Madonna of Montenero.

She was a very local Madonna from the start, and perhaps partly for that reason her cult was often in danger of decay or suppression.

The curious lay order of the Jesuats took it on until they were suppressed in 1668, then the Teatines until they were expelled from Tuscany in 1783. Then from 1792 the Benedictine monks of Vallombrosa, who warded off Napoleon (1810) and the Italian State (1866), expanded the sanctuary, encouraged evidences of their Lady's special favour – hence the paintings – and finally achieved full recognition in 1947, when Pius XII proclaimed the Madonna of Montenero to be the patron Madonna of the whole of Tuscany.

She's a slightly sulky Byzantine lady holding a serious, tired-looking baby Jesus, but on her feast days, on the lucky medals, postcards and gilt-framed miniatures that the nuns sell, she's crowned and festooned with jewellery. Her image hovers in this exotic guise, sometimes enthroned, in the corner of each votive painting – more the kind of thing, people say, you'd expect to find in the south (with all the dark, dubious stress northern Italians put on that word).

And she must indeed owe something of her anomalous character to the weirdly cosmopolitan nature of Livorno itself: a thriving 'free' port from the late 16th century, crowded with Jews, Muslims, Protestants (it had the first and, for a long time, the only Protestant cemetery in Italy); a seamy emporium (coral, cloth, slaves and, in the early days, 'Leghorn' hats, hides, soap, rags). It can't have been a pious town, and it certainly wasn't beautiful – 'colourful' perhaps, violent too, but lacking a culture of its own. Except for a semi-pagan devotion to its own Madonna on the hill. To her, observed Her Britannic Majesty's Consul in Livorno in 1900, 'the least principled have some attachment'.

Sailors, for instance. The shipwreck from which one escaped with one's life is probably the most insistent single theme among Montenero's 9,000 or so *ex voto* paintings, naturally enough. Many of the 19th century examples are gloomily obscure: a particularly splendid one – evidence of the range of the Madonna's prestige – is an oil-on-glass virtuoso piece contributed by a thankful Polish captain called Luca Mergovitch.

The stylised rents in the sails of his ship conspire threateningly with the curly waves, and the legend underneath in pidgin Italian leaves no doubt of his peril. At five in the morning on 28 December 1859 'latitude 46:48, longitude 5:10 ... hit by a hurricane of wind', but through the intervention of the Blessed Virgin arrived safe at the port of Falmouth on 4 January.

The monks' own favourite among the blue and black seascapes, however, is the wreck of the steamer 'Montegrappa' in the Atlantic in 1922, given by Giacomo Sassano 'For Grace Received'. It's unmistakably more home-produced – Captain Mergovitch's painter missed out the hovering Madonna – and in many ways typical of the Montenero vision of the sea: the smart ship on its side still belching smoke, huge swathes of water, lifeboats so small you hardly see them at first glance.

The shipwrecks bring the human scale up against God's in time-honoured fashion. They also exactly occupy the dividing-line between those awful but inevitable events that have to be accepted, and those lesser assaults of circumstance – perhaps equally awful, equally common – which you can survive if you're lucky, if the Madonna intercedes for you, if you're wearing her medal, if . . .

There are very few paintings at Montenero that deal with the perils of childbirth or sickness or war. These things, it seems, you greet with resignation, unless you can feel there's some special ingredient in your particular case – a miraculously successful operation, a shell-burst in North Africa that only failed to kill you by some fluke.

Thus, though Livorno was half flattened in 1943, there are no paintings giving thanks for escaping from bombed houses, but there are – in surprising numbers, throughout the last century and this – pictures of people falling through the floors of jerry-built tenements, or crushed under collapsing ceilings. (Whole families sitting down to supper descend to the next storey in stiff postures of surprise. A housewife who looks at first as though she's leaning on a kitchen counter turns out to be clinging for dear life to a beam, above a void in which a seagull hovers.) You thanked the Madonna of Montenero for your escape from the essentially avoidable calamities that befell you at work, at home, in the street. She wasn't too grand to tinker with the arbitrary details of existence.

Dry land isn't a great deal more stable than the sea. The painters' primitive techniques and the absence of perspective emphasise the queasy sense of vertigo. Even if your apartment building stays up, it's full of dangers. In picture after picture tiny doll-like figures plummet from high windows: 'Laira Angiolini, 12 years old . . . on the day of 12 November 1871 from the third floor, escaped unharmed, catching herself on a clothes-line on the second floor, from which she fell to the ground.' The lucky clothes-line itself is coiled inside the frame.

The ground floor too has pitfalls: 'Giuseppe Puccini, 22 months, fell into a sewer. After about four minutes of desperate struggle he was pulled to safety with the help of the Most Sacred Virgin of Montenero, whose miraculous medal he wore on his breast . . . Pieve S. Paolo (Lucca) 13.9.53'. The painter here has made Giuseppe far too big for once. His rescuers look rather as if they're trying to fit a giant boy into a small black hole, but a photograph in the corner sets things right.

Recent donors, though, do seem specially anxious about authenticity. Alvaro Ceccarini, gored by the bull while he was cleaning out its pen ('perforating his stomach so that his intestines came out . . . saved from certain death by the grace of the Most Sacred Madonna . . . 8.10.50'), offers his bloody vest and a passport-style photograph as well as proof of his good faith. Whereas Angiola Chionzini, who was attacked by a cow on the last day of December 1837, was content to let the painting speak for her. Which it does: the cow is very definitely a cow, it's happening in an empty street, and the odd-sized houses stacked on each side seem at once claustrophobically close and – if you're looking for a refuge – unhelpfully distant.

Traffic accidents account for some of Montenero's most memorably horrid offerings. You see small humans lying under the hooves/wheels of every form of conveyance since 1800: carriages, traps, trucks, bicycles, trams, cars, buses – plus the odd train. Not all of them are harrowing – the party of eight ('counting the driver') who squeezed into a cart on the blue, blue evening of 4 July 1851, to go hunting in the Maremma, and who overturned at speed on a pile of stones somebody left in the road, seem to have had rather a jolly spill.

Not so Giuseppe, 4, and Fortunata, 16, who ran to save him, 'both children of Rosa Polesi': they lie pathetically scrambled under a smart cab, outside the butcher's shop, in June of that same year. Nor 'Santi

Martelli of Livorno, 53, carter by profession, who fell off his wagon when he was unloading at the Finochielle Steps on 26 April 1893, and gave no sign of life . . .' He recovered 'in a month, by the Grace of the Madonna', but you can see he was at that moment – and felt himself to be – a dead man.

There are other street dangers that might strike one as less accidental. Antonio Navi thanks the Madonna for his recovery from 'having been mortally wounded by treachery' on 15 January 1863, between 10 and 11 at night. He's seen being stabbed in the back, quite literally, by a brisk enemy on a black street with dark doorways straight out of nightmare.

Violence erupts in broad daylight too. Cesare di Michele Tocchini's narrow escape took place under the eyes of the butcher, the baker, the cooked-meat man. His story is appropriately breathless: 'Chased by his brother with a knife', it begins, 'his sister-in-law appeared, grabbed the poor boy by the hair, took the bread knife from the counter, and began stabbing him pitilessly, as if he was a barbarous foreigner. He fell to the ground, and the neighbours disarmed the cruel woman . . .'

'This all happened,' he ends, 'in Via del Giglio on August 1st of the year 1840.' It's not a bad phrase – 'this all happened' – to sum up the feeling the paintings express, including the less sensational ones: a mixture of acceptance and outrage, faith, fear and resentment. Life was bloody murder, is murder, you reflect, peering at illustrations of other people's bad luck.

Montenero is a 'human document', and like many things cushioned and sanitised by that label its fascination is rather grubby. It's not about the dignity of suffering at all, but about the craven and utterly natural desire to escape it.

If you join the visitors and pilgrims doing the rounds and adding their own pious or pointless graffiti to the walls, you're caught up in a murmur of nasty curiosity, vicarious shudders, sympathetic clucks. It's hard to believe that many people still feel that 'there but for the grace of the Madonna of Montenero . . .' The sanctuary flourishes (they're blasting new holy grottoes out of the rock, building extra wings), but the new *ex voto* offerings seem to be merely bland or expensive or occasionally gruesome. The tradition of painting petered out during the late 1950s, and with it a whole local way of seeing, a whole region of feeling, recedes into the past, or at least into invisibility.

Perhaps when the Madonna of Montenero became the patron of Tuscany in 1947, it was already a sign that she was losing her potency as a local deity who could counteract the malice of events. And perhaps the visual world has changed too much – everyone with a camera; newspaper and television close-ups of world-wide random violence – for local craftsmen to get calamities down the street or round the corner into focus any more. Perspective has, in a sense, intervened at last. Certainly what happens to a Giacomo Sassano or an Angiola Chionzini doesn't appear in the same flat, revealing light.

Unholy ecstasies

Immodest Acts: The Life of a Lesbian Nun in Renaissance Italy

JUDITH C. BROWN

Holy Anorexia

RUDOLPH M. BELL

THE STRANGE STORY OF Sister Benedetta Carlini survives in the
Medici Archives in Florence (filed under 'Miscellaneous') because
she made mystical and visionary claims that the Church authorities felt
obliged to investigate in 1623. What they found – and what Judith C.
Brown rediscovered, quite, she says, by accident – was that Benedetta
and a younger nun, Bartolomea, had been lovers for years. Which
makes her 'case history' more or less unique.

Lesbian loves had no name (though some thought they were a
subdivision of sodomy) and were mostly invisible as a result. *Immodest
Acts* borrows its title from one of the Church's euphemisms; another
authority called it 'the silent sin'. Still, you could be burned for it
(whatever it consisted in), though it seems very few women were. The
problem, suggests Ms Brown, was that most definitions of sinful sexuality were concerned with the spilling of (male) seed in the wrong
places, and although female physiology was widely misunderstood on
the male model, no one was exactly convinced women were capable of
it – or indeed, of being genuinely sexually interested in one another.

Benedetta had already been investigated once, by the local Provost,
who was satisfied that her claims were genuine: people in her village
recalled that she'd been attacked as a little girl by a devilish black dog;
a nightingale took orders from her; and when she began to see elaborate
and disturbing visions (an enclosed garden, visiting angels, attacking
beasts) she'd consulted anxiously with her confessor and tried, on his

advice, to repress them. Like true visions, they returned with full force – she received the stigmata, in ecstasy; Jesus Himself stole her heart, and gave her His in exchange; He then spoke through her, and ordered the nuns to celebrate His mystic marriage to Benedetta in their chapel, saying 'he who does not believe in My bride shall not be saved'.

Her progress, in fact, much resembled that of other women mystics, except perhaps for the arrogance of the claims Jesus made on her behalf. However, mystical experiences were becoming increasingly suspect as signs of heresy and dissent, and could change their meaning overnight. When Benedetta was reinvestigated in 1623 by sceptical Papal officials, the nuns saw things very differently. Her wounds were self-inflicted, with a needle; her magic 'wedding ring' was a mere stain of saffron; and her guardian angels with their strange names – Splenditello, Tesauriello Fiorito, and such – were demons. This last evidence came from Bartolomea, her nurse and companion, and it was accompanied by revelations the officials were quite unprepared for (even the scribe's handwriting, says Judith Brown, falls apart): that Benedetta, in the guise of Splenditello, had persuaded her into bed again and again, and clutched and touched her so that they both 'polluted themselves' with pleasure.

According to Bartolemea, it was 'the angel . . . who did these things', she was 'forced'. And this the investigators accepted, as they also, with much hesitation, seem to have accepted that Benedetta was 'possessed' by a beautiful, male – and fallen – angel. She may have been a conscious fraud as a mystic, but her 'immodest acts' were best explained by a genuine haunting: this was probably easier than to envisage the relationship as simply itself, especially since the women went along with their interpretation.

Benedetta agreed her angels were devils, and (perhaps) saved her skin by doing so. It's possible, though, that she believed it herself. Ms Brown speculates: 'In this double role of male and of angel, Benedetta absolved herself from sin and accepted her society's sexual definitions of gender.' At any rate, her visions ceased, her stigmata healed, and she fell into the silence reserved for her non-act, sentenced to be 'imprisoned' within the convent for the rest of her long life.

Ms Brown's detective work has produced a splendid study in ambiguity. It's not that the things done were ambiguous, but that their meaning was and is. The cultural assumptions, the available language, shift and change before your eyes, rather as attitudes to visions like Benedetta's were shifting in the seventeenth century. And of course, it's a later twentieth-century shift that made these documents 'visible' again: Ms Brown wasn't looking for Benedetta, but the fact that she's a general editor of 'Studies in the History of Sexuality' doubtless had something to do with spotting these manuscripts among the 'Miscellanea Medicea'.

Rudolph M. Bell in *Holy Anorexia* is more explicit about it: he has looked into the lives of Italian female saints, blesseds and venerables, to find evidence that they had this supposedly faddy modern disease. This makes the book less tentative, and less intriguing, though he does uncover some persuasive parallels.

His prize example is St Catherine of Siena (circa 1348–1380), whose anorexia was terminal, and whose much-mythologised 'Life' does sound eerily recognisable: a favoured child (anorectics come from stable, well-off families) locked early into battle with her parents over her determination not to marry, retreating defiantly into self-mutilation, silence (she lived at home for three years without speaking, for penance) and self-starvation. Eventually she won her father's and the Church's approval for her 'troubled, aggressive, individualistic spirituality', so that her refusal to eat (she vomited when she did) became a sign of God's special grace and her transcendence of 'female' weakness.

Gradually, though (here Mr Bell's thesis converges with Ms Brown's), such assertiveness became suspect as heretical. St Veronica Giuliani (born 1660) found a crazy Jesuit confessor who was even odder about food than she was, and who ordered her to lick the floor and walls of her cell and swallow spider's webs. But increasingly women who tried to define their autonomy, and to expiate the original sin of being born female by fasting (one side-effect is that menstruation stops), were accused of perversity or diagnosed as insane.

An Epilogue by anorexia expert Dr William N. Davies draws a possible moral – that feminist psychologists may be right to question the use of anti-depressants and the search for biological causes; and that 'holy anorexia' may illuminate the contradictions women find in the female vocation. 'You are My vessel and My bride,' said Jesus to Margaret of Cortona, as she starved herself to death.

The vegetable paradiso

Sotto il sole giaguaro

ITALO CALVINO

MR PALOMAR, THE LAST of Italo Calvino's books to appear before he died, was about a looker-on, all eye. The posthumously published *Sotto il sole giaguaro* would have given each sense its own story, and would have been called 'I cinque sensi', except that this time he really did leave something unfinished, a fitting footnote to a writing life devoted to the study of beginnings and the cunning postponement of endings. As it is, we have three pieces out of the intended five, each secreting its own diversionary sub-plots: first 'Il nome, il naso', snuffling enjoyably back and forth through cultural history on the track of a smell (or rather, Smell) from demi-monde to jungle to the new jungle of groups and groupies; then the title story, about Mexican menus (parodic shades of Lawrence's 'Woman who Rode Away'); and 'Un re in ascolto', an inverted fairy tale about the kingdom of the inner ear, its king imprisoned in a whispering labyrinth. They are by way of being 'exercises', as Giorgio Manganelli points out on the dust-jacket – studies in displacement, the body in words.

The title story once upon a time had another title, 'Sapore Sapere', playing on the link between taste and knowledge. It's a theme Calvino touched on in his last tribute to Barthes, whom he praised for inventing (or making it seem possible to invent) a methodology that didn't lose touch with the 'living and mortal' subject. *Sotto il sole giaguaro* looks this rather daunting project straight in the teeth – if taste is knowledge, then to eat is to know. The narrator and his wife Olivia, tourists in Mexico, have worked out a gourmet theory of travel:

the true journey . . . implies a complete change of diet, swallowing whole
the country you're visiting, its flora and fauna and culture . . . passing
through your lips and your oesophagus . . .

Eating is all: their sexual life is conducted across the table, their
excursions into the ruined temples suggest taboo questions about cook-
ery – what happened, wonders Olivia (licking her lips), to the human
sacrifices . . . ? Does the taste for chilli not perhaps recall a time when
spices were used to conceal an unspeakable taste for 'the food of the
gods'? The narrator finds himself watching her mouth at work ('her
tongue pressing me against her palate, cocooning me in saliva, then
easing me under the points of her canines'), and only rescues himself
from the heart of darkness inside by the kind of conjuring trick possible
to narrators. He remembers the magic of words. Eating is not a case
of 'Olivia – food – me' but of 'Olivia – food – *names* – me': 'It was the
name "*gorditas pellizacadas con menteca*" that I was savouring above
all . . .' And so he has his Mexico and eats it. The trick is to remember,
as Calvino the essayist puts it elsewhere, that language, once it exists,
pre-empts the inarticulate gods and their rituals. You can eat without
being eaten – if you're content to eat words.

Or at least, that's one (optimistic) version, which transforms Olivia
back into the partner in a dialogue, the familiar provocative Muse/
Reader (compare Ludmilla in *If on a Winter's Night a Traveller*) whose
demands for ever spicier and more elaborate recipes keep the writer
alive. When Olivia says 'I'd like to eat *chiles en nogado*' the ink starts
to flow, he and she are members one of another, part of 'the universal
cannibalism that . . . cancels the boundaries between our bodies and
the *sopa de frigoles . . . the enchiladas . . .*' It's a very funny story, not
least because that carnivorous jaguar sun invoked in the title courts
comparison with alternative Mexicos (like Lawrence's) that lurk darkly
in the background, trying to confuse ink with blood. Calvino's favourite
analogies in this line were always, anyway, vegetable or mineral. He
has a splendid phrase about the 'perpetuità del vegetale', and it's a sap
or chlorophyll that one imagines running through the veins of his
branching stories, at least from the 'family trees' of the *Our Ancestors*

trilogy in the 1950s on. It was there (and in the eye-witness accounts of cosmic origins in *Cosmicomics* and *Ti-Zero*) that he staked out his territory as a specialist in beginnings and fictional foreplay, his brand of vegetable love (vaster than empires and more slow) – replacing, as he pointed out, an early 'neo-realist' flirtation with Hemingway's *For Whom the Bell Tolls*. He convicts his youthful self not of being second-hand and literary, but of not being literary enough: 'I conjured up', (he wrote in the preface to *Ancestors*) 'the book I myself would have liked to read, the sort by an unknown writer, from another age and another country, discovered in an attic.' The result, of course, was (*pace* Barthes, or at least the Barthes of that era) a newly 'readable' kind of book, the romance of reading – familiar now, though it is worth recalling the euphoria of his *Baron in the Trees* all those years ago, finding his feet above the ground:

> The holm oak was near an elm: their two crests almost touched . . . From the elm, by a branch elbow-to-elbow with the next tree, he passed on to a carob, and then to a mulberry tree. So I saw Cosimo swing from one branch to another, high above the garden.

This moment is echoed here in the ripe jungle episodes on the sense of smell – and both (on the book-from-the-attic principle) echo Edgar Rice Burroughs's Tarzan who, one recalls, learned to write and read before he could speak. And as always the writer's progress from branch to branch depends with a comic and vertiginous frankness on collusion with the reader. 'Il nome, il naso' is about following a woman's special scent, which is (perhaps) the smell of her mortality: to be unique is to be singular and irreplaceable, hence the pleasure (and the pathos) of stories *in the plural*, the ramifications of narrative. (One point about the vegetable analogy is that it's a modest myth about immortality – or perhaps better, continuity – that knows its limits.) The 'Re in ascolto' locates at last a city and a landscape in the whorls of his own ear – but only (again) by following the tenuous thread of a voice from outside. The reader (whether or not 'in' the story) is the necessary conspirator, held at the intimate distance that keeps the stories coming (another analogy here is cat's cradle):

'The novel I would most like to read at this moment,' Ludmilla explains, 'should have as its driving force only the desire to narrate, to pile stories upon stories, without trying to force a philosophy of life on you, simply allowing you to observe its own growth, like a tree, an entangling, as if of branches and leaves . . .

Now that the *oeuvre* is complete (or rather, permanently incomplete), the extent of the confidence trick becomes perhaps clearer: Calvino's Reader – so eloquent, so exigent, so endlessly, suggestively unsatisfied – was his greatest, most irreplaceable invention, his most irresistible flattery to mere actual readers, and may not outlive him. He has joined the ancestors, fixed now on his branch of the family tree, and as he reflected, in one of the Mexican pieces that belong with 'Il sole giaguaro' (reprinted in *Collezione di sabbia*, *TLS*, July 12, 1985) family trees in general have an increasingly ominous way of burgeoning backwards;

> Contemporary anthropology looks for roots further and further back, millions of years away, scattered across continents. (What seems to draw nearer is the end, the lopping of all the branches one by one or all at once, the threat of a demographic or technological catastrophe, of starvation . . .)

Narrowing the analogy inexcusably to literary life, one could say that Calvino's improbable achievement was to fill the last parenthesis with new stories, stories within stories, new ways into the woods.

Man who put the cult in occultism

Interview with Umberto Eco

THIS TIME THE PROFESSOR has gone too far: he's a phenomenon, a scandal, a traitor to the intellectual classes. Umberto Eco's
second novel, *Il Pendolo di Foucault*, has broken the records set by his
first, *The Name of the Rose*: all over Italy you can buy it at news-stands
and in supermarkets.

It has sold more than half a million hardback copies already, before
translation, and even those who forgave him his earlier success have
succumbed to snobbish sneers. Producing one bookish bestseller might
be regarded as a fluke. Doing it twice is uncanny, and in very bad
taste. Newspapers have run polls to see how many readers have got to
page 50, page 150, page 509 . . .

Meanwhile, Eco goes on with business as usual – teaching at the
University of Bologna, living in Milan, visiting the US to lecture on
strictly academic topics. His silence, however, has proved to be an
additional titillation, and now he has given up even on that. Whatever
he does, his bridging of the traditional gap between the minority and
the masses is bound to disturb people's world-pictures.

He is by turns ironic, cross, cool and funny in the face of all the
fuss. When I went to see him he was about to embark on a fortnight's
'cure' at a grand spa hotel (whipped-cream *art nouveau*, but nowadays
nouvelle cuisine) on Lake Maggiore, limbering up for the American
publication of *Foucault's Pendulum* and trying to shed the four extra
kilos which he reckons the book is already to blame for.

Not that he's changed much on the outside – he's naturally stocky
and a bit rotund, and though the beard shows traces of grey, that's to

be expected at 57. The new novel has a mini-dissertation on beards, and in terms of his own classification you'd rate Eco's as an ex-radical beard, bristly but benevolent. He's a man of great energy, and the lake, he says, is like a tranquilliser: it makes him sleep.

This particular evening is the Last Supper before the lettuce-leaf diet, and he orders a fillet steak that's served on a slab of black stone and cooks itself as he eats. He drinks white wine with his steak, indeed with everything, is pleased to discover I always drink red, and suggests I have it with the fish. Such small transgressions amuse him. He tells me about a friend who never smoked in his life, but now puffs away diligently on every trip to the States, just to make a point. We both puff away for less high-minded reasons, as he talks about what happens on the frontiers of the world of books.

For instance: he has just been served an injunction by a man in Cyprus who claims that he wrote *The Name of the Rose* in 1964, and this is just the tip of the lunatic iceberg: 'One of the side-effects of the mass media is that they bring fiction to people who've never read a novel before, and who don't share in the fictional agreement, the suspension of disbelief.' There are probably, he thinks, no more than 50,000 people in any country who belong in the category of novel-readers.

He also received a letter from a man who consulted the newspapers for 24 June 1964 – the date of the narrative climax in the new book – and discovered that there was a fire on the corner of a certain street. Why didn't Eco's character mention it: he must have passed close by as he left the scene of the crime? 'It's a shocking experience to realise we belong to such a small company. The last king of Italy, Victor Emmanuel III, allegedly not a cultured person, visited an art exhibition where he admired a particular landscape, and asked: 'How many inhabitatants does this village have?" You enter this *terra ignota*, where people do not distinguish between fiction and reality.'

For all the jokes, this country where fiction joins reality is a frightening place. Eco's experience relates to Salman Rushie's. He was an early and unhesitating counter-protester – 'It is immoral to kill a man for a book' – but sees the habits of misinterpretation and over-interpretation spreading on all sides. Indeed, his new book is all about that, and in particular about the plunge into occultism he observed in the generation of 1968: 'It was a great disillusion in my life. Half are neo-capitalists, half in some way involved in mysticism.'

The *Pendulum* plot is about Templars, Rosicrucians, Masons, and their groupies' crazed attempts to interpret the world as though there was a buried Enigma: 'Everything I tried to invent is true, I have a drawer full of letters saying "you told us the real secret", a special drawer marked "Diabolicals".' Reading signs is a complicated business, there are levels of interpretation – 'With an X-ray photograph, for instance, first we assume that a spot on the X-ray relates to an event on the body, then that the spot represents a symptom, then that the symptom is a clue to the particular sickness. A radiologist once said to me, "Now I understand why I killed so many people".'

He's very serious man, and thinks that laughter has a serious function. In Anglo-Saxon cultures, he says, 'a smile is a value, if you smile you are a serious person. In Italy, if you don't smile you are serious.' This was a formative discovery for his generation brought up on the idealist philosophy of Croce, where works of art were timeless mental events, not subject to the contingencies of history. P. G. Wodehouse was a particularly effective antidote.

'I am not an Italian writer – my idea of narrative owes a lot to Anglo-Saxon traditions, to French, German. In Italy the novel was seen as a poem. In a poem language comes first, but in a narrative it's the story, the ideas, the narrative functions, and language must cope with them. My work is contrary to Italian ideology.' This is why his work travels so well in translation – 'Narrativity is based on narrative structures, which are international. If the man in Cyprus is right, it's because we're both using fictional archetypes, the curse of the abbey, the criminal abbot.

His novels are fictional answers to philosophical questions – 'Fiction is a *pis aller*: if you cannot be Francis Bacon, at least be Shakespeare.' He regards the theory that Bacon wrote Shakespeare as a prize example of the perverse, conspiratorial frame of mind. He also loves out-of-the-way books, and since *The Name of the Rose* made him rich he has become a collector. When in a new city, he searches the yellow pages for a bookseller 'with a middle-European Jewish name: you can't be called John Smith'. His eyes light up as he describes finding a copy of Trithemius (a fine diabolical) in Vancouver.

Books, for Eco, are not sacred icons but material things, and there's a special pleasure in these obscure collectors' items that confide the Secret of the universe. He thinks the past should teach us a kind of vital modesty – 'if history is dead, then I want to commit suicide'. The motifs of fiction are never new, 'even our meeting is already written in a book'. All you can do is to tell a story in a way nobody told it before, exactly. Perhaps, he suggests, we're in a novel by David Lodge. But no, not quite.

For my part I came away thinking that the British novel could do with an infusion of Eco. He jokes, but never against the serious task of understanding how we get things wrong; and he really is one of fiction's frontiersmen, in the most practical sense, someone who takes the books out of the libraries.

From the mind's balcony

La strada di San Giovanni

ITALO CALVINO

Calvino and the Age of Neorealism: Fables of Estrangement

LUCIA RE

IN HER PREFATORY NOTE to *La strada di San Giovanni*, Italo Calvino's widow says that he told her in the year of his death (1985) that he had a dozen or even fifteen books up his sleeve. One of them was certainly *Lezioni americane (Six Memos for the Next Millennium* – Calvino's title – published by Harvard University Press in 1988, but so far, mysteriously, unavailable in Britain), the Charles Eliot Norton Lectures of which he completed five. Another would have been, according to Esther Calvino, a series of 'esercizi di memoria', to which he intended to add various new pieces. Those, however, were never written so that *La strada di San Giovanni* contains only previously published material. It's far from being a mere assemblage, but it's not quite *his* book either. One can see the patterns and cross-references which linked these texts written between 1962 and 1977. At the same time, the missing pieces of the jigsaw are a palpable loss – Calvino would surely have produced a richer associative weave – and of course it's simply a disappointment that there's nothing here that has not seen the light before.

The title story (1963) introduces the themes of memory and mental geography, retracing the path his father took every day from their house up through the terraced vineyards and garden plots to the family farm. This San Remo landscape, fertile, crowded, precipitous, is the basic backdrop in Calvino's memory-theatre – all the more so since, characteristically, he makes it the scene of estrangement. All the ingredients of pastoral abound, he does not stint on description. However, the very vegetation speaks to him of his own disaffection, the son who followed in his father's footsteps only literally, never metaphorically. Father was a horticultural expert, also an obsessive practical farmer who climbed the steep paths every day and came back laden with his own produce. The son was employed to help fetch and carry – already a recognized alien: 'io era già quello che sono, un cittadino della città e della storia' ('I had already become what I am, a citizen of the city and of history'). This sounds, out of context, a grand claim for a pretentious confession, but in fact the binary oppositions – father son, country city, front door (leading down to the town) back door (leading up to the farm) are presented from the outset as raw material, not the story's point or meta-language. The contrasts are as clear as they look, but a lot more complex than they seem.

Father has his own contradictions. His professional skills are bringing about the end of the traditional farm, with its Edenic variety, its pastoral promise of self-sufficiency. Soon the hillsides will be covered in greenhouses, where flowers are grown on an industrial scale (as now); and the complicated maze of irrigation channels, walls and terraces will be rationalized into a glass and concrete carnation-factory. Still, father retains his conviction that, however bullied, Nature remains unsubdued, 'viva e intera' ('alive and whole'). The son's paradoxes are more subtly marked. As you gradually realize, his indifference to green and growing things ('Di fronte alla natura restavo indifferente, reservato, a tratti ostile': 'to nature I remained indifferent, reserved, occasionally hostile') is being transformed in memory, and in writing, into a kind of love affair. Now, on the page, all that he was blind to is present too. He re-enacts a small skirmish with father by refusing to put down the correct botanical names that were the old man's favourite words; nevertheless, he enumerates with wonder and eloquence the contents of the baskets he used to carry: 'le trombe verdi degli zucchini, le pere "coscia di monaca", i grappoli d'uva Saint-Jeannet, i fichi-fiori, la peluria dura del *chavote*, le spine verdiviola dei carciofi . . .' ('the fluted green zucchini, "nun's thighs" pears, clusters of Saint Jeannet grapes, fig flowers, the hard silken skin of the *chavote*, the purple-green spikes of the artichokes'). Now, when in place of all that plenty there is only a blank sheet of paper, he is eager to fill up the space with name upon name. The 'leaves' of writing-paper replace the greenery gone. And so they bring him back to his difference and distance, for a list is a list is a list . . . His young self was inattentive enough sometimes to lose his way in the labyrinth of paths he trod so often. The writer now would be able to point it out to him 'dell'alto degli anni' ('from the vantage of an older self'), and also from the privileged vantage-point of his vocation, which (for Calvino) requires always the knowledge that writing's presence depends on other absences.

It is a point that all these memory-exercises make in their different ways, modulating – or rather levitating – into artifice. The force of his heritage is never denied in this case, for instance, the verticality of his mental geography (his 'world'): 'per me il mondo, la carta del pianeta, andava da casa nostra in giù . . . non . . . solo le vie e le luci della nostra piccola città, ma *la* città, uno spiraglio di tutte le città possibili . . .' ('my world, the map of the planet, extended from our house on down . . . not . . . only the streets and lights of our little city, but *the* city, a glimpse of all possible cities'). Already we are in the territory of *Invisible Cities*, his childhood's gift to him is a sense of burgeoning permutations and possibilities. 'Autobiografia di uno spettatore' ('Autobiography of a Spectator') (a preface to Federico Fellini's *Quattro Film*, 1975) picks up the same idea, recalling his adolescent addiction to the (American) cinema, and the delights of the unreal (much enhanced by Italian censorship and dubbing). Since he was only able to see so many movies clandestinely, by playing truant, he often had to see the end before the beginning (the murderer unmasked before the crime was committed), and sometimes never saw the middles at all. The very randomness of the experience, as well as its glamour, helps explain why his flirtation with 'neorealism' after the war was so brief.

In short (as we already knew) his reflexiveness is inveterate, ingrained, a kind of destiny: but one very different from the historically 'determined' formula that dominated the post-war years when he began his career. *La strada di San Giovanni* includes a piece on his experiences in the Resistance, 'Ricordo di una battaglia' ('A Battle Memoir': 1974), which takes place mostly 'in the dark', an unheroic (though never mock-heroic) encounter with the confusions of fighting in the hills, on the run. Writing thirty years on, he's saved from the epic perspectives of the Liberation, saved too from assuming that memories stay intact. The gestures of piety towards dead comrades are there, but isolated and in a way powerless, not any longer part of a shared rite. By violent contrast (would he have softened it if he had put the book together himself?) this fugitive text is juxtaposed with a playful *tour de force* about putting out the (Partisan) garbage ('La Poubelle agréé', 1977), where there is nothing to restrain his humour and imaginative opportunism. It is a splendid piece of 'recycling' that starts from the official, approved rubbish container (the point at which private and public life meet, sign of civic rationality) and ranges through absurdity, pathos, polemic, domestic politics, anthropology, mythology (the gods of the underworld), and the writer's own waste-paper basket, in which lie the notes for the piece we are reading – headings like 'the hell of a world in which nothing was thrown away', 'defecation', 'refuse as autobiography', and 'autobiography as refuse'. On reflection (reflection he so expertly provokes) you can see that this piece does belong with the others, since the whole topic of 'purification' is intimately connected with getting memories 'out', and getting rid of them – 'scrivere è dispossessarsi non meno del buttar via' ('to write is to dispossess oneself, no less than throwing things away'); and then again, nothing really goes away, even before recycling became fashionable there was always 'l'eterno ritorno dell'ephemera' ('the eternal return of ephemera'). In a sense 'La Poubelle agréé' is the most engaging – because the most freely ingenious, the least 'necessary' – text in the book. The endpiece, 'Dall'opaco' (1974), is abstract and 'serious', the piece that more than any of the others deserves to be called an exercise – a description of 'the world', no less. He starts from San Remo:

> Se allora mi avessero domandato che forma ha il mondo avrei detto che è in pendenza, con dislivelli irregolari, con sporgenze e rientranze, per cui mi trovo sempre in qualche modo come su un balcone, affacciato a una balaustra ...
>
> (If I had been asked then to describe the shape of the world I would

have said that it consists of an irregular slope with projections and indentations, so that somehow I always find myself on a balcony peering over a balustrade.)

We are on the mind's balcony, in the theatre of consciousness, high up, looking out. This is the beginning of a set of meditations that looks as though it is about to deconstruct external reality, but/and does the same for the self, for good measure. A fitting conclusion for a memory-book, though somehow – because it's designedly so cerebral – it feels less fresh than the other texts. On the whole, however (though some in Italy have been openly irritated by the attempt to interpret his legacy this way), this book vindicates the attempt to follow his intentions, rather than heap his leavings into a mere chronological pile.

The order of his *oeuvre*, none the less, has its own significance. Lucia Re's densely documented and fascinating study, *Calvino and the Age of Neorealism: Fables of Estrangement*, looks back to the 1940s and to his first novel, *The Path to the Nest of Spiders* (1947). It is a book that should become compulsory reading for all students of his work, since it explores the difference – and the continuity – between the communist Calvino writing his Resistance novel, and the later seeming-fantasist. She devotes three long chapters to setting the scene, sharing out the space between political, historical and narratological contexts, and analysing the shades of 'neorealism' in the work of (among many others) Pavese, Vittorini, Moravia, Rossellini, Visconti and De Santis. There's also a continuous barrage of contemporaneous theory (Lukács, Gramsci, Adorno, Sartre, Barthes), along with analysis of early essays in which Calvino spells out his understanding of the politics of literature, defining himself not exactly *against*, but always at a sophisticated remove from literal-minded myth-making. For example, this quotation from 'Ingegneri e demolitori' ('Engineers and Wreckers': 1948), as she says, sketches out the world of his 'ironic imagination':

> It will be necessary to give birth to a range of characters who will unveil a whole world of new fantasies, of new contacts with life, death, love, the city, nature . . . it should be possible to make fun of these characters and to take pity on them as much as to admire them.

Her reading of *The Path to the Nest of Spiders* is all about his 'distancing
. . . decentering . . . defamiliarisation' of realist strategies, and she argues
that he was, already, a thoroughly dialogical writer, interweaving (but
never synthesizing) a range of codes.

So the novel is revealed as 'a historical novel, a fable, a *Bildungs-
roman*, and a quest-romance', while never exactly being any of these
things. Each code 'projects a totalisation in its own right', and conflicts
with the others. Calvino 'acknowledges the possible political value of a
complex teleological vision of history as a totality, while simultaneously
disclosing the idea of totality itself as a myth without foundation'. This
brilliant balancing-act (if she is right, and she's certainly convincing),
anticipates the later connoisseur of cosmogonies. It also suggests that
readings of Calvino which emphasize only his 'estrangement' from the
real are mistaken. He is a sceptic who doubts doubt too: and thus at
a vital distance from the atmosphere of exhaustion and hypertrophied
acting-out that characterizes contemporaneity under the sign of international postmodernism.

Freedom fighter

Interview with Oriana Fallaci

Though she lives a lot of the time, these days, in New York, Oriana Fallaci is still thought of as a kind of national heroine in Italy – a Florentine Joan of Arc in a war correspondent's helmet and flak jacket. On the international scene, too, she made her reputation as a female Quixote who tilted fearlessly at the great and the bad, from Kissinger to Khomeini, exposing their alarming visions and grotesque pretensions in magazine interviews famed for their passion, irreverence and sheer bloody-minded cleverness. Fallaci also became a world-wide bestseller as a novelist with the publication, in 1979, of *A Man*. The result of all this success is that she has found herself more and more on the receiving end of other people's curiosity, envy and scepticism. Droves of ordinary readers idolise her, while writers and critics are often cool, dismissive, distant. One veteran journalist who wrote a sympathetic piece about her reported back in some bemusement that his postbag was suddenly overflowing with letters of rapturous appreciation from Fallaci's fans. It was like opening a door, he said, on to a different world, the world of celebrity inhabited by actors, footballers, pop people and gurus.

Fallaci hasn't responded very gracefully to this role reversal, having always seen herself as the observer, the questioner of other people's myths. Intensely present on the page she may be – not for her the pretence of 'objectivity': 'On every professional experience I leave shreds of my heart and soul,' she boasts. But she prefers to think of herself as someone in a sense invisible, outside the frame, her own woman.

Writing, for her, was a blow struck for freedom, and freedom was her fetish. When people tried to pin her down, she was horribly disconcerted. In *Playboy*, of all places, she was hoist with her own petard, 'For the first time in my life,' said interviewer Robert Scheer in 1981, 'I found myself feeling sorry for the likes of Khomeini, Qaddafi, the Shah of Iran and Kissinger.' She still doesn't like giving interviews at the best of times. And this isn't the best of times, because she has been seriously ill. Oriana Fallaci is consequently even more furious with the world than usual, since the first rule of this woman's personality, the trait that gives her her reputation as a holy terror, is to despise weakness.

She wasn't wearing all of her armour when we met in Florence. Bright red nails, yes, and a purple T-shirt with (in English) the legend 'Good girls go to heaven. Bad girls go everywhere', exactly matching her purple pants. But she was wan and without the make-up she always wears – often along with a big hat, dark glasses and a cloud of cigarette smoke – to confront the photographers. Her gravelly voice I'd already got used to on the phone. She talked with dramatic emphasis, sitting on an uncomfortable-looking leather sofa. This was her parents' house: the small sitting-room is decorous in the stiff, decent, unlived-in way of middle-class Italian families like hers. Later I heard about her father (who died in 1988), but we started, as agreed, with strictly literary topics – in particular of course her latest epic novel, *Inshallah* (Chatto & Windus, £15.99). I knew, however, as doubtless she did too, that it was unlikely we'd be able to separate work from her private life so neatly, since her writing is intensely personal. *A Man*, for instance, is a blow-by-blow account of the life and death of Alekos Panagoulis, hero of Greek resistance to the Colonels and, from 1973 until fascist hit men forced his car off the road in 1976, her lover. *Inshallah*, 800 pages set in Beirut, with a cast of hundreds, doesn't overlap with life in the same sense, but its very style and structure grow out of her ingrained obsessions: with living as an adventure, with heroism, with dying, with books as babies.

Gradually she slipped more and more into Italian, the tongue she swears by, and swears in – *Che cazzo! Che stronzo!* She caresses her words or spits them out with equal zest; italics are her natural mode, and her favourite punctuation mark looks like this: !?! 'On every word I left a drop of blood. I *hate* writing, I hate this book and I hate writing. I hate this book because it has taken too much of my life, it has stolen from me the blue sky, the sun . . . Writing is a very masochistic activity. Colette says it should be punished like any other crime, because it's a crime against ourselves. And she's right. What is ugly in writing is the solitude; and that you have to take the water from your own well. And then there is the immobility. You cannot move, you sit down at the bloody table and you are there in a state of hysteria, silent hysteria . . . and you're doing something which is absolutely unnatural. I do not understand writers who adore their books, are even satisfied with their books . . .' But woe betide critics who declare themselves unsatisfied: 'When they speak badly of my books I'm like a tigress. My books are my children. Others cannot touch them. I can beat them, I can destroy them, I can kill them . . .'

There's a strange contrast people have often remarked on, between the aggression in her voice and her tiny (five-foot-nothing), photogenic frame. She is glamorous in a conventional way, but comes on like a tragic heroine. No wonder she caught Kissinger napping, so that he confided that he saw himself running American foreign policy like a lone cowboy in a Western – a revelation of the quality of his daydreams he was never allowed to live down. (Now that I've met Fallaci, however, it strikes me that she herself probably didn't find the Lone Ranger image as ludicrous as others did.)

Her speech is full of bardic figures: patterns, repetitions, fierce images. 'I'm a Florentine. When you listened to a local peasant talk, his way of speaking was metrical by instinct. He chose words that gave the phrase an elegant phonetical movement.' In the novel Fallaci has tried for the same effect through artifice, using assonance, alliteration and even rhyme, composing her lines in blocks of sound. She did classics at school – 'We were *imbued* with the *Iliad* and the *Odyssey*' – and that's part of the formula too, a recipe for getting the physical body and the life of action and conflict on to the page. The best novels about war in our times have been anti-heroic, mock-epic, blackly comic and carnivalesque – Heller's *Catch 22*, Vonnegut's *Slaughterhouse Five*,

Farrell's *Singapore Grip*. But Fallaci takes the heroic approach, defiantly. As a journalist she first found her real subject in war, and as a novelist she's inspired by the old epic motives: to immortalise the fallen, overcome death, defy fate. She is, she readily agrees, a child of war; the 1939–45 war was her school.

Her partisan father, Edoardo, was a fanatical libertarian. He encouraged her to learn English, and when Italy signed the Armistice in 1943 she came in very handy for guiding stranded allied servicemen to safety. Other things too. 'My father used me – cynically, my mother said: "You'd use a newly-born child for your ideas!" He used me, "Take this gun to Mr So-and-so." I would hide it inside the salad in a string bag, hand grenades too. When you do these things, even if you are very young, they form you morally. The first twenty young men who were executed here in Florence by the Germans, I saw them. I was passing by and I saw these guys against a kind of wall near the railway, and then . . .' She mimes the machine gun's *rat-at-at-at*. 'Many remained alive and the German officer went over to finish them off. I was sitting on my bicycle, one foot on the ground, and I was petrified, like Lot's wife in the Bible. Thirteen. It's too little. When the partisans did the same thing to the fascists – it wasn't really the same thing, most of them escaped to Argentina – I didn't see that, but I heard it, all day long. It's a trauma I'll never forget. I remember very well the 11th of August 1944, when all the bridges were blown up. I was with my father. *Vroom!* "That was Ponte alle Grazie," he said. *Vroom!* "That was Ponte Santa Trinità." That night I saw the withdrawal of the Germans, led by an officer on a white horse – reality is always more fantastic than imagination – and the white horse kept slipping on the asphalt in Via Senese. We are living in *un'epoca di pentiti* – an age of turncoats, fascists who turned communist, who turned capitalist. Maybe mine is a sad case of immobility, but I have never changed. I remain substantially what I was on the night of the 11th of August 1944. I don't know if I was very unlucky or very lucky. I think I was very lucky, because I started understanding things very early.'

She was the eldest of three sisters, the precocious, serious, tomboy one, very much her father's creature. In 1946, at sixteen, two years ahead of her peers and with a brilliant school record, she went to university to study medicine. But before long, the journalist's job she'd taken to earn the necessary cash became her profession and medicine was left behind. As for her rise through the ranks, being hard up and female, she's always said, merely honed her determination. Also, she clearly wanted, and enjoys, the good things in life. She has a second home in New York – the top half of a brownstone – and a rambling country house here in the Chianti mountains where, like the good anarchist and libertarian she is, she keeps the chapel in good order for the local priest. (She respects other people's beliefs – but only if they are held with as bold a conviction as her own.)

'I may be intolerant. It's typical of people who are obsessed with freedom that they are intolerant. My father, this symbol of freedom, he was a tyrant with me. Panagoulis was a tyrant in a daily relationship.' Her father died in her arms, refusing a priest. 'I didn't know what to do at the moment of his death. He knew very well that he was dying, and I wanted to do something. Finally I found the thing. '*Cazzo!*' I said to him, '*Che uomo coraggioso sei!* What a brave man you are, you've always been brave, and you are now! *Quanto ti ammiro!* How I admire you!' And he looked at me with eyes full of happiness. He died smiling.'

In *Inshallah* she plays God. Starting from horrific images of dismembered bodies, bloody bits and pieces, in the aftermath of the 1983 kamikaze attacks on the American and French peace-keeping contingents in Beirut, she pieces together, Frankenstein-style, her monster story of protest on behalf of life, following the fates of the surviving Italian contingent to their bitter end. The novel digests all the wars she's reported, Vietnam, the Indo-Pakistani war, the Middle-eastern wars, all the revolutions in Latin America. 'I was stealing the souls of the soldiers, those little guys. They're so young, and they are condemned to die and to kill.' The book is a military romance, not at all (as you might expect) journalistic or documentary in feel, but more like a panoramic painting in oils by a war artist – a giant canvas crowded with more than eighty individual character studies. Her techniques are reminiscent of nineteenth-century classic novels, and of one popular novel which she admires inordinately, Margaret Mitchell's *Gone With the Wind.* 'It's a masterpiece of narration,' she says: 'that woman really knew how to build a story.'

She has no Rhett Butler, though, and no Scarlett either. Her people are citizens of now, caught up in the contemporary kind of civil war where there are not two sides but – as she nastily says – a whole cathouse of factions. The old larger-than-life figures have gone AWOL, and this serves if anything to accentuate Oriana Fallaci's own epic ambitions. Her love affair with life and her flirtations with death are the real subject. Though she takes with great seriousness the time-honoured metaphor of the book having a life of its own – 'When a book is so elaborate, so ambitious, so full of characters, et cetera, at a certain moment it is no longer you who is writing the book' – you sense that this book, her brain-child, is really her surrogate self.

She once wrote, in *Letter to a Child Never Born* (1975), about the dilemma of whether or not one should give life. 'It is a book about the *right* of giving life or not. The woman asks the child permission – and the child refuses.' I asked her what she thought now about never having had children of her own. 'I tried more than once, but I lost them. It's certainly a great consolation when you die to leave another human being that's flesh of your flesh. You die much less when you leave a child. But – I hope it's not pretentious, what I'm saying – I hope there will be at least one work, at least one . . . I need to believe that *these* children will outlive me, because otherwise . . . I'm in trouble, I really die. But all the same, rationally speaking, no son or daughter on paper can substitute for a son or daughter in the flesh, and I feel that I've been deprived of something. I feel offended with destiny in that sense, yes I do.'

Inshallah has taken on an added significance for her since it was published in Italy two years ago: its theme of destiny (which is what, in Arabic, the title means) is something she has had bitter reason to rethink. 'The more I age, the more I believe in this destiny thing. Listen, I don't want to talk about this, at the same time I cannot get free of it because it's part of my life. I am firmly convinced that in March of last year something fatal happened to me. I wrote a story in the *Corriere della Sera*, at the end of the Gulf war, and it started with these words,

"*Da questa guerra sono tornata con una ferita che non si vede.*" I have come back from this war with an invisible wound. I was with three marines, and we were smothered in a black cloud for more than an hour, the Platonic idea of black. When you say it's dark in the night you always see something. This was solid. It was one of the most frightening experiences of my life.'

And yes, there is the story, date line March 26, 1991, by-line Oriana Fallaci. She wrote exactly those words, and more: 'Because it is not an external wound, a wound that bleeds and leaves a scar, it is a hidden wound which will reveal itself who knows when. In six months, a year, two years?' She proved horribly prophetic.

'Why was I at that time in that place, why did the wind change ... Destiny? So many of your family die of cancer, you don't, but then you go, of all the bleak places on this planet, to Kuwait, on that day, on that road, at that hour. I'm not scared. I'm angry. To be angry with your enemy is very different from being scared by your enemy, and I am determined to defeat the bloody bastard. I may be stupid, but I'm determined to win, or at least to delay things as long as possible.'

Her courage is daunting. And you can see why – though much of the intellectual establishment wants to dismiss her as a brilliant journalist grown over-ambitious – her popular readership responds to the way she lays her life on the line. You know what writing is *for*, for a moment: for refusing to go quietly, to do as you're told, to accept your lot. The heroic approach. '*Inshallah* does not mean acceptance, or resignation. No, no! *Al contrario!*' The other side of destiny is chance; things only look inevitable with hind-sight, at the time the roads branch outwards. When she interviewed ex-CIA director William Colby years ago, she asked him what was on her file. He wouldn't tell, but did let slip that the last word was 'Unpredictable'.

As I was leaving, when the tape was off, she said that her horror was of weakness. She needn't worry, I thought; or not about that. The paradox of her strength is that she feels fully alive only when she's fighting: enlisted still among the motley troops of the old partisan, her father, but with no heroes left to worship. Freedom, I thought, really has been a tyrant for her.

On the seas of story

L'isola del giorno prima

UMBERTO ECO

Umberto Eco used to tell people that he wrote his second novel *Foucault's Pendulum* because 'One could have been an accident'. But surely three are a sign of a serious vocation? A vocation, anyway: the new novel, *L'isola del giorno prima*, is lighter and less laboured than *Foucault*, but again clearly belongs to the curious genre of palimpsest, occult history in which he has carved out such a distinctive corner. It's another quest, a detective story even – if you count the search for a way of measuring longitude as a kind of maritime whodunnit. We're in the seventeenth century, 1643 to be precise, in the fictional territory Defoe will colonise eighty years later in *Robinson Crusoe*, the sort of place Swift will turn into a setting for misanthropic satire in *Gulliver's Travels* – a still-uncharted Antipodean land where the plants and animals aren't yet named and labelled and classified in European tongues; where living corals confound the distinctions between animal, vegetable and mineral; and where the birds and flowers look like the creations of a master-jeweller who probably isn't the Christian God. And to compound disorientation, our hero Roberto de la Grive is a man whose mind is a baroque melange of pious, magical and scientific orders of explanation, none of which at all suffices, though they all (teasingly) seem to fit in some ways.

So Roberto is shipwrecked in more senses than one, and to rub it in, to underline just how much he is the creature of a history that has no lodgement yet on this island, he's actually shipwrecked *on a ship*. The wooden table he was lashed to when his own ship, the *Amaryllis*, went down has landed him on a rival explorer's barque, the *Daphne* –

mysteriously deserted, but anchored safely just outside the reef that surrounds the unreachable shore. (Roberto, heir to a modest, landlocked north Italian estate – and at the service of Eco's plot, besides – has never learned to swim.) Alone with his fears and his memories, he writes letters to the Lady Lilia, whose Parisian salon was the finishing-school where he acquired the last word in fashionable notions, before being blackmailed by Mazarin to turn spy on the English Dr Byrd, and join his South Sea voyage. . . . We're not given his letters, mostly. A narrator looking over his shoulder in the confident manner of a Walter Scott, or a Dumas (two Eco favourites) recounts his history, intercut with his experiences aboard the eerily unpeopled vessel, which reveals all sorts of strange cargo: a hold full of clocks, an automatic organ powered by water, a naturalist's collection of new plants, an aviary. But no clue to the whereabouts of the crew, no sign of violence, or panic. Like Crusoe's island, however, Roberto's ark has an Other, an Intruder, who materialises halfway through, just when we're ready to put his fears down to paranoia.

Roberto's Other is no innocent Man Friday: if we haven't worked out by now that Eco is interested in introducing his hapless European explorer to his *own* heritage, then the advent of aged Jesuit Caspar (who's been hiding on board) makes the point tragi-comically clear. He's a marvellous creation, an erudite, eloquent and shamelessly opportunistic apologist for theology-as-science, convinced that Galileo is a heretic, and yet at the same time an inventor on his own account, who has designed a leather skin-diver's face-mask and a one-man, leg-powered submarine. Though Roberto is inclined to scepticism, he can't cast Caspar in the role of the evil Other for long. In fact, he has already encountered something much worse on his earlier ship, where the Englishman Byrd had turned a tortured dog into an organic clock.

This is a piece of genuinely baroque nastiness, all about weapon salve: the idea was that you treated the steel that wounded the patient with your magical unguent, or if you were a bad medicine man stuck it into the fire, to cause either healing or pain. Vivisector Byrd has invented a version of Greenwich Mean Time which involves someone back in London torturing a knife at certain times of day, whereupon the dog on the ship the other side of the world howls. Or perhaps, given he has an open wound, he just howls anyway.

Caspar, a benevolent bumbler by comparison, explains to Roberto what happened to the crew – they thought the Jesuit had the plague, left him to die, went ashore taking his most indispensable machine, the Specula Melitensis, with them, and were eaten by passing cannibals – and persuades him that what we now know as the International Date Line runs between ship and land, so that on the island it is yesterday. Hence the title, 'The Island of the Day Before'; and hence the necessity of either Roberto learning to swim, or Caspar testing his own sub. Both plots happen (this book is a Borgesian garden of forking paths), but Caspar's ends first. He really does become part of yesterday, though not in the way he meant. And of his bones are coral made. . . .

Roberto's loneliness enters a new dimension now, and he becomes an author for real, in order to try to take charge of this dangerous new world. But Eco is interested in demonstrating how to get lost in your plot, then Roberto's climactic adventures on the ocean of story stage the Death of the Author with spectacular ingenuity, several ways at once. Earlier he's dreamed of the island as 'a place where every human . . . like a boy lost in the forest, would find a new language capable of being born out of a new contact with things', and at last he learns the secret of going back to the maternal beginnings of life, where he'll even perhaps find his lover after all, no longer unobtainable. He quotes Donne – 'come i rigidi gemelli del compasso' – and there are shades too of Marvell (our vegetable love). He doesn't share their penchant for brevity and compression, though, any more than *his* author. The book is a crammed compendium of tales, and I've missed out (just for example) a whole chunk of the thirty years war, an elaborate narrative about Roberto's Double, an intrigue involving Richelieu, and an icono-graphic, punning history of the Dove (Colombo). The whole thing conspires against any paraphrase or overview, we're pulled down into the undersea world of branching digressions where there are always new beginnings.

And it has all been meticulously planned, of course. Eco's Charles Eliot Norton lectures, published by Harvard University Press under the title *Six Walks in the Fictional Woods* earlier this year, were written largely in praise of 'lingering':

> fictional texts come to the aid of our metaphysical narrowmindedness. We live in the great labyrinth of the actual world ... a world whose paths we have not yet entirely mapped out and whose total structure we are unable to describe.

Fiction – to simplify and moralise, which indeed here he does – is 'a form of therapy against the sleep of reason', because it enables us to understand something of the mechanisms by which we overinterpret the world. Fiction mimics the world, and mirrors us back to ourselves, in the role of the reader, like Roberto in the novel. And like Roberto too, the model reader described in the lectures learns to become more interested in beginnings than ends: on the very last page Eco recalls the strange bliss of being shown, in a planetarium in Galicia, 'the sky that had appeared over my birthplace, Alessandria, Italy, on the night of January 5–6, 1932 ... the first night of my life. ... That was a fictional wood I wish I had never had to leave. ...' His sense of the function of fiction in our time is that – by being self-conscious – it enables us to lose ourselves.

It's a deliberate conflation of the roles of writer and reader – something that's underlined in the lectures, which pay homage to Italo Calvino's unfinished series of eight years before (*Six Memos for the Next Millennium*). And the stress on 'lingering' is of course a back-handed allusion to Calvino's praise of quickness and lightness. Calvino in fact once said, in answer to the question, Why do you write? that he wrote books he would like to *read*. This is even more true of Eco, who is, for all his erudition, the most reader-friendly of contemporary novelists. It may seem paradoxical, then, that he is notorious for his distrust of professional reviewers and critics. (The new novel has been ruthlessly embargoed in Italy until the day before publication, October 5th.) But he distrusts them because they insert themselves between reader and writer. *Foucault's Pendulum* was 'dissected' long before it was out, and this time he's taking no chances, trusting instead to the audience who turned that book into a best-seller. Will he pull it off again? Very likely, for he offers – as he says – the traditional *consolations* of fiction, craftily and generously and knowingly, which means that with Eco you can have your postmodernist cake and eat it.

Signs of possession

Out of Florence:
From the World of San Francesco di Paola

HARRY BREWSTER

IN THE EARLY 1900S about a sixth of the population of Florence was made up of foreigners, most of them, like Harry Brewster's family, Anglo-American and German. By the close of the century, which he himself didn't quite live to see, their houses, collections and gardens had all been sold on, dispersed and built on – with a very few exceptions. The ex-monastery of San Francesco di Paola is now, as he wrote, 'the only property in Florence of historical interest that is still the home of a non-Italian family with roots abroad that has owned and lived in it for some generations'. A 'world' has shrunk to a few hectares, a picturesque standing pool of time, these days a listed property, which reduces death duties but forbids development.

The last two major landmarks to go, relatively recently – as Brewster observes, with some hint of *schadenfreude* – had been Violet Trefusis's house in Bellosguardo, L'Ombrellino, now a conference centre, and (on the opposing hills, on the Via Bolognese) Harold Acton's La Pietra, which belongs to New York University. Those were grand, pretentious houses, and their proprietors were both wealthy and famous for their loyalty to the high-camp style in which they embroidered the traditions of housekeeping bequeathed by their mothers. They themselves weren't the marrying kind, and had no children. Brewster here has an anecdote about going to see Violet on her deathbed (she died in 1972): she said, archly and menacingly, 'Harry, I want your blood', though it wasn't clear whether she was thinking of a transfusion, or something more symbolic. He didn't stay to find out, they weren't at all close. Harold Acton, who was closer, if only in a spirit of rivalry, also wrote about

Trefusis's long last months in a story in his collection *The Soul's Gymnasium* (1984) – dying, she teases all her friends by asking them to choose a 'keepsake' from among her fabulous jewels, brought in on a tray by the maid. For quite a while, she is able to enjoy watching them salivate before plumping modestly for the diamond choker, but gradually the game palls, they stop believing her, and anyway are dying off one by one themselves. Her possessions lose their magic to possess.

The really creepy thing about Acton's story, however, is that it was semi-plagiarized from Violet herself, who several times in her novels had staged just the kind of final scene she went on to act out. Parted from the one great love of her life, Vita Sackville-West, she had written pathetically (in 1920) of her 'homeless, friendless condition'. 'All morning I have been making lists of my things . . .' Trefusis and Acton were both aware of themselves as members of a dying breed, and performed accordingly in rococo style. They made inventories of people, mostly long gone. The Brewsters hadn't the money or the inclination to belong to that intensely social world – they travelled a good deal, particularly to Greece, and they only 'improved' their ex-monastery and its farm buildings minimally after the Second World War (when the German half of their ancestry had saved the place from being confiscated), in order to let them to tenants. *Out of Florence*, as a result, is about the mystique of stones and trees, more durable stuff.

It is just as much a matter of possession, however, if in a different style. Brewster's fugitive, posthumous pieces have a pagan aura, invoking the genius of place, and the mostly fictionalized characters who appear in them – mysterious tenants or temporary travelling companions – are like fleshy, mildly comical nymphs, emanations of the landscape. His story of how he helped see off the project to build a Hilton Hotel on the field next door is disappointingly short on detail, partly because it was done by an untidy series of pressure groups he was passionately involved with only while the emergency lasted. And the writing is sometimes vague, the language haunted by displacements – secular trees, for instance, must be an echo from Italian *secolare*, centuries-old; and it is hard to tell whether 'Ian Greenlegs' (Ian Greenlees, sometime Director of the British Institute in Florence) is a